THE CINEMA OF MARTIN SCORSESE

THE CINEMA OF MARTIN SCORSESE

LAWRENCE ▪ S ▪ FRIEDMAN

CONTINUUM ▪ NEW YORK

1997

The Continuum Publishing Company
370 Lexington Avenue, New York, NY 10017

Printed in the United States of America

Library of Congress Cataloging-in-Publication Data

Friedman, Lawrence S.
    The cinema of Martin Scorsese / Lawrence S. Friedman.
        p. cm.
    Includes bibliographical references and index.
    ISBN 0-8264-1004-9 (hardcover : alk. paper)
    1. Scorsese, Martin–Criticism and interpretation. I. Title.
PN1998.3.S39F75   1997
791.43'0233'092–dc21   96-37135
                                                                CIP

All stills courtesy of Martin Scorsese and
Jerry Ohlinger's Movie Material Store, Inc.

Contents

Flashbacks: An Auteur Is Born

"There are no works," François Truffaut once said, "there are only auteurs." Titling a book *The Cinema of Martin Scorsese* apparently ratifies Truffaut's point about the director's pre-eminence. Why not *The Cinema of Robert De Niro,* Scorsese's favorite actor, who has starred in more movies than Scorsese has made? Or how about *The Cinema of Paul Schrader,* Scorsese's sometime scriptwriter, who wrote *Taxi Driver,* rewrote *Raging Bull,* and adapted *The Last Temptation of Christ,* arguably Scorsese's most powerful films? "Marty is fond of saying that *Taxi Driver* is my film and *Raging Bull* is De Niro's and *The Last Temptation of Christ,* is his," Schrader avows.[1] Taken literally, Schrader's words demolish Truffaut's *"politique des auteurs":* the director's preeminence is not definitive but contingent. At the very least they invoke Panofsky's likening of filmmaking to cathedral building: both result from the collective labor of many specialists.

It's a rare moviegoer who knows a film's director. And the ubiquitous video stores whose sales and rentals command a mushrooming share of the movie market, list films chiefly by title, occasionally by star, seldom by director. Moreover, the auteur theory reeks of elitism in an era when the line between high and popular culture has blurred if not disappeared. Intimations of hierarchy—anathema whether artistic or intellectual or both—lurk in its Olympian assumptions. Auteurism smacks of originality at a time when originality yields to imitation and repetition. Nostalgia dampens inventiveness, which increasingly consists solely of whizbang technology. We are excited by how the bad guy gets zapped, not why; it is form that hooks us, not function.

In retrospect, Truffaut's hallowed auteurism looks like cinema's version of the modernism most famously represented in literature by James Joyce. Truffaut's 1954 *Cahiers du Cinema* essay—"On a Certain Tendency of the French Cinema"—rejected the aesthetic of the previous generation of cineastes much as Joyce's *A Portrait of the Artist as a Young Man* rejected the aesthetic of the previous generation of novelists. Truffaut might even have bought Joyce's "I go to encounter for the millionth time the reality of experience and to forge in the smithy of my soul the uncreated conscience of my race" with its implication that hitherto authenticity had gone unconfronted and uncreated. Joyce's personal pronouns fix the author as source and center of a text that derives its meanings from his manipulations. His theory of art is a theory of control—of the means *and* the ends of creation. Out of bits and pieces of experience the artist forges a unified artifact susceptible to (his) consistent interpretation. Film auteurists endlessly invoke this unity and consistency, claiming that a true auteur's "signature" is discernible even when his "authority" is compromised by the economics and/or politics of filmmaking. Orson Welles's "signature," for example, is apparent in all his films, even though he lost total control of his oeuvre after *Citizen Kane*.

Yet auteurism seemed more plausible in Truffaut's day than it seems in ours. A modernist conceit, the theory faces rough going in a postmodern world that values diversity above unity, repetition above originality, and surface above substance. Most postmodern art is as fragmented as its audience(s), reduced to imitating moribund styles when it is not contemplating itself. And postmodernity may be even more uncongenial to the would-be film auteur than to the presumptive writer, painter, or composer. The prohibitive cost of movies militates against creativity: financiers prefer surefire formulas to risky originals. And television—the indisputable source of the cultural lives of nearly everyone born after Truffaut's 1954 auteurist manifesto—all but demands obeisance to the "reality" it at once incarnates and reflects. Successful TV shows now spawn movies, much as successful movies some time ago began spawning "novelizations." A creative filmmaker must distance himself from the banality of television but not so much as to alienate an audience weaned on the medium. And he faces formidable competition: once upon a time everyone wanted to write the great American novel; now everyone wants to make the great Hollywood movie. Applications to film schools multiply, and academics from other disciplines trip over each other in their rush to teach film courses.

The many fragmentations of postmodern American society, the advent and triumph of television, the prohibitive cost and competition of making movies would appear to offer the *politique des auteurs* slim prospects for survival. Add the demise of the sometime stultifying but frequently sustaining Hollywood studio system, and the likelihood of an American New Wave is remote. Yet in the mid-1970s, along came a group of brash young directors whose sudden emergence and revolutionary filmmaking evoked memories of the French *nouvelle vague* of the late 1950s and early 1960s. Like Truffaut and his famous cohorts—Jean-Luc Godard, Claude Chabrol, Eric Rohmer, and Jacques Rivette—the new American auteurs—Francis Ford Coppola, George Lucas, Brian De Palma, Steven Spielberg, and Martin Scorsese—made intensely personal films that bore their sometimes quirky but always unique signatures. What film historians David Bordwell and Kristin Thompson conclude about the French auteurs is no less true of their American counterparts: "In retrospect the New Wave not only offered several original and valuable films but also demonstrated that renewal in the film industry could come from talented, aggressive young people inspired in large part by the sheer love of cinema."[2]

It's this "sheer love of cinema" that animates the films of American and French auteurs alike. Truffaut and his colleagues began as critics, writing for the Paris film journal *Cahiers du Cinema* in the mid-1950s; the Americans emerged from film schools in the mid-1960s. Both groups were products of a film culture, unlike their respective predecessors who had drifted into filmmaking from other fields, most notably theater. In the years between the death of neighborhood movie houses and the birth of video stores, film schools were the chief American repositories of film history. At UCLA, USC, and NYU respectively, Coppola, Lucas, and Scorsese in the 1960s emulated Truffaut and company in the 1950s at "the Cinémathèque under the direction of Henri Langlois, where the film fanatics spent the better part of their waking hours under the spell of motion pictures from every nationality and period."[3]

Many New Wave films became featured "texts" on the "syllabi" of American film schools: a latter-day generation of film fanatics would master the cinema of the French auteurs along with the classic Hollywood cinema that so inspired those Cinémathèque regulars. Scorsese, for example, knows Truffaut's movies as well as Truffaut—who once claimed to know *Citizen Kane* by heart—knew Orson Welles's. As Scorsese says, there are certain Truffaut shots "I will never get out of my system. There's a shot in *Shoot the Piano Player*. . . . He cuts three times, coming closer each time. That shot's in every picture I make, and I don't know why."[4] It's not only the restless, often handheld camera but the deliberately casual mise-en-scène, the intricate homages to favored auteurs, the socially marginal and/or alienated heroes, and the resistance to narrative closure that Scorsese inherits from the *nouvelle vague.* Yet these stylistic tics, useful for spotting the director's "signature," are rather the shadow than the substance of auteurism. What the auteur theory finally boils down to is personal vision more than technical mastery. George Lucas and Steven Spielberg, for example, are peerless technocrats; yet neither has created an intensely personal cinema on the order of Martin Scorsese's.

As much as the Italian immigrant culture he was born into or the movies he grew up on, it was the Roman Catholic Church that shaped the young Martin Scorsese. Like the young James Joyce, Scorsese imbibed a sacramental view of the world along with the bread and wine of the Eucharist. Mary Pat Kelly claims that Scorsese, like Joyce, creates "moments of epiphany" that reveal the "potential significance" or "radiance" of objects. Both men are "priests of the imagination" who want their works experienced on a spiritual level.[5] "*Mean Streets* (1973) is a religious statement," said Scorsese of the film that first won him widespread recognition. And its method no less than its message reflects a sacramental cast of mind: "I wanted to give all the hints about what I wanted to say, but not make the statement." Although he is a lapsed Catholic, Scorsese cannot get the religion out of his blood or keep it out of his work: "The whole idea of faith fascinates me. . . . I guess it's the same type of feeling someone else might get from taking an acid trip."[6]

Spiritual experiences, including the feeling of communicating directly with God, carry over from Scorsese's Catholic boyhood. A retreat he went on as a high schooler culminated in a "fright vision" that triggered a never-to-be-forgotten spiritual crisis. "Exactly like *Portrait of the Artist,*" Scorsese remembers the retreat, complete with "the old fire and brimstone sermon." So powerfully does Joyce's preacher invoke the boundless fire and eternal torture of hell that Stephen Dedalus feels his brain "simmering and bubbling within the cracking tenement of the skull." Eerily reminiscent of Stephen's trauma was Scorsese's "auditory hallucination" triggered by a similar sermon: "I heard crickets that got louder and louder and louder until they made me feel like I was going to burst."[7] Like Joyce, Scorsese appropriates the quintessentially Catholic imagery of the retreat for artistic purposes. In "Jerusalem, Jerusalem," a fifty-page outline for a film he never shot, Scorsese recapitulates his own retreat experience, fire and brimstone sex sermon, hallucinatory vision and all. J.R., transparently Scorsese, suffers the same fate as his creator: "I wound up in a very bad state for which the priest's only advice "was to see . . . a very good Catholic psychiatrist."[8] Like the young Scorsese, J.R. is beset by the sexual demons that seem particularly to target adolescent Catholics. Paul Schrader's line—"'Jerusalem, Jerusalem' was the diary of a masturbator"–struck a chord in Scorsese who recognized himself in J.R. "Exactly. . . . The point is, you can't live with that guilt, you can't live with that guilt." That repeated phrase and its follow-up—"Nine years of analysis. It's a matter of learning how to live with it"—hark back to the sermon at the retreat and the priest's parting advice.[9]

"Guilt. A major helping of guilt, like a lot of garlic," remains the strongest legacy of Scorsese's Catholic youth.[10] And it is guilt, conceived in masturbation and prolonged in maturer symptoms of sexual bad faith, that is a recurrent motif, perhaps *the* recurrent motif, in Scorsese's life and art alike. Yet the epigraph to "Jerusalem, Jerusalem," borrowed from French director Robert Bresson's *Diary of a Country Priest* (1950), hints that for Scorsese the Church represents more than guilt and pain: "God is not a torturer. . . . He only wants us to be merciful with ourselves." It is even possible that Scorsese was looking beyond Bresson's film to its source in the eponymous 1936 novel by Georges Bernanos. For Scorsese, the vision of Bernanos, whose love–hate relationship with the Church combined the impassioned Catholicism of the believer with the equally impassioned anti-Catholicism of the apostate, might have seemed apposite to his own. Turned off by Church dogma, Scorsese remains under the spell of Catholic ritual and iconography. First Communion and the plaster statues and crucifixes in St. Patrick's Old Cathedral that constituted his first images of Christ retain their hold on Scorsese's adult imagination. So powerful was his early fascination with religion that Scorsese long aspired to the priesthood. At thirteen he went to Cathedral College, a preparatory seminary on Eighty-Sixth Street, only to be expelled for the poor grades he would later attribute to the distraction of falling in love with a young girl from another school. Next stop was Cardinal Hayes High School in the Bronx, "run by parish priests and brothers . . . rough guys." Yet even the school's harsh regimen failed to deflect Scorsese from his chosen vocation: "Up until 1960, I had wanted to finish at Cardinal Hayes, maybe go to the university for a few years, and then go into a seminary and become a priest."[11] But Fordham turned him down because of bad grades, and Scorsese, lured by the promise of film courses, "settled" for NYU.

By 1960, the eighteen-year-old Scorsese had not so much renounced the Church as rechanneled his religious impulse into film. It is probable that his early zeal had always been animated less by burning faith than by ritual and imagery. Scorsese has argued retrospectively that he embraced the priesthood as the surest means of salvation, "wanting that vocation, selfishly, so that I'd be saved. . . . I wound up finding a vocation in making movies with the same kind of passion."[12] So filmmaking turns out to be a religious vocation devoted no less than the priesthood to the quest for salvation. Predictably, it is Scorsese's earliest films that evoke Catholicism most overtly—and most passionately. *Mean Streets* trumpets its obsessions up front: "You don't make up for your sins in church. You do it in the streets. You do it at home." In a November 1973 *Time* interview, Scorsese called the film a "religious statement" that asks, "Can you really be a saint in this day?" It is the word made flesh: Catholic dogma's fix on sin, penance, and redemption rendered visible on film. Sainthood turns out to be impossible in *Mean Streets;* but its intimations haunt Scorsese's later films, nearly all of which reflect on how to lead a moral life in an immoral world. Many of his male protagonists erupt into senseless violence, their aspirations to spiritual purity frustrated by a squalid world they never made.

Although Scorsese was inspired to make movies—"to put my feelings into action really"—by Haig Manoogian's 1960 NYU lectures on film history, the knack of translating a religious vocation from the priesthood into filmmaking began much earlier. Asthmatic as a child, Scorsese was dragged endlessly to the movies by parents who did not know what else to do with him. After the age of three, when his asthma worsened, the boy's nearly nonstop moviegoing and television watching—the Scorseses were one of the first families on their block to get a television set in 1948—conjured up images whose power would rival those of the Church. A Trucolor trailer for a Roy Rogers movie he saw at three produced Scorsese's earliest movie memory: he dreamed of becoming a cowboy and Westerns remained his favorite movies for the next several years. Sacred and profane images already began to converge in Scorsese's grammar school drawings. A would-be painter, he drew what he saw on the movie screen along with pictures of Christ on the cross that he imagined from the nuns' stories. As a child he was so fascinated by movie aspect ratios, claimed Scorsese many years later, that he "would do little drawings in 1:1: 33."[13] Thus enamored of the matter and the manner of film production from childhood, it is no wonder that the mature filmmaker habitually thinks and speaks in visual images. What Pauline Kael once remarked of Bernardo Bertolucci seems equally true of Scorsese: "movies arc as active in him as direct experience—perhaps more active, since they may color everything else."[14] Here, for example, is Scorsese recalling the noxious atmosphere of an oppressively hot New York summer night when he was shooting *Taxi Driver:* "It reminds me of the scene in *The Ten Commandments* portraying the killing of the first-born, where a cloud of green smoke seeps along the palace floor and touches the foot of a first-born son who falls dead."[15]

Recounting the important films in his life, Scorsese separates those he saw before from those he saw after entering film school in 1960. His early passion for Westerns proved more than puppy love. *I Shot Jesse James* (1949), Sam Fuller's first movie, introduced Scorsese to a director whose films "influenced me so greatly; *Park Row* (1952), *Pickup on South Street* (1953), these are some of the strongest things I've ever seen. Later I saw *Forty Guns* (1957), which is my favorite. . . . I very much liked the Westerns. John Ford is my very favorite director, I love all of his films. . . . *The Searchers* (1956) became one of my favorite films."[16] It was Fuller and, especially, Ford who first revealed the director's shaping hand, although in retrospect Scorsese gives equal billing to the stars—John Wayne, Maureen O'Hara, Henry Fonda—for instilling in him the critical aware-ness that the same people made the films he liked. Besides Westerns, other 1950s films that he grew up on stick in Scorsese's mind: *On the Waterfront* (1954); *East of Eden* (1955); *Giant* (1956); and one of the first foreign films he discovered, Ingmar Bergman's *The Seventh Seal* (1956). Of course a whole new world of film opened up for Scorsese in the 1950s via the fledgling medium of television.

Because the big American studios would not sell their movies to tele-vision in the 1950s, foreign films were regularly shown. Scorsese remem-bers his family clustered around the television set crying over the Italian films—*The Bicycle Thief, Open City, Paisan*—that were featured on Friday nights. But British films aired more frequently and apparently affected Scorsese more profoundly. He recalls seeing Michael Powell and Emeric Pressburger's *The Tales of Hoffmann* (1951) for the first time on "Million Dollar Movie," a program that showed the same films twice on week-nights and three times on Saturday and Sunday. Although he saw it in a mutilated black-and-white version bristling with commercials, Scorsese was "mesmerized by the music, the camera movements and the theatri-cality of the gestures by these actors who were mostly dancers."

Repeated television viewings of *The Tales of Hoffmann*

> taught me about the relation of camera to music: I just assimilated it
> because I saw it so often. Even now there's hardly a day when the
> score of the picture doesn't go through my mind, and of course it
> had an effect on the way I handled the musical sequences in *New
> York, New York* and the fights in *Raging Bull.* There was another les-
> son I learned from it too: When we were doing the close-ups of De
> Niro's eyes for *Taxi Driver,* I shot these at 36 or 48 frames per second
> to reproduce the same effect that I'd seen in the Venetian episode of
> *The Tales of Hoffmann,* when Robert Helpmann is watching the duel
> on a gondola.[17]

That Scorsese was so "mesmerized" by a film he would not see uncut
and in color until many years later testifies to the incantory power of *The
Tales of Hoffmann,* even on television. *The Red Shoes* (1948), another
Powell/Pressburger collaboration and the first of their films he saw in
color, "hypnotized" Scorsese when he went to see it with his father at the
Academy of Music on 14th Street. "I don't think anything had struck me
as that powerful . . . except perhaps another film I had seen in the same
theater with my father, Renoir's *The River,* which also had a dance
sequence." Struck by the dancing, he was even more intrigued by the
"mystery" and shocked by the "hysteria" of *The Red Shoes.* When it came
on television, he watched it repeatedly in black and white before seeing
it again in color and becoming "fascinated" by the character of the
impresario "whose dedication destroys everything around him. What
appealed to me was the cruelty and the beauty of his character—especially the scene where he smashes the mirror, filled with self-hate."[18] It is
not surprising that Scorsese was fascinated by the impresario, a character
whose destructive rage eerily prefigures the pathologies of Scorsese's
own protagonists. And there is more than a little of the impresario in
Scorsese himself. In late 1978, too much "high living" landed him in the
hospital with internal bleeding just when he had to decide whether to
direct *Raging Bull.* "I said yes. I finally understood that for me I had
found the hook—the self-destructiveness, the destruction of people
around you, just for the sake of it. I was Jake LaMotta."[19]

Already bewitched by *The Red Shoes* and *The Tales of Hoffmann,*
Scorsese fell under the spell of still another Michael Powell film—
Peeping Tom (1960)—in 1962 at NYU. At first Scorsese "couldn't believe"
that this "extraordinary" film had been made by one of the collabora-
tors on the two earlier ones. In its savagely ironic juxtaposition of

voyeurism and murder, *Peeping Tom* resembles a far more famous 1960 release—Alfred Hitchcock's *Psycho*. And like *Psycho,* it is an early version of the slasher film, shocking (at least for its time) in its gruesome treatment of equally gruesome subject matter. Scorsese's fascination with *Peeping Tom,* however, lies not so much in its gruesomeness as in its protagonist, a photographer obsessed with recording the most intimate of private moments. Read "director" for "photographer," and *Peeping Tom*'s photographic images evoke for Scorsese "a sense of the actual nuts and bolts of film-making":

> I have always felt that *Peeping Tom* and *8½* say everything that can be said about film-making, about the process of dealing with film, the objectivity and subjectivity of it and the confusion between the two. *8½* captures the glamour and enjoyment of film-making, while *Peeping Tom* shows the aggression of it, how the camera violates. These are the two great films that deal with the philosophy and the danger of film-making. From studying them you can discover everything about people who make films, or at least people who *express* themselves through films.[20]

If the reverence for *Peeping Tom* seems quirky, the invocation of Federico Fellini's *8½* (1963) is practically de rigueur for a film school graduate of Scorsese's generation. Indoctrinated with the auteur theory at NYU, students were nonetheless taught to apply it pretty exclusively to European directors. Still, it is a measure of *8½*'s impact that Fellini's is the one movie by an acknowledged European master that Scorsese invariably lists—*Citizen Kane, The Red Shoes,* and *The Searchers* are others—among his personal favorites. It's probably because movies have always been Scorsese's life that he is so obsessed with *8½,* a film about filmmaking whose protagonist is himself a filmmaker and whose subject is ultimately itself. But although he views *8½* primarily as a triumph of *personal* filmmaking, its style and symbolism may influence Scorsese more even than its reflexivity. Fellini's restlessly prowling camera and his (Guido, the director–hero of *8½,* is transparently Fellini) yearning for emotional and/or spiritual transcendence are equally Scorsese's. Guido's obsession with a symbolic girl in white, for example, is replayed by Travis Bickle *(Taxi Driver)* and Jake LaMotta *(Raging Bull),* albeit in an earthier and more problematic fashion. Like Fellini in *8½* but even more compulsively in *La Dolce Vita* (1960), Scorsese zeroes in on the collision between sensuality and spirituality, most obviously in his depiction of a conflicted Jesus in *The Last Temptation of Christ* (1988).

Yet despite its retrospective allure, *8½* appeared only at the tag end of Scorsese's film school days. By the time *8½* was released in 1963, he had seen countless foreign films, most notably those of the French New Wave. Between 1960, when he entered NYU film school and 1963, when he got his M.A. and wrote and directed his first movie—a nine-minute 16 mm short called *What's a Nice Girl Like You Doing in a Place Like This?*—Scorsese saw no American films. Although he later caught up with American films on television, Scorsese— and his entire generation of filmmakers—were chiefly inspired by the startlingly innovative works of the *nouvelle vague*. To be in film school at NYU in the early 1960s, when the New York Film Festival began screening French New Wave films that rarely made it to the West Coast, was to be in cinematic heaven. Jean-Luc Godard's *Breathless* (1959) and Alain Resnais's *Hiroshima Mon Amour* (1959) are Scorsese's oft-cited examples of films whose "influence stays with you." But it is to the early films of François Truffaut—*The 400 Blows* (1959); *Shoot the Piano Player* (1960); and *Jules and Jim* (1961)—that he owes his greatest debt. A takeoff on *Jules and Jim* fills the first two minutes of Scorsese's first short, the nine-minute *What's a Nice Girl?* And homages to the New Wave in general and to Truffaut in particular abound in Scorsese's excruciatingly personal early features, *Who's That Knocking at My Door?* and *Mean Streets*. Even as late as 1990, Scorsese invoked Truffaut's style in explaining his own: "I wanted *GoodFellas* to move as fast as . . . the opening of *Jules and Jim* and to go on like that for two hours."[21] The ambiguous freedom and uncertain future of a male character at the end of *The 400 Blows, Shoot the Piano Player,* and *Jules and Jim* as well as the narrative role of music in establishing a scene and evoking its mood recur as often in Scorsese's films as they do in Truffaut's own later ones.

Still, the Truffaut influence is more a matter of feeling than of form. Asked by film critic David Ansen in a 1987 interview about the impact of Godard and Truffaut, Scorsese replied that they "taught me a sense of freedom. Especially *Jules and Jim,*" which, unlike Godard's "too cerebral" films, made you "just feel emotion, you feel incredible love." In the same interview, Scorsese singled out Bernardo Bertolucci's *Before the Revolution* (1964), which he saw "maybe thirteen, fourteen times" and "studied . . . over and over again" as the film that directly inspired his own first feature. "Bertolucci was everyone's idol then," recalls Scorsese. Only twenty-four when he made *Before the Revolution,* Bertolucci was barely older than Scorsese and his NYU classmates. Scorsese's decision to make a feature while still at film school undoubtedly reflected the sense of urgency that Bertolucci's precocious work triggered in ambitious young American filmmakers of the 1960s. Ironically, it was not what Bertolucci is conventionally noted for—the convergence of sexual and political passions—that so inspired the American sixties generation. Politically illiterate by comparison to Bertolucci, the young Americans paid far more attention to his visual style than to his Marxist ideology. Bertolucci's traveling shots, as lyrical as they are eccentric, were far more influential than the ideas that inspired them. It is "his feelings for the sensuous surfaces of life," then, that leads Pauline Kael to call Bertolucci a "born filmmaker." And it is no coincidence that Kael likens Scorsese's "operatic visual style" to Bertolucci's in a review of *Mean Streets* that is every bit as laudatory as her earlier review of *Before the Revolution*. She specifically compares the score of *Mean Streets*—"the background music of the characters' lives"—to the "motley score" of *Before the Revolution*.[22] But if there is a single moment in Scorsese's cinema that clinches his affinity with Bertolucci's sweepingly "operatic" mastery, it's the opening shot of *The Age of Innocence* (1993). Panning a nineteenth-century New York opera audience, Scorsese's mobile camera establishes the social definitions and distinctions that, as Kael says of Bertolucci's movies, "transport us imaginatively into other periods of history."[23]

To evoke the formative influence of the French and Italian New Waves is not to deny the impact of American films. When Andrew Sarris applied the auteur theory to American directors in the early 1960s it came as a revelation to Scorsese. Many of the films he had loved as a boy, but was taught at NYU to downplay, were thus "rehabilitated," including such favorites as the Westerns of John Ford and Howard Hawks. Few films haunt Scorsese's imagination more relentlessly than *The Searchers*. *Taxi Driver* is commonly read as an urban take on the Ford Western. And Scorsese has often cited Hawks's *Red River* (1948) and *Rio Bravo* (1959) among American films he most admires. What is so curious is not that he thinks so highly of Ford and Hawks but that such a quintessentially urban filmmaker as Scorsese should be drawn to Westerns in the first place. Maybe it is the centrality of macho loners, men who typically rage against real and/or imaginary enemies and even against themselves in Western narratives. After all, Scorsese's mobsters are really urban cowboys: they're like Western gunslingers, shooting up New York City instead of Dodge City. Still, the director who was Scorsese's closest mentor was no more Ford or Hawks than Truffaut or Bertolucci.

John Cassavetes was the filmmaker whose example, encouragement, and friendship most profoundly inspired Scorsese's early work. *Shadows,* Cassavetes' first feature, was *nouvelle vague* filmmaking American style. At the crest of the European influence, when Scorsese and his film school cohorts burned to make New Wave–ish movies, Cassavetes showed them how to do it. "Cassavetes had used a lightweight 16 mm camera for *Shadows* in 1959, so there were no more excuses. If he could do it, so could we!"[24] An uncompromisingly personal film shot in documentary fashion for a paltry forty thousand dollars, *Shadows* won the plaudits of film cognoscenti and the Critics Award at the Venice Film Festival. Cassavetes was an actor's director. He began as a popular television actor in the 1950s and later acted in movies—mostly to finance his own directing projects, à la Orson Welles. Cassavetes' films invariably focus on the dynamics of interpersonal relationships. Because his wife, Gena Rowlands, and his close friends, Peter Falk and Ben Gazzara, were typically his principal actors, Cassavetes' cinema of intimacy is burnished by their real life affection for one another. The quirky mix of narrative and documentary styles; the voyeuristic handheld camera; the ensemble acting; above all, the uncompromising commitment to a cinema of personal assertion were inherited from Cassavetes.

Even more serendipitous for Scorsese than the consciousness-raising *Shadows* was Cassavetes' interest in his career. Theirs was not the conventional mentor/protegé relationship: Scorsese needed filmmaking opportunities more than lessons. But Cassavetes was there when Scorsese needed him most. Between projects in 1971, Scorsese "begged John Cassavetes, who had become a friend, to give me some work. He put me on *Minnie and Moskowitz* as a sound editor at $500 a week for doing nothing! I even lived on his set for a week ."[25] A year later, Cassavetes, who had loved *Who's That Knocking at My Door?,* saw a rough cut of *Boxcar Bertha,* a violent exploitation film that Scorsese had just finished directing for schlockmeister Roger Corman, and hated it. "You just spent a year of your life making a piece of shit," Cassavetes told Scorsese, warning him "not to get hooked" on exploitation films and urging him to go back to making films like *Who's That Knocking?*[26] Thus chastised—and inspired—Scorsese dusted off an oft-rejected and long-shelved script called *Season of the Witch,* a putative sequel to *Who's That Knocking?,* and rewrote it. The result was *Mean Streets,* Scorsese's breakthrough movie.

A mentor of a different sort was Haig Manoogian, Scorsese's film teacher at NYU. They did not always agree on movies: Manoogian dismissed *The Third Man,* a film Scorsese loved, as "just a good thriller"; and the teacher never shared his pupil's enthusiasm for Hitchcock. After *Who's That Knocking at My Door?* was released, Manoogian read *Season of the Witch* and begged Scorsese not to make any "more pictures about Italians," a classically bad piece of advice that Scorsese wisely ignored. Without *Mean Streets,* to say nothing of *Raging Bull* and *GoodFellas,* Scorsese's oeuvre would be drastically impoverished. Yet it was Manoogian who instilled in his students his own passion for film. "Haig really inspired us: he had this almost religious zeal, so that if you had an idea, before you knew it you were out on the streets and in the middle of filming."[27] When students complained that they had no scripts to direct, Manoogian told them to write their own, a prescription Scorsese followed in his earliest screenplays. *Mean Streets,* which he cowrote with NYU buddy Mardik Martin, was the last script Scorsese put his name on until *GoodFellas* (1990). Not surprisingly, *GoodFellas,* like *Who's That Knocking?* and *Mean Streets,* treats the New York street world of the early 1960s that Scorsese grew up in. Every Scorsese film is a personal statement, but these three best reflect Manoogian's insistence that his students value their own experience. "Thanks Haig," reads the closing title of *Raging Bull.* Hard on the heels of a citation from John 9:24—26 about the man who "once was blind but now . . . can see," it is Scorsese's final tribute to the man who made *him* see, and who died just before the film's release.

Manoogian's help had not been confined to the classroom. "In 1969 I went back to NYU as an instructor —Haig gave me the job because I was broke," Scorsese admits.[28] Manoogian even became his first producer, raising the $37,000 that enabled Scorsese finally to complete *Who's That Knocking at My Door?* Without Manoogian's encouragement and faith— part of the $37,000 was his own savings—the film that jump-started Scorsese's career might never have been made. And it was Manoogian who talked Joseph Brenner, an old army buddy and sexploitation film distributor, into distributing *Who's That Knocking?* Because Scorsese was in Europe filming commercials at the time (1968), Manoogian even negotiated the nude scene that Brenner demanded and that finally got the movie released. From its earliest incarnation at NYU as *Bring on the Dancing Girls* (1965) to its premiere at the 1967 Chicago Film Festival to its commercial release as *Who's That Knocking at My Door?* (1969), Scorsese's first feature owed its life in good part to Professor Haig Manoogian.

2

....

Our Gang: From Elizabeth Street to Mean Streets

aig Manoogian's advice to make it personal did not so much reveal hidden truth as confirm Scorsese's basic instinct. Little Italy, the neighborhood where he grew up, provides the geography; the Catholic Church the morality; and the New Wave(s) the aesthetic for Scorsese's projected Italian-American trilogy: the aborted "Jerusalem, Jerusalem," *Who's That Knocking at My Door?*, and *Mean Streets*. The two that finally got made are, as Bernardo Bertolucci once said of his own films, "desperately autobiographical." They are coming-of-age movies whose protagonists are barely disguised stand-ins for Scorsese himself. In these early evocations of Italian-American life on the Lower East Side, what is chiefly remarkable is its insularity. Little Italy comprises no more than about ten blocks, of which three—Elizabeth Street, Mott Street, and Mulberry Street—are the most important. So sharply defined were the "boundaries" that people kept to their own block. Elizabeth Street, where Scorsese's parents were born and where he lived from 1950 to 1966, was mainly Sicilian. "Growing up down there was like being in a Sicilian village," Scorsese remembers.[1] Greenwich Village, a few streets away, was another world into which Scorsese never ventured until he enrolled at New York University in 1960. Not that the denizens of Little Italy burned to get out: their hearts and souls, like Scorsese's, were stuck there. Light years away from Elizabeth Street, ensconced in a posh seventy-fifth floor midtown apartment in the 1990s, Scorsese still insists on the formative role of the world he left behind: "The bonds that you made, the codes that were there, all have an influence on you later in life."[2] *GoodFellas* (1990) preserves undiluted that fidelity to the vanished world of his parents invoked in his earliest films.

Italianamerican (1974), Scorsese's forty-nine minute paean to his parents and their way of life, stresses the centrality of the family in Italian immigrant culture. Although it is hardly Scorsese's best film, as he periodically claims, *Italianamerican,* in depicting the nitty-gritty of family life, is a reminder that the Catholic Church and the Mafia were not the only power elites in Little Italy. The family, more than any other institution, wove the fabric of everyday life. What better than Mama's spaghetti sauce as the symbol of Italian family—and communal—culture? Catherine, Scorsese's mother, shuttles between the couch where she sits by her husband, Charles, and the kitchen where the sauce simmers throughout *Italianamerican.* And it's the recipe for that spaghetti sauce, appended to the movie's credits, that triggered a standing ovation when *Italianamerican* was shown at the 1974 New York Film Festival. Like any good documentary, *Italianamerican* captures the typical in limning the particular. Set in the Scorseses' Elizabeth Street apartment and shot in six hours around a couple of dinners, it's replete with cultural signifiers: plastic-covered living-room furniture; garish kitchen wallpaper; food-laden dining table (Scorsese's hand furtively enters the frame, reaching for tidbits of salad, as his parents talk); a half-emptied bottle of red wine. Catherine and Charles Scorsese, charmingly spontaneous after an awkward moment or two, talk movingly about life in Sicily where their parents came from and life in Little Italy on Elizabeth Street where they were born and where they still remain. His story about lighting Sabbath candles for the Jews who once shared the neighborhood; hers about long ago in Sicily when her father, dashing in blue uniform and white-plumed hat, and her mother, spying him from her balcony, fell in love at first sight and were married twenty-two days later, are the stuff tradition is made of. And Scorsese embellishes that tradition, fleshing it out with brief snippets of black-and-white archive footage of turn-of-the-century immigrants arriving and settling in New York. As his family's emotional history comes alive, Scorsese "discovers" Catherine and Charles: "I had seen them as parents, not as people. . . . Suddenly they became people. And I saw the story of their life as a love story."[3]

Italianamerican was made for "Storm of Strangers," a television series commissioned by the National Endowment for the Humanities for the 1976 American Bicentennial. Scorsese's "doing" the Italians conformed to the series design of treating a different ethnic immigrant group—Irish, Jews, Poles, and others—in each of its installments. In eschewing the usual stock footage and voice-over narration, however, he created a documentary that transcended its nominal purpose even as it fulfilled it. According to Scorsese, *Italianamerican* is not only his best film but the one that freed his style. Thus the subverting of conventional documentary form in *Italianamerican*—"rather than dissolving from one image to another so as to soften the cuts, to jump around until I was free of the form"—prefigures the radical stylistic freedom of *Raging Bull*.[4] More obviously, *Italianamerican* complements Scorsese's barely fictionalized "neighborhood" films such as *Who's That Knocking at My Door?* and *Mean Streets,* which similarly blend documentary and narrative conventions.

Being herself in *Italianamerican* was not Catherine Scorsese's debut in her son's films. A decade earlier she had played the mother of Murray, a small-time hood, in Scorsese's second student short, *It's Not Just You, Murray!* (1964). This fifteen-minute account of a comically inept Mafioso was Scorsese's first film incursion into the Little Italy of his childhood. Although Catherine never speaks a word, she is everywhere in the movie, silently bearing a plate of spaghetti to Murray in prison (she feeds him between cell bars), keeping vigil in the hospital. She thus personifies the family values more fully articulated in *Italianamerican*. Still, it is not so much family life—Murray endlessly refuses his mother's spaghetti—as street life that is anatomized in the film. And far from romanticizing street life, Scorsese satirizes it in the person of Murray whose succession of dim-witted capers makes gangsters more farcical than sinister. Shot in Scorsese's grandmother's and uncle's apartments and in cellars on the Lower East Side, *It's Not Just You, Murray!* is on one level a quasi-documentary account of Italian-American life in the sixties. Yet it is also a freewheeling spoof of Hollywood genres from Warner Brothers gangster films *(Roaring Twenties, Public Enemy)* to Paramount road pictures. The Murray–Joe partnership, apparently inspired by the Bob Hope–Bing Crosby friendship in *The Road to Zanzibar* (1941), is the prototype of the buddy combinations that constitute the primary relationships in many of Scorsese's later films. It is of some significance that the macho male bonding Scorsese is famous for originates in the zany melding of Hope and Crosby. A comic subtext often lurks beneath the scarifying surface of gangster films such as *Mean Streets* and *GoodFellas* where more sinister tough guys echo Murray's nonsequiturs and malapropisms.

It's Not Just You, Murray! is Murray's own account of forty-odd years of wheeling and dealing in the rackets culminating in the good life of fancy ties and fancier cars that he is now (1964) enjoying. But his narration unknowingly conceals what Scorsese's camera insistently reveals: Joe, whose lifelong friendship Murray extols, actually betrayed him at every turn, letting him take a rap that lands him in Sing Sing; sleeping with his wife; even fathering his children. It is conceivable that Murray catches on at last but chooses to "believe" Joe's various denials anyway. After all, the fast-talking Joe had always explained away his every double cross of the slow-witted Murray. And besides, Murray is "living good" and cannot see rocking the boat. So Murray's version adds up to a self-portrait of the mobster as buffoon; it figures that Scorsese got the name Murray from a Mel Brooks movie. Yet Murray is also a Sicilian nickname, and his escapades derive from Scorsese family stories of the kind retailed in *Italianamerican*. It's the seriocomic seasoning of Mel Brooks movies and Italian immigrant sagas, of gangster films and road pictures with a soupçon of Fellini, that gives *It's Not Just You, Murray!* its savor. And for a fifteen-minute student short, Murray's story remarkably previews vintage Scorsese material: the hood as hero; the neighborhood as locale; the "good life" as suspect. Even more remarkable— and equally prescient—may be its evocations, revisions, and subversions of film genres. Scorsese's encyclopedic film "vocabulary" is already on display along with his habit of "quoting" famous films for his own purposes. When the characters from Murray's life dance around his new white Cadillac, the transcendent symbol of his "achievement," to the accompaniment of circus music, their parody of the joyous dance around a circus ring at the end of *8½* spotlights the distance separating Scorsese's hero from Fellini's and constitutes the ultimate satire on the life and times of Murray. *It's Not Just You, Murray!* catapulted Scorsese to the promising young director ranks, winning the Jesse C. Lasky Intercollegiate Award for the best student film of 1964; playing the 1966 New York Film Festival; and even running commercially in a blown-up 35mm version.

If *It's Not Just You, Murray!* had done nothing but establish Scorsese's characteristic mise-en-scène, it would have been achievement enough for its twenty-two-year-old creator. "In fact," Scorsese would claim years later, "of all my films *Murray* is the one that shows the old neighborhood, the way it looked in the early sixties, right before it began to die out. . . . And the old, or the actual living neighborhood, is kind of gone now. In *Murray* and *Who's That Knocking?*, a dramatic version of *Murray,* there was an attempt to portray "just the way I was living."[5] This insistence on the way it was—equally explicit in Scorsese's tagging *Mean Streets* "an anthropological study"—implicitly blurs the conventional distinction between documentary and feature filmmaking. And Scorsese's handheld camera and rapid-fire oblique editing add to the documentary look of *Who's That Knocking?* and *Mean Streets.* Still, the intensity of these early films derives less from their setting and style than from Scorsese's identification with their protagonists: the guilt-ridden J.R. of *Who's That Knocking?* and the slightly older but similarly afflicted Charlie of *Mean Streets.*

Sometime in 1965, around the time *Who's That Knocking?* was gestating, Scorsese stopped going to Mass and made his last confession. "I've been confessing most of the time since then on film. . . . Still, I can't help being religious. I'm looking for the connection between God and man," he revealed as late as 1991.[6]

Scorsese's autobiographical soul-searching originates in "Jerusalem, Jerusalem." J.R., one of a group of eighteen-year-old Catholic boys on retreat, incarnates the young Scorsese's moral sensitivity and sexual guilt. Only with the greatest difficulty does he manage to confess his most grievous sin—masturbation—and then only by euphemistically labeling it "self-impurities." That most of "Jerusalem, Jerusalem" is taken up by the boys' recitation of the Stations of the Cross and Father McMahon's fire-and-brimstone sermon on Marriage and Sex testifies to Scorsese's obsessions. Graphic accounts of Christ's excruciating suffering on the Cross are rapidly crosscut with J.R.'s vision of blood spurting from a young man's spike-punctured wrists and Father McMahon's parable about a young boy and girl who, unable to wait for marriage, "burned to death in each other's arms" in an auto accident. The staying power of these episodes in J.R.'s imagination manifests itself in the climb up a hill to view the surrounding countryside in *Who's That Knocking?,* an abbreviated replay, minus the religious trappings, of the tortuous hillside progress through the Stations of the Cross in "Jerusalem, Jerusalem." And in one of *Mean Streets's* crucial scenes, Charlie is taunted by his buddies for (still) believing a retreat parable identical to Father McMahon's about the fiery wages of premarital sex. At the end of "Jerusalem, Jerusalem," J.R. is back home from the retreat and lying in bed when suddenly his room is bathed in light, and "glorious and beautiful" music bursts forth, followed by a closing title: "For the greater glory of God." Although the joyous ending of "Jerusalem, Jerusalem" belies most of what preceded it, there is no whiff of irony in its Jesuit dedication. Apparently a sincere celebration of J.R's spiritual struggles, the ending suppresses "Jerusalem, Jerusalem"'s many religious downers: it is Scorsese's *Ode to Joy.*

In 1981, fifteen years after he had finished writing "Jerusalem, Jerusalem," Scorsese was still so haunted by its narrative that he spoke of making it for television. That it never got made is probably just as well. The too-good-to-be-true sweetness and light resolution of J.R.'s spiritual crisis may have been a hard sell in the late sixties, much less in the early eighties. Basing a spiritual crisis on masturbatory guilt edges the crisis—and its resolution—toward banality. When J.R.'s sexual hang-ups finally reach the screen in *Who's That Knocking at My Door?*, at least they are related to fornication, not masturbation. No longer the teenage student of "Jerusalem, Jerusalem," J.R. (Harvey Keitel in his first movie role) is several years older but no less guilt-ridden: he refuses to have sex with his obviously willing girlfriend and later walks out on her when he learns she is not a virgin. Scorsese now calls the sexual conflict of this film *medieval*, marveling that he made a movie about sexual repression in the age of sexual revolution. Still more remarkable was his compulsion to make it in the first place. "Yeah, but that was my way of life," he explains, as though he *had* to get his life on film no matter what.[7] The raw power and visceral excitement of *Who's That Knocking?* and *Mean Streets* stem from their nakedly autobiographical urgency: Martin Scorsese *is* J.R. and Charlie.

Who's That Knocking at My Door? is shot in black-and-white film stock that reflects the film's documentary exactitude and its hero's either/or morality. For J.R., women are Madonnas or whores. Ideal womanhood, predictably incarnated in the Italian–American wife and mother, is established in the opening scene: Catherine Scorsese serves her homemade bread to a group of young children gathered around her kitchen table. Close-ups of a votive candle and a statue of the Virgin Mary seal the identification of the ideal woman with motherhood, nurturing, and the Catholic Church. Throughout the scene, the Virgin Mary's symbolic presence is intensified by repeated and extreme close-ups of the presiding statue. Catholic iconography multiplies in a bedroom scene in which J.R. and his new girlfriend kiss before a statue of the Madonna and Child, a cross hanging over the bed. There's a tenderness—and a sensuousness—in their initial embrace that is seldom, if ever, matched in Scorsese's subsequent films. But J.R.'s fitful lovemaking—punctuated and explained by crosscuts between the lovers on the bed and the statue of the Virgin on the bureau—ends not in consummation but in frustration. Technically, it's not the roomful of religious artifacts that unmans him: "Call it anything you want—old fashioned, or what. . . . If you love me you'll know what I mean," he tells the incredulous girl. What he means, however, is rooted in the Catholic doctrine that his mother's religious artifacts emblazon. A woman is either a saint or a sinner: "A broad isn't exactly a virgin. You play around with a broad. You don't marry a broad."

The early strategy of the movie is to idealize the boy–girl relationship. That she's referred to simply as "the girl" spotlights her generic status as the first of Scorsese's blond dream girls. Zina Bethune (the girl) radiates purity in her shy smiles and demure glances. And her halo of blond hair, accentuated in black-and-white and invariably backlighted, enhances her Madonnalike ethereality. She's a virginal temptress, a grownup edition of the little girls who so excited Scorsese in grade school that he was always

> wondering what was underneath [their] uniforms. Those uniforms became very striking to me, so that later in *Who's That Knocking?* and in *Taxi Driver* I had them wear what look like parochial school uniforms. A blazer and a pleated, Scotch plaid type skirt–Cybill Shepherd wears that in *Taxi* as a kind of joke.[8]

But Cybill Shepherd's "look" is far more knowing than Zina Bethune's. Shepherd is a wolf in sheep's clothing, her ripe sexuality displayed rather than dampened by her demure outfit. There's no such "joke" in *Who's That Knocking?* Bethune's appearance is unmediated by the irony that hedges Shepherd's, perhaps because in *Who's That Knocking?* Scorsese, as his cinematic alter ego J.R. reveals, was still too uptight to joke about his sexual obsessions. If Bethune's little-girl clothes *did not* reflect the essential innocence of parochial school uniforms, J.R. would probably have run for cover. That's pretty much what he does when he concludes that her innocence has been fatally compromised by her rape.

It is the girl herself who tells J.R. about the rape, but it is his conceptualization of her story that appears in flashback on the screen. So violently is the sequence filmed that Scorsese's lunging camera seems implicated in the rape if not the actual rapist. Its repeated enactment on the screen reflects J.R.'s compulsive replaying of the scene in his mind. Slow motion, stills, and a pulsating sound track amplify his fixation. His turning a brutal sexual assault into a lurid sexual fantasy that brands the girl a "broad" relieves him from loving her. J.R.'s "I can't understand it. . . . How can I believe you?" casts more doubt on his own adolescent view of women than on her veracity. Of course, there is no reason to believe the girl is lying; but even if she is, it is not her story but its effect on J.R. that is paramount. On the one hand, his disbelief embodies the same fear of mature sexuality shown earlier in his refusal to make love to a "nice girl." On the other hand, it's logically absurd: if you "play around" only with a "broad" and a broad is what she is now, why not play around with her instead of causing her to leave? In any event, a contrite J.R. later shows up at the girl's apartment at 6:30 in the morning, confessing that he misses her and raising the possibility that at least he perceives the folly of stereotyping women. "You know I love you," he tells her after hefting her copy of *Tender Is the Night* in what looks like a not-so-subtle visual signal that love is here to stay. Alas, it is not to be. J.R. is as obtuse as ever, and his subsequent offer of marriage is as insulting as his previous reaction to her rape: "I understand now and I forgive you. . . . I'm gonna marry you anyway." When the girl replies, "No it's not enough, it's not good enough," J. R. reverts to type: "Who else is gonna marry you, you whore?" He even accuses her of leading him on by letting him in "at this hour of the morning . . . what kind of broad does that make you?" Throughout the episode J.R. casts the girl as a fallen woman in need of forgiveness: she is Mary Magdalen to his Jesus Christ. Finally, she has had enough: "go home, go home," she tells him.

But J.R.'s headlong charge down nine flights of stairs ends not at home but in church, the fount of his sexual inhibitions. It is St. Patrick's Old Church where as a child Scorsese sought the acceptance he could not find in the streets. Now J.R., Scorsese's alter ego, seeks similar solace, first in the confessional, then prostrate before a statue of the crucified Christ. Extreme close-ups of the pierced side of Jesus and the stigmata of saints underscore J.R.'s identification with Jesus in particular and with the martyred in general. "Who's that knocking at my door, all last night and the night before? Bang, Bang, Bang, I can't stand this awful pain. Who's that calling my name?" blares the sound track, echoing J.R.'s mental equation of Jesus' agonies with his own in a grotesque parody of the crucified Christ calling out to God the Father. As he twice kisses the nail-punctured feet, J.R.'s mouth fills with blood, a bit of cinematic overkill that nonetheless pinpoints the pathology of his sexual hang-ups.

All during the climactic church sequence, Scorsese cuts rapidly back and forth between religions icons and sexual encounters. One of the sex flashbacks is J.R.'s compulsive re-creation of the girl's rape story; the other is the infamous nude scene demanded by the film's distributor and inserted into *Who's That Knocking?* after the film's apparent completion.

Variously derided as incongruous and/or intrusive and obviously irrelevant to the film's original design, the nude scene works surprisingly well. Whether J.R. has lived the scene or merely dreamed it is not important. What is important is how it dramatizes his muddled sexual ideology. The nude women he cavorts with are clearly "broads," not nice girls. Yet the sequence's climactic shot of a fully clothed J.R. showering a deck of cards on a naked girl in bed—an ejaculation but not a sexual one— implies that "playing around" with "broads" is no less frustrating than cooling it with "nice girls." Even if J.R.'s card flinging is a gesture of contempt rather than a sign of impotence, sex with broads is not notably satisfying. Moreover, the scene's evocative positioning belies its arbitrary conception. Scorsese sandwiches it initially between two episodes that elicit J.R.'s familiar distinction between *nice girls* and *broads.* The first follows J.R. and the girl out of a theater where they have just seen *Rio Bravo* and *Scaramouche,* an action double feature whose swashbuckling heroes embody the macho ethic so dear to J.R.'s heart. No sooner does J.R. call a female character a broad than Scorsese cuts away to the nude scene with its *broads* on parade. Then it's back to J.R. and the girl for his self-righteous conclusion: "You don't marry broads."

The theater marquee that advertises *Rio Bravo* and *Scaramouche* as it frames the exiting couple suggests J.R.'s outlook even before he speaks. It is not the first time that movies define character in *Who's That Knocking?* Immediately before the theater sequence and immediately after the unconsummated lovemaking bout, J.R. parties with a group of like-minded male friends. Visibly relaxed with the boys, J.R. shows none of the tension he felt with the girl. What passes for fun consists mainly of brandishing, examining, and pointing a gun. The party's biggest laugh comes when one of the gang grabs another around the neck and, in an agonizingly protracted slow motion sequence, jams the gun against his head in mock threat. When the gun finally goes off, it is only whiskey bottles that shatter in emulation of a similar episode in *Rio Bravo,* which Scorsese invokes with a quick cut to a mock-up of a gun-toting John Wayne, and a montage of stills from the movie. J.R.'s identification with Wayne, and implicitly with the uncompromising morality that Wayne incarnates, is signaled initially in J.R.'s first meeting with the girl. She is reading a copy of *Paris Match* opened to a photo of John Wayne in *The Searchers*. Staged on the Staten Island ferry, the ensuing boy-meets-girl sequence begins when she catches J.R. staring at the photo, and they start talking about *The Searchers*. At first the girl cannot recall anything about the movie. Then she recalls it but hesitates to admit that she cares for Westerns until, coaxed by J.R., she finally agrees with his contention that everybody should like them. "Ever seen *[The Man Who Shot] Liberty Valance?*" he asks her, invoking another classic John Ford Western, which, like *The Searchers,* stars John Wayne.

It is only in retrospect that the apparently harmless movie chatter on the Staten Island ferry reveals its potentially harmful subtext: the polarized view of women embodied in John Wayne and embedded in J.R. Perhaps the girl's initial reservations about westerns reflected an instinctive suspicion of a genre that valorizes macho heroics. (J.R. even gushes over the crudely aggressive title character played by Lee Marvin in *The Man Who Shot Liberty Valance.)* In *The Searchers,* John Wayne's Ethan Edwards is an embittered ex-Confederate soldier whose niece Debbie (Natalie Wood) has been kidnapped by the Indian chief Scar. Edwards's obsessive search for her is complicated by his fear that she has been sexually contaminated as Scar's squaw—a fate worse than death for a white woman. Although Scorsese will quote John Ford more fully in *Taxi Driver,* the sexual geometry of *The Searchers* is equally relevant to *Who's That Knocking?* Debbie's lost innocence threatens to become a greater issue than her whereabouts. It is not so much whether Edwards will find Debbie as whether he will kill her when he does that becomes the burning issue of *The Searchers.* Of course, it is J.R.'s comparable obsession with the girl's "corruption" that destroys their relationship. Never mind that her debasement is no more voluntary than Debbie's: that she's no longer a virgin condemns her. J.R.'s refusal to accept her account of the rape comes across as nothing more than a smarmy attempt to blame the girl for his own sexual insecurity.

J.R. is most secure with the boys. Just after the Staten Island ferry sequence plants the macho ethic via *The Searchers* and *The Man Who Shot Liberty Valance,* its implications are enacted in an otherwise throwaway scene. One of J.R.'s buddies, Charlie, steals forty dollars from a girl he is making love to; he then generously hands the unsuspecting victim five dollars for cab fare. It is the sort of casual degradation of women that is taken for granted in J.R.'s circle. Then there is the party scene where gunplay with the boys replaces foreplay with the girl, and where the *Rio Bravo* flybys forecast the distinction between "girls" and "broads" that J.R. reveals outside the movie theater. Another minor but revealing episode with the boys takes place between the theater and rape-story scenes with the girl. J.R. and his buddy Joey accompany an unnamed young man to upstate Copake where they head immediately for the nearest bar. They're doing what they habitually do in Manhattan: killing time in a bar as a recurrent example of their kind of male bonding. But the third man wants to show J.R. and Joey "something beautiful" ("OK, what's her name?" Joey predictably exclaims)—the view from atop a nearby hill. A comically arduous climb culminates with J.R. and Joey huffing and puffing their way to the summit well behind their fitter companion. For Joey, the landscape spread before them is no big deal. But J.R.'s rapt gaze from on high recalls "the beauty of the view from the top of the hill" in *"Jerusalem, Jerusalem"* after he and Bud and Mikey—another trio of climbers—had completed the Stations of the Cross. Flanked in *Who's That Knocking?* by scenes between J.R. and the girls, the climbing episode recapitulates the male camaraderie that overshadows the heterosexual relationship. Yet its primary function may be to indict the church as the source of J.R.'s sexual hang-ups. And it is to the church that J.R. flees for solace after the climactic scene of their breakup in the girl's apartment. From the ensuing montage sequence filmed in the church—arguably the most powerful moments in *Who's That Knocking?*—Scorsese flashes back to the nurturing mother before closing with a shot of J.R. and Joey parting on a shadowy street. According to Michael Bliss, "these male characters are condemned to pass into the darkness of ignorance, isolation, and death," victims of "the Catholic-corrupted, Catholic-appropriated Jesus, the God of pain and destruction. . . ."[9] Perhaps. But Bliss's (over)heated interpretation ignores the crucial epigraph to "Jerusalem, Jerusalem" that defines Scorsese's God: "God is not a torturer. . . . He only wants us to be merciful with ourselves." If the Jesus of *Who's That Knocking?* is Bliss's "God of morbidity," He is the creation of J.R., the product of J.R.'s failure to be merciful with himself. Still, the conflation of maleness with church and home in the closing images of the film, offers scant hope of J.R.'s sexual maturation. "I'll see you tomorrow," J.R. and Joey reassure one another: the adolescent drama of male bonding and female stereotyping has yet to run its course.

To read impending desolation and death into *Who's That Knocking at My Door?* risks equating adolescent confusion with adult trauma. Although Catholic imagery and ritual saturate the film, the church functions as little more than sexual arbiter. Catholicism may have warped J.R.'s attitude toward women, but his condition is neither fatal nor necessarily incurable. That is not to trivialize J.R.'s burden of sin and guilt, simply to keep it in perspective. It is not J.R. but Charlie, his successor as

Scorsese's alter ego, who in *Mean Streets* (1973) must face up to the tragic fallout from a Catholic morality that pits his spiritual yearnings against his worldly ambitions. J.R.'s beeline from the girl's apartment to the church—for refuge?, for solace?, for absolution?—shows his inability to find, or even to seek, any but a religious solution. In *Mean Streets,* the Catholic solution is explicitly rejected in an opening soliloquy that Charlie apparently directs to God: "You do not make up for your sins in Church, you do it in the streets." It is an existential manifesto. I'll do penance, but I'll do it my way. And Charlie's sins—he is a small-time collector for his Mafia uncle's loan shark operation—are potentially graver than those of J.R., a between-jobs former bank teller whose transgressions were as often imagined as real. For Charlie (Harvey Keitel again), a would-be saint whose aspirations to spiritual purity clash incongruously with his desire for Mafia advancement, the stakes are higher than they were for the younger and simpler J.R.

Charlie's belief that penance comes from actions in the street and not from prayers in church invokes the age-old dilemma of how to live a moral life in an immoral world. And the fallen world, so often hazily metaphorical, is grittily palpable in the lurid nightscape of *Mean Streets.* Fitfully illuminated by the red of neon signs and gaudy nightclub interiors, Scorsese's latter-day inferno is a nightmare world of smoky rooms and shadowy streets. Although the mob rules by night, its domain is subterranean and claustrophobic. Charlie and his friends may swagger through Little Italy's mean streets, but they are trapped in them as well. To make it in criminal society, Charlie must cozy up to his Mafia boss uncle (Cesare Danova) even as he fears divine retribution for doing so. To placate a watchful God, he periodically holds his hand to the flame, symbolically invoking hellfire and damnation. But despite his soul-searching protestations, Charlie is wed to the mob. When Teresa (Amy Robinson), the girl he is involved with, dreams of moving uptown and begs him to join her, Charlie stalls by claiming that he has "got something going in the neighborhood." What he has got is Uncle Giovanni's implicit promise of a failing restaurant whose aging proprietor cannot keep up his protection payments to the syndicate. A product of his constricted society, Charlie seems to fear the loss of his uncle's favor more than the wrath of God. Charlie's version of doing penance in the streets is to reassure God of his good intentions without renouncing his self-serving actions. Scorsese explicitly rejects the conclusion that Charlie's professed sincerity distances him from his fellow mobsters: "No, in *Mean*

Streets we're all rotten, we're all no good in a sense, but we're still people, we're still human beings. And the lead character, being me, has to grapple with a sense of guilt because of this, because it isn't the way it is said in church."[10] This curious disclaimer suggests that Charlie wants not so much to mend his sinful life as to cauterize his guilty conscience.

Charlie's ambivalence infects his two closest relationships. With the epileptic Teresa, he reverts consciously or unconsciously to J.R.'s bifurcated view of women. When she asks him why he never says he loves her, Charlie replies, "Because you're a cunt." When the shocked and angry girl retreats from the bed where they have just made love, he hastily assures her that he was only joking. Still, it appears that for Charlie a woman who is not a virgin is a whore. Later, after refusing to move uptown with Teresa, he tells her that he cannot see her for a while: Giovanni has told him to stay away from her, and Charlie will not risk his uncle's anger for Teresa's love. "Just let me get the restaurant first," he tells her. Charlie realizes that getting the key to the restaurant compromises his getting the key to heaven. And there is always a convenient flame—a votive candle in the church, a stove burner in the restaurant—to plunge his fingers into as a reminder of the fires of hell. Scorsese even reprises the retreat priest's homily about the unmarried couple who died in a fiery car crash while making love. Recalling his own retreat when another priest told the same story two years before Charlie heard it, Tony concludes that the church is no different from any other "organization." "Why do you let those guys get to you?" he asks Charlie. "You gotta be more like me." But Charlie accepted the story in the belief that priests are not "guys"; only priests offer the means of salvation, and "I want to be saved."

Questions of salvation or damnation likewise animate the second of Charlie's close relationships, that with Teresa's cousin Johnny Boy (Robert De Niro). The cousins are routinely lumped together by Uncle Giovanni who advises Charlie to stay away from both of them. Again Charlie must choose between conflicting loyalties. Johnny Boy owes more money than he can ever repay to Michael (Richard Romanus), a neighborhood loan shark whose threats of violence escalate with Johnny's every evasion. Johnny Boy is convinced that only Charlie's uncle can bail him out and pesters Charlie to intercede. But Charlie is no more willing to risk the restaurant for Johnny than for Teresa. Although it is easy to read his rejection of the cousins as a simple choice between their welfare and Giovanni's patronage, the issue is more complicated than that. Charlie never actually abandons either of the cousins: Johnny Boy and Teresa are with him in the harrowing car crash that concludes *Mean Streets*.

What Charlie wants is to get along with everybody: he is always the peacemaker, stepping between angry punks in vain attempts to head off the brawls that regularly erupt wherever the gang gathers. Moments before a fight breaks out in Fat Joey's poolroom, he calls Charlie "St. Charles"; and a scene in Tony's bar begins with Charlie playing the priest and offering benedictions to a couple of his buddies. During the same beach scene in which he rejects Teresa's plea to move uptown with her, Charlie lists sand and sea among his dislikes. Asked what he does like, he laughingly cites spaghetti and movies and, more seriously, St. Francis of Assisi. The ambitious, calculating, and materialistic Charlie reveres the saint whose life so profoundly contradicts his own.

To admit the sincerity of Charlie's religious gestures—from invoking the saints and mortifying the flesh to yearning for redemption and confessing his sins—is not to deny his self-serving motives. His voice-overs regularly inform God of his good intentions that his subsequent actions negate: he is negotiating with God, not serving Him. Charlie mollifies God and Mammon (Giovanni) alike, hoping to dodge the wrath of both. Giovanni instructs his nephew in the art of calculation whenever they get together. Loyalty to himself excepted, Giovanni counsels a strategy of noncommitment that values playing it safe. Ever the compromiser, Charlie accepts his uncle's advice while surreptitiously circumventing it. Ordered by Giovanni to keep an eye on Teresa without becoming involved with her, Charlie responds not by ending the relationship but by concealing it. But in the macho environs of *Mean Streets,* where heterosexual love invariably takes a back seat to male camaraderie, the key relationship is the friendship between Charlie and Johnny Boy. Whether Charlie is drawn to Johnny because of Teresa or vice versa, the macho imperative is dominant. Faced with the choice of remaining with Teresa when she is having an epileptic seizure or chasing after Johnny Boy to make certain he meets with Michael as promised, Charlie abandons her to the ministrations of a neighbor woman (Catherine Scorsese). It is not that the friendship with Johnny is safer than the affair with Teresa: for Uncle Giovanni, whose belief that Teresa is "sick in the head" applies equally to Johnny, they are both off-limits to Charlie. Given his uncle's opposition to the cousins and his own reluctance to jeopardize his prospects, it is a wonder that Charlie sticks with Teresa and especially with the increasingly volatile Johnny Boy.

When he suffers with Teresa and Johnny Boy in the bloody denouement of *Mean Streets,* it is Charlie's way of "making up for your sins . . . in the street." Arising from the depths of Charlie's psyche, this theory of doing penance is pronounced in voice-over while the screen is still dark before the film begins. Charlie gets out of bed, passes in front of a cross displayed prominently on the wall, and stares into a mirror as though to plumb the depths of his soul. Soon he is in church, contemplating a pietà as he holds his fingers to the flaming candles in the first of many evocations of hellfire. It's Charlie's way of buttonholing God, of opening negotiations on redemption. What he tells God expands the implications of the opening voice-over and establishes the rationale for many of Charlie's otherwise implausible actions. "If I do something wrong, I just want to pay for it my way. So I want to do my own penance for my own sins. What do you say?" A preview of what "my way" will involve occurred in the preceding scene when Johnny Boy entered the film by gratuitously blowing up a mailbox. The blasted mailbox symptomizes the recklessness that leads Johnny Boy into starting barroom brawls and, more dangerously, into welshing on his debts. Befriending Johnny Boy is a formula for self-sacrifice that to a lesser degree also applies to loving Teresa, a neighborhood outcast by virtue of her epilepsy as Johnny is by virtue of his wildness. Thus Charlie's dream of sexual climax with Teresa ("I came blood") and his crucifixion posture on the bed where they make love represent more than Scorsese's familiar conflation of sex and death: they are tokens of self-sacrifice as well.

Teresa may inspire the odd self-sacrifice, but Johnny Boy is the cross Charlie must bear. Sporting a porkpie hat and checking his pants at the door, Johnny swaggers into Tony's bar between two girls he picked up in the Village. It is an absurd entrance shot in slow motion to the accompaniment of another of Charlie's interior monologues addressed to God: "Thanks a lot, Lord, thanks for opening my eyes. We talk about penance and you send this through the door. Well, we play by your rules, don't we?" Of course Charlie's credibility requires Johnny's imbecility: the greater Johnny's faults, the greater Charlie's sacrifice. What is credible in a would-be Catholic saint, however, is suspect in a would-be Mafia bigshot. By allying himself with losers, Charlie risks the disfavor of Uncle Giovanni, the arbiter of mob ethos, who values normative behavior above all else. Because it is in the various transactions (particularly financial ones) between mobsters that fidelity to the norm is largely demonstrated, Johnny Boy's confession that he owes not only Michael but practically everyone else advertises his deviance and compromises Charlie's reputation. For Charlie, who has vouched for Johnny, debts are obligations to be discharged; for Johnny, debts are nuisances to be finessed. Fleecing outsiders is all right—Tony and Michael dupe a couple of Riverdale kids out of twenty dollars shortly after the barroom scene—but welshing on buddies is anathema.

A cavalier attitude toward borrowing money is only one symptom of Johnny Boy's flakiness. His senseless acts of violence flout the code of moderation implicit in Giovanni's patience with the restaurant owner who misses a payment. Violence is a last resort not a willful indulgence. Moreover, Johnny's brand of violence calls attention to itself: it is the sort of self-display that the careful mobster avoids. Blowing up mailboxes and shooting at the lights of the Empire State Building epitomize Johnny's recklessness, but what gets him into real trouble is his big mouth. After a typically pointless brawl in Fat Joey's poolroom winds down, Johnny Boy calls Joey a "scumbag" and violence flares up again. Talking too much proves costlier later when Johnny goes out of his way to insult Michael in front of the gang at Tony's bar. Arriving hours late for his meeting with Michael, Johnny Boy buys drinks with twenty of the thirty dollars Charlie gave him to placate the loan shark. Johnny then caps his insulting offer of the remaining ten dollars by telling Michael that he is the single creditor stupid enough to keep lending him money. "You're a fuckin' jerk-off," he shouts at Michael (who had called Johnny Boy a jerk-off in an earlier barroom confrontation), and when Michael goes for him, Johnny pulls a gun and taunts him again. Although the gun is empty, Johnny Boy could hardly have done more to provoke the homicidal vengeance that Michael attempts at the end of *Mean Streets*.

It is Johnny Boy's manic pas de deux with Michael that finally forces Charlie's hand. So far Charlie has managed to steer a politic course between Giovanni's expectations and Johnny's demands. "Everybody loves Charlie, a fuckin' politician," sneers Johnny when Charlie prods him to meet Michael. And after the damage is done and Michael exits the bar vowing revenge, Johnny tells Charlie, "You got what you wanted." As Johnny Boy sees it, what Charlie wanted was just such an excuse to wash his hands of him. But he has not reckoned with Charlie's guilt-ridden conscience and tortured religiosity. There is more than a whiff of deliberate sacrifice in Charlie's borrowing Tony's car and driving out of town with Johnny and Teresa in tow. Even as he heads for Greenwood Lake, a destination whose ironically idyllic name suggests its unattainability,

Charlie must know that mob "justice" is inescapable. No sooner do they cross over the bridge to Brooklyn than a car driven by Michael overtakes them, and a gunman fires a salvo of shots, wounding Johnny Boy's neck and Charlie's hand. Charlie's car skids out of control, demolishing a hydrant and jetting water skyward. Miraculously, nobody is killed: Johnny Boy weaves down the street clutching his neck; Teresa slumps in the car, a hand protruding from the shattered windshield; and Charlie sinks to his knees, the posture of prayer reinforced by his wounded hand raised in apparent supplication.

The violent climax is as ambivalent as it is inevitable. Inevitable because the mob ethos and hermetic environment of *Mean Streets* permit no escape. Even the specific wounds are foreshadowed in Charlie's many hand-to-neck gestures, not to mention his habit of holding his hand to the flames. And Uncle Giovanni, avatar of the gangster code that triggers the shooting, watches a television film of an injured woman being rescued from a car wreck, a preview of Teresa's being led away from Charlie's smashed car. Several times Giovanni had warned Charlie not to get involved with Johnny Boy, and Michael had once threatened to "break his [Johnny's] legs." As in *Who's That Knocking at My Door?*, there are several instances of pointing a finger as a gun. Such mock gunplay resembles Johnny Boy's shooting at the lights of the Empire State Building and waving an unloaded gun at Michael: apparently harmless macho displays, they prefigure the murderous gunfire of Michael's hit man. The sense of foreboding is intensified by Scorsese's manipulation of film noir standbys such as rain-slicked streets and shadowy alleys.

What separates *Mean Streets* from the typical noir imitation goes beyond Scorsese's technical mastery of a form that most directors can only feebly copy. It's the (omni)presence of religion, a key element of Scorsese's cinematic "signature," that singularly sets the film apart. Catholicism powerfully affects Charlie's moral conflict and intensifies the film's atmosphere of looming destiny. Religion haunts Charlie—in the church icons, in the rooftop statue of Christ presiding over the neighborhood, in the ubiquitous Festival of San Gennaro, and most intimately in his fervid apostrophes to God. According to Scorsese, it is the failure to reconcile religious ideality with manifest reality that undoes Charlie:

> See, the whole idea was to make a story of a modern saint, a saint in his own society, but his society happens to be gangsters. . . . Somebody does something wrong, you've got to break his head or

shoot him. It's as simple as that. Charlie became a character who refused to acknowledge that and eventually did the worst thing he could do, which was to put everything off, put all the confrontations off, until everything explodes. It's a whole guilt thing. No matter where he goes, he's lost."[11]

Granted the inevitability of Charlie's fate, its meaning remains ambivalent. If the "worst thing" he does is "to put everything off," he is more sucker than sinner. But Scorsese lays a graver sin than procrastination on his alter ego: "Charlie uses other people, thinking that he's helping them; but by believing that, he's not only ruining them but ruining himself . . . it's a matter of his own pride—the first sin in the Bible."[12] And Pauline Kael, in her rave review of *Mean Streets,* called Charlie "Judas the betrayer," who "talks a lot to Johnny Boy about friendship and does nothing." For Kael, "Johnny Boy is the only one of the group of grifters and scummy racketeers who is his own man; he is the true hero, while Charlie . . . is the director's worst vision of himself."[13] So Charlie, the man who would be St. Francis, turns out to be Judas; and Johnny Boy, the loose cannon, turns out to be "a saintly idiot . . . with his own inarticulate desire to be a free spirit."[14] But valorizing Johnny Boy exalts freedom—however demented and anarchic—for its own sake. And besides, *Mean Streets* is not about Johnny's rage to be free; it is about Charlie's wish to be saved.

Charlie is no St. Francis; but he is no Judas either. "Sold who out?" Scorsese replied to a query about the ending of *Mean Streets.* "Charlie sold them out? No, he never did that. Charlie just waited too long so that everything blows up in his face."[15] If he cannot save himself or his friends, it is not from lack of trying. Whatever else can be said about Charlie's nightmare drive and its violent culmination, it is no betrayal of Johnny Boy and Teresa. On the contrary, it is Charlie's most dramatic effort to shoulder Christ's burden, a bid for sainthood no matter how misguided: "I guess you could say things aren't going so well tonight, but I'm trying, Lord, I'm trying." Like a previous Charlie voice-over—"You don't fuck around with the Infinite"—this one affirms that God is running the show. The climactic car crash manifests not God's terrible wrath but His infinite mercy. Scorsese's lesson is one of hope, not despair: "In his vision Charlie's wound, a shot in the hand, is his 'stigmata,' Johnny Boy's neck wound is not fatal, and Teresa survives—for, as Scorsese envisions the narrative, 'they all learn something at the end of *Mean Streets,* only they have to get it from, again, the hand of God.' "[16]

But it is the hand of Martin Scorsese, playing Michael's hired assassin, that administers God's judgment in a hail of bullets. Although Michael is out to get Johnny Boy, the gunman seems to regard anyone in Charlie's car as fair game. Yet the theory that Scorsese "casts himself as the assassin coming to fulfill God's will and destroy his alter ego, Charlie," is too pat.[17] Wounding Charlie superficially, Scorsese confers upon him(self) the punishment he craves without the destruction he fears. What finally counts in *Mean Streets* is the process, not the payoff. When Charlie staggers away from the car crash, he's still struggling, neither damned nor saved, but surely reprieved. All along, he has been trying to fashion an identity with which he can live. A sharper version of J.R., Charlie senses alternatives that never occurred to his predecessor. *Who's That Knocking at My Door?* ends with a whimper, *Mean Streets* with a bang: J.R. is essentially unchanged, but Charlie "learns something," insists Scorsese, "a kind of enlightenment of some sort."[18] What's in store for an enlightened Charlie is anybody's guess, though Scorsese once alluded to "a blueprint for the third part of *Mean Streets,* which is going to be about Charlie when he gets married, settles down, has a couple of kids and lives on Staten Island."[19] The sequel never got made, but its "blueprint" subverts any doomsday reading of *Mean Streets:* "It was like an allegory for what was happening to me trying to make movies. . . . The picture was for me. . . . I drew from personal experiences about a guy trying to make it."[20] A guy trying to make it: that is mainly what the cinema of Martin Scorsese is all about.

The Way West:
Making It in Hollywood

Mean Streets is an early watershed in the cinema of Martin Scorsese, a film that threatens to exhaust the very subject(s) it apotheosizes. Whipsawed by conflicting claims of church and street, Charlie/Scorsese struggles to "lead a good life . . . when everything around you . . . just doesn't work that way . . . that's the main theme of the picture, since I'd thought that would probably be my only film—I thought I'd be going off to direct other films, nonpersonal films for other people, and that Mean Streets would never be released. That was the one I poured it all into in terms of this religious concept." Shifting penance from the church to the street—the "religious concept" of Mean Streets—decisively secularizes the struggle for salvation. "In the Street could mean Hollywood," Scorsese once reminded an interviewer.[1] After its secular resolution, the church/street conflict that inspired Who's That Knocking at My Door? and Mean Streets becomes a dead letter. Not that moral issues and their attendant religious symbolism disappear from Scorsese's movies. But the institutional presence of the Catholic Church as source and arbiter of morality does. And as the church recedes, so does God: not until The Last Temptation of Christ (1988), and only then, will He reprise his star turn of Mean Streets.

Even as Scorsese fought to exorcise his personal demons in Who's That Knocking . . .? and Mean Streets, he was burning his autobiography behind him. With the release of Mean Streets in 1973, he had pushed self-scrutiny as incarnated in the coming-of-age movie about as far as it could go. Moreover, despite its critical acclaim, Mean Streets appealed to a limited and mostly urban audience, the sort of audience that had responded to the films of Scorsese idols Michael Powell and John Cassavetes. As much as he revered the two iconoclastic directors, Scorsese yearned for the mainstream success that they never achieved. The long gestation of *Who's That Knocking . . . ?* and the lean years of scrambling for any film work he could get in the late sixties and early seventies probably dampened Scorsese's enthusiasm for life in the slow lane. A lifelong outsider by his own admission, he was afraid that few filmmaking chances would come his way. As late as 1991, his reputation both enviable and secure, Scorsese confessed to being "nervous" on the eve of shooting *Cape Fear:* "It's a matter of becoming complacent about the ability to make films."[2] *Mean Streets* multiplied its thirty-year-old director's filmmaking opportunities, vaulting him from the fringes of the movie industry into the mainstream. Scorsese had already relocated to Hollywood, a move as much symbolic as geographic, in the fall of 1970. The quintessential New Yorker, he seemed to be pulling up the roots of his physical and spiritual inspiration. Yet the Hollywood years preceding *Mean Streets* were crucial to his maturation as a director.

During the late sixties, Scorsese had worked on several projects that drew him out of Little Italy and out of himself. In *The Big Shave* (1967), *Woodstock* (1970), and *Street Scenes* (1970) he shared and documented the values of the sixties counterculture. That Scorsese intended *The Big Shave* for "The Angry Arts against the War," a week-long antiwar protest, reveals his political sympathies at a time when the bitter debate over the Vietnam conflict was dividing America. A harrowing six-minute depiction of a young man butchering his face in the act of shaving, the short appeared instead in Jacques Ledoux's 1968 Festival of Experimental Cinema in Belgium where it won Le Prix de L'Âge d'Or. Shot with ten roles of Agfa color film—a grant from the Belgian Cinematheque—*The Big Shave* is a blood-drenched parable of self-destruction written as well as directed by Scorsese. Despite its brevity the film powerfully evokes the senselessness of violence, which ultimately destroys its perpetrator. The fatal shave takes place in a glaringly white bathroom so tiny that the camera could barely be moved. Shaver and spectator alike are trapped, condemned respectively to enact and to witness the apparently unstoppable bloodletting. Bunny Berrigan's 1939 recording of "I Can't Get Started" ironically underscores the lesson of Vietnam: better not to have started than not to stop. Once started, the shaver hacks away at his face, oblivious to his copiously flowing blood. Obsessive, even suicidal, his grisly action emulates America's in Vietnam. Both the shaver's violent obsessiveness and its relevance to Vietnam are respectively invoked in Scorsese's credits: "Whiteness by Herman Melville" and "Viet 67."

Melville's whiteness, famously incarnated in the whale that Captain Ahab so single-mindedly stalks in *Moby-Dick*, evokes the destructive futility of an obsessive quest that resembles America's in Vietnam. An obscure object of desire, the white whale ultimately resists definition, sharing its inscrutability with that of America's longest war whose aims grew cloudier rather than clearer with time. And while the compulsive shaver and the ultrawhite bathroom of *The Big Shave* alone justify the "Whiteness by Herman Melville" credit, Scorsese might also have been thinking of Melville's much-anthologized short story "Bartleby the Scrivener." Like Scorsese's shaver, Bartleby silently self-destructs amidst surroundings (office, prison) which, like the tiny white bathroom, suggest entrapment. Unsurprisingly, Scorsese considered ending *The Big Shave* with Vietnam action footage as well as including it in a week-long antiwar rally in New York. The short actually opened at the 1968 New York Film Festival, minus the war footage and ending with the "Whiteness by Herman Melville" and "Vict 67" credits. Without its cryptic credits, *The Big Shave* might be no more than "a perfectly cinematic and simple exercise in black comedy."[3]

Which side Scorsese was on during the Vietnam imbroglios of the late sixties and early seventies is amply clarified by his loving work on *Woodstock*. This epic documentary of the three-day rock 'n' roll love-in at Max Yasgur's farm near Bethel, New York, in August, 1969, arguably the greatest concert film ever made, radiantly celebrates the definitive counterculture event of the sixties. *Woodstock* director Michael Wadleigh, an old friend and NYU colleague who had photographed the 16 mm sections of *Who's That Knocking . . .?*, enlisted Scorsese as assistant director and supervising editor. *Woodstock* has been conventionally—and justly—praised for telling it like it was; yet its considerable technical achievements, notably in intricate split-screen compositions and brilliantly recorded sound, are mostly overlooked. Writing on the occasion of the twentieth anniversary "Director's Cut" release, critic Jonathan Rosenbaum noted that the "grand mosaic structure" of *Woodstock* belies—and transfigures—its "outward appearance as the simple record of an event. . . . Most impressive is the way these choices [i.e., of camera angles and shots] never slide into stylistic formula," though the cutting and the introduction of multiple images are always geared to the beat and the developments of the music.[4] Yet even as Rosenbaum celebrates *Woodstock*'s cinematic flair, he unintentionally begs the question of its attribution. *Woodstock* turned out to be a one-shot triumph for its putative director, Michael Wadleigh, whose filmmaking career it pretty much began and ended. Martin Scorsese, Rosenbaum parenthetically—and somewhat disingenuously—notes at the end of his article, "was one of the film's main editors as well as assistant director."

According to James Monaco, the "real honors" for *Woodstock,* "still the best of concert music films," belong to Scorsese:

> Direction of *Woodstock* consisted simply of sending out ten or a dozen camera people with as much stock as they could carry and telling them to do their thing, shooting everything that happened during that historic weekend in upstate New York. The crew came back with an overwhelming amount of footage–more than one hundred hours by some accounts. The real creative job lay in reducing this amorphous mass of raw material to a running time of three hours and giving it shape and pace. Scorsese and his crew did a magnificent job, and *Woodstock* remains one of the most notable models of the craft of editing since the Steinbeck editing table was invented. Its thoughtful and moving use of the split screen (which allowed another hour or two of footage to be squeezed in) has never been equaled.[5]

Sharing assistant directing and editing credit on *Woodstock* was Thelma Schoonmaker who had met Wadleigh and Scorsese during a six-week film course at NYU. All three won Academy Awards when *Woodstock* swept 1970 honors for Best Documentary Feature. The politically committed Schoonmaker helped Scorsese edit his next directing project, *Street Scenes,* another counterculture documentary. It was Scorsese's own commitment to a cinema of personal vision that inspired Schoonmaker's devotion. But only after a decade of drifting from one film project to another would she again collaborate with him: "I would have loved to work with Marty, but I wasn't in the union. . . . And then, *finally,* Marty called me about *Raging Bull,* and the lawyers got me in the union."[6] Since winning a 1980 Oscar for her work on *Raging Bull,* Schoonmaker helped Scorsese cut every one of his [ensuing] films. That the two of them, who would go on to form one of the great editing teams in contemporary American cinema, collaborated on *Woodstock,* may account for the "grand mosaic" of the finished product.

Among the most haunting of *Woodstock's* brilliantly edited sequences are the relatively sedate, nearly painterly, composition of Joan Baez's mesmerizing rendition of "Joe Hill" and her a cappella "Swing Low, Sweet Chariot," sung before a raptly silent audience of half-a-million; Joe Cocker's "With a Little Help from My Friends," featuring the singer's falsetto response to his own vocal on the other half of the split screen;

Crosby, Stills, and Nash filling a triple-screen, its two red-filtered fore-grounds bisected by a dimmer background on their first number before mirror images and drifting mikes frame a black midsection on the group's finale; Santana's triple-screened drums, cymbals clashing side-to-side around the centered drummer; Sly and the Family Stone's piercing "I Want to Take You Higher," a melee of gyrating bodies emerging from the blue-filtered night. Only infrequently does editing inspiration flag, notably on Jimi Hendrix's very long guitar solo that concludes the "Director's Cut." Far from Rosenbaum's "invaluable addendum," the Hendrix number (a significant chunk of the forty minutes Wadleigh tacked on) evidences the flaccidity of material unmediated by the editing magic of Scorsese and Schoonmaker.

Scorsese's politics of the Vietnam era may be inferred from the allegory of *The Big Shave* and the music of *Woodstock*. But only in *Street Scenes* did he wear his political heart on his sleeve. This seventy-five minute documentary coverage of the student demonstrations roiling college campuses in 1970 Scorsese artfully assembled from bits and pieces of 16 mm footage shot by his politically fired-up NYU students. Although *Street Scenes* was Scorsese's brainchild, its achievement, like *Woodstock*'s, lies more in its editing than in its conception and directing (Scorsese admits to shooting only the final sequence). It was the May 1970 slaughter of four students by overzealous state troopers who fired on a crowd of anti-war demonstrators at Kent State University that sparked the widespread protests chronicled in *Street Scenes*. Sickened by the Kent State killings, Scorsese and a group of his NYU students and friends, among them Harvey Keitel, joined the stream of like-minded activists flooding into Washington, for one of the Vietnam era's largest antiwar rallies. The march on Washington is the climactic event of *Street Scenes* that begins with conventional antiwar rhetoric and moves on to document a Wall Street demonstration before zeroing in on its definitive Washington episode. The finale, a sort of coda set in a Washington hotel room and the only sequence Scorsese acknowledges shooting, features a raucous debate about political commitment and artistic integrity that predictably solves nothing: "I used footage that showed nobody knew what to do, neither radicals nor conservatives. Everybody was yelling at everybody and the picture ends in the middle of an argument because that was when the film literally ran out! I just left it that way. I thought 'Perfect,' it was God-sent."[7] So *Street Scenes* expires in gusty rhetoric and political posturing: a Tower of Babel whose loudly competing voices subvert the humanistic values Scorsese sought to capture. The frustration of its final sequence mirrored Scorsese's eventual disillusionment with the entire *Street Scenes* project. Working with inexperienced students and makeshift equipment; condemned for being too political or not political enough; weakened by a particularly severe asthma attack that forced him to take cortisone for the first time, Scorsese all but disavowed the finished product. Although *Street Scenes* was screened to some acclaim—whether due to its intrinsic merit or its political timeliness remains unclear—at the 1970 New York Film Festival, it soon dropped from sight. Since its limited release—it is now nearly impossible to find—Scorsese has further downplayed his role in *Street Scenes* and resisted its inclusion in his filmography. More significantly, the documentary may have soured him on political filmmaking: "At the end, all we saw was utter hopelessness . . . not futility, but the impotence of the people."[8] Changing times, shifting priorities, economic imperatives—or "utter hopelessness": whatever the cause(s), the ensuing cinema of Martin Scorsese lacks the political urgency of *The Big Shave, Woodstock,* and *Street Scenes.*

By the end of 1970, Scorsese seemed to be spinning his career wheels, teaching at NYU and latching on to whatever film work came his way. He might easily have gone the way of two idols, John Cassavetes and Michael Powell, filmmakers who, despite their undeniable talent, remained on the outskirts of the movie business. Always scrounging for financing, Cassavetes made several highly personal low-budget films respected by movie buffs but largely ignored by the general public. And Powell was unable to make even a single feature during the last thirty years of his career. For Scorsese, however, to remain an independent New York filmmaker dedicated to art for art's sake was not in the cards. As ambitious for mainstream success as for critical acclaim, he immigrated to Hollywood at the behest of Fred Weintraub, a Warner Brothers vice president and one of the money men behind *Woodstock.* "Freddie had another rock film called *Medicine Ball Caravan* . . . and there was nine hours of footage. Some of it was on 8 mm, most of it on 35 mm Techniscope, and the rest on 16 mm. He brought me out as an editor to put it in some kind of order; it was meant to be a two-week job."[9]

For Scorsese, moving to Hollywood was as much a spiritual and psychological uprooting as a geographical displacement. Magnifying the difficulty of adjusting to a radically different lifestyle was the emotional trauma that followed him West. The late sixties had been "a very bad period." Haunted by the autobiographical material that he was fashioning into *Mean Streets,* plagued by recurring asthma attacks, his career apparently on hold, Scorsese seemed to be self-destructing: "Our wives hated us," Scorsese recalls of the days when he and NYU buddy and collaborator Mardik Martin would "sit in my Valiant and write *Mean Streets,*" unwilling to go home and face their wives' derision.[10] Personal and professional angst converge subtextually in *The Big Shave* where the shaver slicing his face to pieces reflects more than Scorsese's outrage about Vietnam. "Consciously it was an angry outcry against the war. But in reality something else was going on inside me, I think, which really had nothing to do with the war. It was just a very bad period, a very bad period."[11]

Nearly divorced, sharing a depressing apartment with Harvey Keitel, and leery of *Medicine Ball Caravan* and its nine-hour mishmash of footage that he had to wrestle into some semblance of order, Scorsese seemed to have traded misery in the East for misery in the West. Still, he won a measure of respect for his editorial salvaging of *Medicine Ball Caravan* and began a relationship with Weintraub's daughter, Sandy, who would live and work with him for the next four years. Then came Scorsese's big break: a meeting with Roger Corman, "King of the Bs." Corman, producer of low-budget money-making exploitation films for American International Pictures, had seen *Who's That Knocking at My Door?* when it opened in Los Angeles as *J.R.* and had liked it well enough to hire Scorsese to direct *Boxcar Bertha,* the projected sequel to *Bloody Mama* (1970). Although most of the more than two hundred features he produced and/or directed since 1953 are eminently forgettable, Corman became famous for spotting talented young directors and advancing their careers. Not only Scorsese, but Francis Ford Coppola, Peter Bogdanovich, Jonathan Kaplan, and Jonathan Demme were one-time Corman protégés. Confessing his own early addiction to Corman movies, Scorsese maintains that the producer is "one of the best, but he's underrated in America—just alone, what he has done for others is amazing."[12] Shot at breakneck speed on penny-pinching budgets and larded with gratuitous sex and violence, Corman's films virtually define the exploitation genre. Yet so long as a movie met its shooting schedule and budgetary strictures and contained the mandatory exploitation scenes, Corman gave his directors leeway: "Corman did leave you alone, provided you played it within the genre and didn't get too crazy," recalls Scorsese.[13] Without this creative space, Scorsese and other young talents might not have been drawn to Corman projects. How exploitation films can transcend their generic boundaries is apparent in *The Little Shop of Horrors* (1960), shot by Corman in a record two days. That this macabre tale of a man-eating plant may be read as a swipe at rampant capitalism—human blood alone sustains the little florist shop—squares with Corman's 1979 avowal of the underlying seriousness of his work: "My films are very committed—personally, psychologically, and politically. . . . But I'm very careful to make this a subtextual commitment. I prefer the audience to go to see a commercially oriented film, and find to their surprise—and hopefully to their delight—that there is more there."[14]

Whether there is more to *Boxcar Bertha* than the escalating violence that wipes out most of the cast is debatable. Conceived as a sequel to Corman's *Bloody Mama, Boxcar Bertha* shares its predecessor's focus on a strong woman and its Depression Arkansas setting. Both films shamelessly exploit the *Bonnie and Clyde* formula that revolutionized the American cinema of the late sixties and early seventies. Protagonists are antiheroes whose values clash with those of the traditionally respectable pillars of society. Society is sterile and corrupt, its defenders grim and humorless foils to the free-spirited rebels that they so relentlessly chase down. Although the protagonists are inevitably crushed by the Establishment, their defeat or death is more apotheosis than capitulation. This reversal of moral values, the sine qua non of *Bonnie and Clyde* and its imitators, particularly resonated in the Vietnam era that spawned them. Like *Bonnie and Clyde, Bloody Mama* and *Boxcar Bertha* evoke the thirties to reflect the familiar social and political unrest of the sixties. *Bloody Mama,* however, merely exploits the sensationalism of the *Bonnie and Clyde* scenario for its own sake. Lost are the subtextual inferences that confer significance on the otherwise banal resemblances between thirties and sixties America. Unlike Bonnie and Clyde, Ma Barker and her cretinous brood are neither romanticized nor mythologized. Ma's psychopaths lack the Robin Hood charisma of the Barrow gang: the Barkers initiate more social injustice than they ever rectify. Essentially a vehicle for unfettered mayhem, *Bloody Mama* is chiefly memorable for Shelley Winters's flamboyant Ma Barker and, particularly, for Robert De Niro's Lloyd Barker, Ma's youngest son. In its spiritual vacancy and crazed intensity, De Niro's portrayal foreshadows several of his future roles in Scorsese movies. Because Lloyd was supposed to waste away before he finally got killed, De Niro starved himself during the five and a half weeks of shooting, a process he would famously reverse more than a decade later as Jake LaMotta in *Raging Bull.*

Boxcar Bertha falls somewhere between *Bloody Mama* and *Bonnie and Clyde,* retaining alike the exploitation film structure of the former and the social and political implications of the latter. As a matter of fact, *Boxcar Bertha* dramatizes the inferential politics of *Bonnie and Clyde,* translating subtextual reference into textual action. When young Bertha Thompson (Barbara Hershey) bears horrified witness to the fiery crash of her father's crop-dusting plane in the film's opening sequence, the political battle lines of *Boxcar Bertha* are already firmly drawn. Because he had been ordered into the air by his greedy boss despite mechanic Von Morton's warning about the plane's sputtering engine, Thompson *père* becomes a martyr to capitalist exploitation. Henceforth, Bertha will cast her lot with the poor and the downtrodden, the have-nots who are mercilessly exploited by the haves and further victimized by the Great Depression. The rich, represented chiefly by Sartoris the railroad boss, wanting only to get richer, employ vicious henchmen to guard their property and to cow or kill union organizers and members. Because it is the Depression and jobs are hard to come by, the fat cats never lack for willing workers. In this ideal climate for capitalist exploitation, workers are commodities and unions are crushed, their members marginalized at best, persecuted and murdered at worst. The social message of *Boxcar Bertha* may be drenched in the blood and gore that are de rigueur in Corman movies, but its depiction of capitalism run amok is not altogether inaccurate. On one level at least, *Boxcar Bertha* reflects the same anti-Establishment perspective Scorsese had shown in *Street Scenes* and *Woodstock.*

The working-class sympathies of *Boxcar Bertha* are incarnated primarily in Big Bill Shelley (David Carradine), a railroad worker and labor leader. A union man with a social conscience, Shelley "evolves" into an outlaw who robs the railroad to fund the union. His companions in crime—the orphaned Bertha; the black mechanic, Von Morton (Bernie Casey); and the Jewish cardsharp from the East, Rake Brown (Barry Primus)—run the gamut of exploited types. As generic victims of oppression, the woman, the black, and the Jew amplify the us-versus-them scenario of *Boxcar Bertha* beyond the class warfare expressed in the struggle between Shelley the union man and Sartoris the railroad magnate. Scorsese cleverly measures the gap between workers and bosses by casting as Sartoris John Carradine, the real-life father of David Carradine who plays Shelley. Their differences are instantly apparent when the unctuous voice and polished look of the elder Carradine confront the flat diction and scruffy demeanor of his son. The casting serves also to highlight the generational nature of the war between haves and have-nots, valorizing the rebellious Shelley gang at the expense of their repressive elders. Shelley is himself a latter-day Robin Hood, intent on diverting railroad profits into union coffers. Only after an upright union official rejects Shelley's ill-gotten cash is plunder divorced from purpose and the gang's motivation rendered indefensible. Yet even when little pretense of altruism remains, Shelley reflexively echoes his earlier refrains: "I ain't cut out for this kind of life," and "I'm not a criminal, I'm a union man."

Because *Boxcar Bertha* is a Corman film, Big Bill Shelley must periodically raise Bertha's skirt along with her political consciousness. Yet despite the genre's demands for sex as gratuitous as its violence, their love scenes display a romantic tenderness rare in Scorsese's subsequent films. While the poignancy of the love scenes reflects the Hershey/Carradine real-life affair at the time, it also owes something to Scorsese's reading of the film's central relationship. Raising the stakes of the exploitation script he inherited, Scorsese expands its several religious signifiers into a surprisingly coherent symbolic pattern. Bertha becomes Mary Magdalene to Shelley's Christ, seeking in him political if not spiritual salvation. Like her biblical counterpart, Bertha is a sometime prostitute whose devotion to one man belies her promiscuity with many. Scorsese seals this symbolic identity in a lingering shot of a Magdalene painted on the back wall of a black fundamentalist church where the Shelley gang momentarily hides out. The mural shows a woman gazing devotedly at a redeemer dressed in white robes with a small river flowing between the two larger-than-life figures. According to biblical tradition, Jesus appeared first to Mary Magdalene after his burial; and in black American fundamentalism, Mary Magdalene has been celebrated in spirituals such as "Is There Anybody Here Like Weeping Mary?" Scorsese accidentally discovered the church mural while on location in Arkansas and used it to match both his own Italian tradition and Bertha's character with religion practiced by the socially oppressed.[15]

The evocation of Magdalene and Christ in Bertha and Shelley was not lost on Barbara Hershey and David Carradine who at the time gave Scorsese a copy of Nikos Kazantzakis's *The Last Temptation of Christ*, Hershey putting in a bid for the Magdalene role she would play when Scorsese eventually filmed it. Kazantzakis's stress on the human identity of Jesus appealed to Scorsese whose Big Bill Shelley would apotheosize into Christ in the film version of *The Last Temptation*. Shelley's more immediate apotheosis occurs at the end of *Boxcar Bertha*, when he is nailed to the side of a boxcar in a crucifixion scene whose shots Scorsese would repeat verbatim in *The Last Temptation of Christ*. Although the crucifixion scene wasn't his idea—it came with the original script—Scorsese took it as "a sign from God," reflecting his own obsessions in the interval between *Who's That Knocking?* and *Mean Streets*. Its serendipitous appearance in the script gave Scorsese the perfect opportunity to stamp his personal signature on *Boxcar Bertha*. "I liked the way we shot it, the angles we used, and in particular the way you saw the nails coming through the wood, though they were never seen piercing flesh."[16] Shelley's crucifixion climaxes a savage beating inflicted by Sartoris's goons before they nail him to the boxcar, a fate that actually befell several labor leaders in the 1930s. Thus linked to those fallen heroes of the union movement as well as to the crucified Christ, Shelley completes his metamorphosis from outlaw to martyr. As the train starts up, gathering speed as it begins to roll away, Bertha runs alongside the moving car crying, "Don't take him, don't take him." Intimations of transcendence trail her cry, converting it into a plea that her Savior be allowed more than his brief sojourn on earth before being translated into Heaven. Because the crucifixion and its aftermath are shot mostly from behind Shelley and above Bertha gaping up at him, the ascension effect is magnified. A closeup of the outstretched hand of the crucified Shelley and a final shot of the same hand protruding from the corner of the frame complete the allusion/illusion.

Premonitions of death had haunted Shelley's last days. "I'm finished," he tells Bertha when she discovers her captured lover working on a chain gang. And when she is taken to Shelley shortly after his escape, he looks old and tired, peering at her from behind glasses and talking of nothing but impending death. "You don't have to rush it," she pleads even as the railroad thugs who will beat and crucify Shelley burst through the door. Not only in the manner of his death but in its premonition and acceptance Shelley reenacts the drama of Christ's last days on earth.

If *Boxcar Bertha*'s religious and political signifiers challenge the limits of the exploitation genre, its nearly nonstop violence is vintage Corman. So extravagant is the carnage that it overpowers the love story and subverts the characters' motivation. Thus the lovemaking scenes between Bertha and Bill barely punctuate the spiraling mayhem. And the

Shelley gang's Robin Hood premises give way to self-serving impulses as indefensible as those of their capitalist opponents. Although the gang's first holdup is a chance affair—a train they hop happens to be carrying money that they lift almost as a lark—Shelley and company compromise their working-class solidarity in mimicking the actions of the robber barons they deplore. When a comically overdressed Bertha and Rake—she in a fancy gown, he in a tuxedo—crash Sartoris's party to rob the assembled guests of cash and jewels, they are parodying the affectations of these pompous fat cats. Maybe the ill-fitting clothes stress the unalloyed working-class affiliation of the awkward wearers. Yet in their flashy getups Bertha and Rake revel in the trappings of the class enemy: dressing up wishfully emulates a lifestyle they theoretically condemn. Bertha suggests a similar blend of childish delight and wishful emulation when, dripping with heisted jewelry, she later makes love with Shelley. Not that Bertha and the gang ever make common cause with Sartoris and his ilk; but the moral gap between good guys and bad guys narrows when labor activists turn social bandits. Shelley's "I'm not a criminal, I'm a union man" refrain rings increasingly hollow as he completes his transformation from working man to train robber. Robbery loses its apparent rationale, however, after the union rejects the fruits of the gang's criminal labors. Stripped of moral justification, the gang henceforth robs for the hell of it, not so incidentally filling the formulaic bill of the exploitation film.

So explosively accelerating is the violence of *Boxcar Bertha* that violence itself threatens to become the subject of the film. While not denying Corman's formulary requirements, Scorsese puts his own spin on the action of *Boxcar Bertha:* "Mostly I attempted to show the characters as people acting like children, playing with violence until they start getting killed—then they're stuck in a real game, a life and death game. I used the element of surprise violence to emphasize that when you least expect it, things are destroyed, people are killed—that's very important to the picture.[17] Scorsese's analysis is more than an arty recipe for nonstop slaughter; the same could be said of the violence in *Boxcar Bertha*'s successors from *Mean Streets* to *Casino.* And if "surprise" violence is an early component of Scorsese's signature, so is the explicit religiosity that attends it. Aspects of *Boxcar Bertha*'s violence may be redemptive and/or cathartic, and not only in the climactic crucifixion of Shelley/Christ but in the contrasting fates of his followers/disciples Rake and Von as well. Rake's shotgun death releases the displaced Yankee gambler from a troubled role he was not fit to play; and black Von shotguns Shelley's killers, avenging his martyred leader and ridding himself of his (white) oppressors. There's even a certain symmetrical elegance to the violence: the capitalist exploitation that destroyed Bertha's father in the beginning is itself destroyed by Von in the end.

Still, it is not necessary to applaud the violence of *Boxcar Bertha*. It is even arguable that the film's economic, political, and religious allusions drown in buckets of blood. *Boxcar Bertha* is no masterpiece; but neither is it the "piece of shit" John Cassavetes called it. Cassavetes actually went on to admit that it was a "good picture" though unworthy of Scorsese's time and talent. But *Boxcar Bertha* got Scorsese into the Director's Guild and proved that he could work within the Hollywood system. So pleased was Roger Corman with the film that he offered to back *Mean Streets* to the tune of $150,000 on the condition that Scorsese make all the characters black. Even after Scorsese told him it wouldn't work, Corman agreed to distribute the film anyway and, grateful to the man who "really got it started," Scorsese quoted a scene from Corman's *Tomb of Ligeia* (1965) in *Mean Streets*.[18] Because the $300,000 Scorsese eventually scraped together for *Mean Streets* would mandate no-frills filmmaking, the Corman connection paid off again. Paul Rapp, Corman's associate producer, persuaded Scorsese that for $300,000 the film could only be shot in Los Angeles: "Go to New York, shoot some background stuff for five days and then come back here and we'll do all the interiors here."[19] So, with the Corman crew from *Boxcar Bertha,* Scorsese wrapped up *Mean Streets* in a Cormanesque twenty-seven days, barely exceeding his meager budget. Except for the climactic "Brooklyn" car crash shot in downtown L.A., all the exteriors were New York, Scorsese squeezing out several more than Rapp's allotted four days in order to capture as much New York atmosphere as possible. When Robert De Niro's Johnny Boy spews gunfire from a rooftop, the Empire State Building looming in the background sites the roof in New York; its window, however, is in Los Angeles. Johnny Boy blows up a "Mott Street" mailbox in San Pedro; a man gunned down in a bar (L.A.) staggers out to fall in the street (New York). That *Mean Streets* drew critical kudos for its "authentic" location reflects not so much the blindness of reviewers as the skill with which Scorsese assembled the pieces of his jigsaw puzzle. Perhaps ironically, the film shot mostly in Los Angeles proved successful only in New York, bombing elsewhere including L.A. where it again got favorable reviews but did only two weeks' business.

Without *Boxcar Bertha,* there most certainly would have been no *Mean Streets* and probably no *Alice Doesn't Live Here Anymore* (1974), its immediate successor. *Mean Streets* had transformed the youthful New York director in search of a project into a Hollywood hotshot deluged by scripts. Among those scripts was *Alice Doesn't Live Here Anymore,* a star vehicle that Ellen Burstyn hoped to parlay into a Best Actress Oscar. Fresh from her popular if not notably artistic success in William Friedkin's *The Exorcist* (1973), Burstyn had the clout to specify the director of her next picture. Because an established director might easily balk at making a film so blatantly designed to showcase its leading lady, Burstyn asked Francis Ford Coppola to recommend a young director who would do justice to her project. When Coppola suggested Scorsese, Burstyn had to be persuaded that the apparently macho director of *Mean Streets* was right for a "woman's film." Paradoxically, it was her actual screening of *Mean Streets* that propelled her toward Scorsese: "It was a movie with a life and a reality of its own," said Burstyn, who was "very impressed" by the film. "I thought Scorsese would be perfect for *Alice,* which needed to be roughed up. I wanted to make it the story of women today, with our consciousness as it is now, not a Doris Day film."[20] Meanwhile, after *Mean Streets,* Scorsese no more wanted to be typecast as a director of gangster films than he had previously wanted to go on making exploitation films à la *Boxcar Bertha.* Scorsese's "I wanted to make a film which was completely different and yet rough, the way I always like it. Rough in camera movement, rough in impact," meshed seamlessly with Burstyn's need for *Alice* "to be roughed up."[21]

After a six hour confab with Burstyn ended in a meeting of minds regarding the film's emotional thrust and character portrayal, Scorsese was hired to direct *Alice Doesn't Live Here Anymore.* Given major studio backing, name stars, and most importantly, a million-dollar-plus budget, he had made it into big-league filmmaking. Money bought several weeks of rehearsal time prior to shooting during which Scorsese had actors improvise key scenes while screenwriter Robert Getchell took notes and modified his script accordingly. Money also bought an eight-week shooting schedule, nearly all of it on location in Tucson, plus the added luxury of shooting three hours and sixteen minutes of footage for an eventual running time of one hour and fifty-three minutes. So comparatively lavish was his first studio-financed budget that Scorsese, ever the film buff, was able to indulge himself in a highly stylized $85,000 set (the *total* cost of *Who's That Knocking at My Door?* was $35,000) for the opening sequence of *Alice.*

An elaborate homage to William Cameron Menzies whose *Invaders from Mars* (1953), a cult classic in which adults and extraterrestrials alike are seen through a child's eyes, the sequence also invokes *Duel in the Sun, Gone with the Wind,* and, especially, *The Wizard of Oz.* Alice as a little girl made up to look like Dorothy in *The Wizard* poses before what looks like the familiar Kansas farmhouse, now transplanted to Monterey, California, circa 1948. A garishly red-filtered and back-lit Hollywood sunset backgrounds Alice skipping across an idealized bridge and singing snatches of "You'll Never Know," the lushly romantic song Alice Faye warbles on the song track. Young Alice Hyatt dreams of becoming a second Alice Faye, singing her way to the stardom associated with the flamboyant movies Scorsese quotes.

Scarlet titles set in plush blue velvet further mimic the look of bygone Hollywood melodramas like those directed by Douglas Sirk. No great admirer of Sirk, Scorsese nonetheless wanted to begin *Alice* like a Sirk melodrama. Russell Metty, the respected cinematographer who shot Scorsese's tests, had photographed three of Sirk's glossy confections of the 1950s: *Magnificent Obsession, Written on the Wind,* and *Imitation of Life.* The "women's pictures" of their day, Sirk's adult soap operas were produced by Ross Hunter whose saccharine Doris Day vehicles Ellen Burstyn had hired Scorsese to avoid emulating. Like Doris Day comedies, Sirk's melodramas seem to falsify the female experience. And Scorsese's Sirklike Monterey flashback is as illusory as Alice's reverie of stardom. The $85,000 that went into this first footage that Scorsese had ever shot on a studio set was money well spent: the memory of Monterey resonates throughout the film—a complex metaphor of lost childhood, impossible dreams, and illusory ideals.

Alice's fairy tale Monterey explodes into the raw reality of Socorro, New Mexico, where a grown-up Alice is the wife of a brutish truck driver (Billy Green Bush) and the mother of a bratty eleven-year-old son (Alfred Lutter). The assertive little girl who challenged Alice Faye's "You'll Never Know"—"I could do better, and if anybody doesn't like it they can blow it out their ass"—has turned into a near-caricature of the model housewife, anxiously plying her sullen husband with his favorite foods. No less than the contrast between Monterey and Socorro, that between Alice the girl and Alice the woman exploits a recurring motif in Scorsese's films: the counterpointing of illusion and reality. What he objectifies in cutting abruptly from Monterey to Socorro is the emotional instability that invariably afflicts his male protagonists. Alice's internal conflicts—expressed in the contrast between the confident girl and the repressed woman—is another version of Charlie's conflict between God and Mammon in *Mean Streets*. At the heart of their respective conflicts is an ideal self-image that real life cannot sustain. By making Alice's Monterey such a patently indoor imitation of the outdoors, Scorsese follows Sirk in suggesting that we look not at life but at an imitation of life. When Scorsese's camera plunges into Socorro, the inset frame of the Monterey sequence expands to full frame. Yet the deliberate artifice of the film-within-a-film vision of Monterey persists in memory, a reminder of the hazy boundary between illusion and reality. So in the palpably real world of Socorro, no sooner does Alice jokingly wish her husband dead than he is obligingly killed off, the victim of a truck crash that launches Alice on Scorsese's version of the yellow brick road. The "hand of God" Scorsese somewhat disingenuously called the fortuitous accident that gives Alice the freedom to find herself. Whether inspired by God or by Douglas Sirk, Alice's fulfilled wish recalls the miraculously granted wishes of countless fairy-tale heroines. In any event, such blurring of generic markers serves to destabilize the mise-en-scène of *Alice Doesn't Live Here Anymore*. It is conceivable that Scorsese is playing around with the ambiguities of the quintessential Sirk film, the aptly titled *Imitation of Life* (1959). Does imitation consist of authentic or counterfeit reproduction? Apropos of *Alice,* does Scorsese faithfully depict a woman's quest for her own identity, as advertised? Or is he, by slyly involving fairy-tale motifs, subverting the very conventions that quest relies on? These questions provoke a profounder one: Whose movie is this, anyway? Richard Dyer cites *Alice Doesn't Live Here Anymore* as one of the "very few" instances in "which the totality of a film can be laid at the door of a star."[22] Although Dyer's "can" is tentative, his point makes sense given Ellen Burstyn's sweeping control of the financing, the directing, the scripting, even the casting of *Alice*. That despite Burstyn's undeniably forceful presence, *Alice* is as much Scorsese's film as hers testifies to an already formidable auteurism. In its awareness and manipulation of convention, spontaneously freewheeling camera work, quirky takes on human relationships, and sudden outbursts of unpredictable violence *Alice* is vintage Scorsese.

The artful juxtaposition of Monterey and Socorro stamps Scorsese's signature on *Alice Doesn't Live Here Anymore* even as it suggests divergent ways of seeing the film. Monterey implies romantic comedy, Socorro more serious stuff. Neither setting is off-limits for a "women's film," but

Socorro and its ilk are more conducive to a "feminist film." Any believable feminist agenda urges the suppression if not the extirpation of Monterey from Alice Hyatt's memory. To persist in Monterey dreaming is to fall short of the summa of women's liberation. Yet Alice's quest is so structured as to compromise the feminist ideals it ostensibly values. It is not the classic feminist epiphany of freedom but the *deus ex machina* of her husband's accidental death that motivates Alice to drop her Betty Crocker act. "If her husband hadn't been killed, she would never have left him," Scorsese affirms. "See, that's the character. It's a very important point," he adds, explicitly denying Alice the consciousness-raising scenario of women's liberation. "She would not have moved unless the hand of God came down and said, 'Bang. This is it. Make your decision. What are you going to do?'"[23] That it is the whim of God—the ultimate patriarchal authority—makes virtue out of mere necessity, all but invalidating the concept of "decision." Moreover, despite the obligatory scenes of female bonding with Bea (Lelia Goldoni), the best friend and confidante she leaves behind in Socorro, and Flo (Diane Ladd), the foul-mouthed waitress she works alongside in Tucson, Alice remains largely dependent on men.

Again, the structure of *Alice Doesn't Live Here Anymore* militates against feminist assertion. A road picture that defines an over-the-rainbow destination in Monterey strands its heroine short of the Emerald City of her dreams. On the way to Monterey, Alice and her son Tommy stop first in Phoenix. As in most road movies, the various stops constitute tests of the protagonist's capacity to endure, to survive, ultimately to prevail. For Alice, Phoenix poses the challenge of making enough money to continue on to Monterey. Walking into a bar as shadowy and claustrophobic as any in *Mean Streets,* she tearfully persuades its soft-hearted owner to audition her for a singing job. That she lands the job testifies less to her talent than to the owner's charity. Scorsese prolongs the audition and subsequent singing scenes just long enough to reveal not only the shakiness of Alice's voice but the hopelessness of her dreams. Not for the first time or the last is the bar Scorsese's site of broken dreams: Alice's singing success is predictably short-lived, and when she stops next it is to work as a waitress, the very job she has been trying to avoid. Even her fleeting success is won with tears, hardly the prescription for women's liberation. Crying, both in and out of bed, was Alice's only means of getting her husband's attention back home in Socorro. It is the last resort of an otherwise helpless woman. Of course Alice's crying can be read by die-hard feminist theorists as a knowing stratagem for enlisting male sympathy by displaying stereotypical female weakness. Still, it is more likely that her instinctive recourse to tears marks Alice as a creature of habit who will continue to depend on the kindness of (male) strangers. Whether her tears are spontaneous or strategic, they suggest that success for women is directly proportional to their skill in manipulating men. Thus, Flo leaves the top of her blouse unbuttoned as she leans over to serve the restaurant's male clientele, a ploy to get bigger tips that she recommends to Alice. And a third waitress, a timorous airhead forever muddling orders, unhesitatingly takes up with a scruffy biker, riding off into the night with the first (only?) man who beckons.

Alice's first love affair multiplies the clichés of male–female relationships. A persistent young stud, complete with cowboy hat and string tie and apparently fascinated by her singing, will not let up until he lures Alice into bed. Once there, she is as sexually turned on as the newly liberated woman figures to be. This sexual (re)awakening and its corollary— that women cannot live without men—are as conventional as the stultifying marriage Alice escaped. And when Ben Eberhardt (Harvey Keitel) turns out not only to be married but a psychopath who brutalizes his wife, Alice learns that victimization, like dependence, is not confined to marriage. The violence latent in her husband detonates in her lover when his pregnant wife shows up. Not a man to be swayed by a woman's tears, Ben pulls a knife on his sobbing wife, slaps her and the shocked Alice around, and even threatens Tommy. (Scorsese fans saw this coming earlier when Ben made the familiar gesture of pointing his finger as a gun.) Ben's explosion is shot in a confined space with a handheld camera that intensifies the violence. No doubt designed to underscore the vulnerability of a lone woman, it is a scene right out of *Mean Streets* or *Taxi Driver*. Further, the inclusion of such a horrific episode serves to destroy any lingering illusions Alice may harbor about the real world. The coda to her less than scintillating singing debut, the maniacal violence she barely escapes emphasizes that for Alice and Tommy life alone on the road may be as intimidating as it is contingent.

Arriving in Tucson (the way to Monterey is oddly circuitous), Alice searches in vain for a singing job. Out-of-the-way Tucson looks like a dismal stand-in for Monterey, an end-of-the-line field of broken dreams where Alice has to settle for the waitressing job she has always equated with failure. Drudging away at the nondescript Mel's Cafe, Alice's dream of Monterey seems no closer to fulfillment than it was back in

Socorro. But dreams endure, and Alice works as hard at convincing Tommy—and herself—that they are still Monterey-bound as she does at the diner. At this juncture of the film, however, grim reality has apparently overtaken wishful thinking. Alice's uninspired singing, her disastrous run-in with Ben, and now her dead-end job look like Scorsese's way of saying the party is over. After all, he—and Ellen Burstyn—had set out to demythologize the Doris Day women's picture and depict modern women as they really are. Yet just when things look bleakest for Alice, along comes a deus ex machina every bit as egregious as the truck that flattened her husband. Into Mel's strides the improbably handsome David (Kris Kristofferson) who spots the frazzled waitress across a crowded room and all but falls in love with her at first sight. Turns out David is a prosperous rancher conveniently divorced from a wife who ran off with the kids, and "so lonesome I could cry." Warm and caring, charming and sensitive, handsome and well-fixed to boot, David is a dream come true. Who needs Monterey? Enough of *Alice Doesn't Live Here Anymore* remains to develop the ensuing relationship between Alice and David, but its outcome is rarely in doubt. True, there is the compulsory misunderstanding—David smacks Tommy after one too many of the kid's vulgar outbursts—that momentarily drives the lovers apart. But it is a manufactured crisis that is as predictable in *Alice* as it would have been in any run of-the-mill "women's film" of an earlier era.

In fact, *Alice* looks more and more like an old-fashioned romantic comedy as the relationship between the lovers plays out. Alice's soul-searching speeches practically trip over each other as Ellen Burstyn emotes for all she is worth in a (successful) bid for an Oscar. It is a bravura performance made possible by a succession of set pieces that feature Alice in one-on-one situations calculated for maximum dramatic effect. Shrill arguments with David and with Tommy and a couple of affecting heart-to-hearts with Flo allow Burstyn to pull out all the stops. The downside of seizing every such opportunity to let loose emotionally is most apparent in the banal and all but interminable gabfest between Alice and David after they first make love. And it is precisely in Scorsese's (and/or Burstyn's?) handling of the Alice/David relationship that the contradictions of *Alice Doesn't Live Here Anymore* are most apparent. Mise-en-scène conspires with emotional overkill to confuse if not subvert the film's intentions. A quasi-idyllic picnic scene at David's ranch, for example, restages the Socorro family dinner tableau. Alice easily reassumes her homemaker role, fixing lunch for the men (David and Tommy) in her life. Clearly more comfortable cooking than singing, Alice does not so much regress—her food figures to be better than her voice—as reaffirm. And what she is reaffirming is the old-fashioned notion that women without men remain unfulfilled. Not that there is anything wrong with Alice wishing to reconstitute a family. What is fishy, however, in a film that claims contemporary relevance, is the implication that a woman cannot do without a man. Women's work, be it singing or waiting on tables, lacks intrinsic value: it is simply a more or less desperate holding action until a man comes along. Alice's confession to Flo—"I don't know how to live without a man"—deflates her earlier vow never "to live through another man" again. Of course it is possible that the end of her quest was not liberation from but acquiescence to the old order. And the quest is therefore a (qualified) success ending as it does in the self-understanding that makes virtue of accommodation.

Beginning with the traumatic argument at the ranch that ruptures the lovers' relationship, the movie eddies between genres. The realistic intensity of the breakup dissolves into the parodic staginess of their makeup: Alice and David fall into each other's arms, cheered on by an applauding lunchtime crowd at Mel's. The tonal clash between the breakup and makeup scenes reflects the difficulty of resolving the conflicts built into *Alice Doesn't Live Here Anymore*. As the script underwent countless revisions, versions of closure ranged from Alice's marrying David and living happily ever after in Tucson to Alice's refusing David and pushing on to Monterey with Tommy. Ellen Burstyn explains the restaurant reconciliation scene in light of the studio's demand for a happy ending, a demand that rankled her and Scorsese: "Marty and I were disgusted. The end they wanted was a *movie* ending, not a *real* ending—which was why Marty had everybody applaud, because that was *his* way of acknowledging that this was the *movie* ending."[24] Thus the cafe scene evokes the corny resolutions of earlier "women's pictures" to underscore their theatricality, not to suggest their viability. Still, the scene does reunite Alice and David, apparently locking in domesticity in Tucson and locking out singing in Monterey. According to Burstyn, "We were all very disgruntled, because she was giving up her dream" until "Kris Kristofferson made the contribution that saved us all." Improvising during rehearsal, Kristofferson/David tells Burstyn/Alice, "You want to go to Monterey? I'll take you to Monterey, let's go!"[25] Hard on the heels of Alice's plaintive "I was happy in

Monterey" and David's generous offer to give up his beloved ranch for her, Kristofferson's improvisation resolves the either—or predicament. Alice gets David without relinquishing Monterey: she can put her dreams away for another day secure in the faith that David will take her to Monterey if and when she wants to go.

Although Kristofferson's inspired ad lib seals the cafe scene reconciliation by (re)defining the Alice/David relationship, it does not end the movie. Another inspiration, art director Toby Rafelson's, led to the closing follow-up shot of Alice and Tommy alone together, which had initially preceded the cafe scene. Rafelson's idea of switching the order of the scenes was pounced upon by Scorsese: "You're absolutely right because it's a matter of her main relationship in the film being with the kid."[26] All along, Tommy was the film's catalyst, mediating Alice's various relationships either overtly or subliminally. It is concern for Tommy, for example, that precipitates Alice's flights from men. No sooner does Ben storm out of the motel room after threatening Tommy than Alice starts packing; and she in turn storms out of David's house after he strikes her son. When she is working Alice is forced to leave the bored and resentful Tommy cooped up in their motel room. Predictably he gets in trouble, falling in with the precociously rebellious Audrey (Jodie Foster, affecting in a minor role that prefigures her appearance as the adolescent hooker Iris in Scorsese's next film, *Taxi Driver)* and getting so drunk on cherry wine that he lands in the hospital where his by now frantic mother is called to pick him up. On the road as elsewhere Tommy's moody whining and nonstop bidding for attention fray Alice's nerves. His endless retelling of an unfunny joke about a great gray gorilla almost sadistically persecutes his mother. And although theirs remains an essentially loving relationship, Tommy's acerbically willful behavior effects a dominance over his mother that mirrors the adult male–female relationships of *Alice.*

Scorsese's reordering of the film's last two scenes does more than emphasize the primacy of the mother–son relationship. *Alice Doesn't Live Here Anymore* concludes with mother and son walking down a Tucson street toward a sign that reads "Monterey." Incredibly, the sign was not planted by Scorsese but loomed serendipitously before the walkers: "It was like God put it there. I said, 'Oh then, we can't change it, can we?'"[27] A multifaceted signifier, the telltale sign clarifies the apparent closure of the cafe scene. By (re)invoking Monterey the sign insists upon the contingency, rather than the certainty of the Alice–David relationship. With or without David, who is pointedly absent from this last scene, Monterey remains an option for Alice and Tommy. Whether this synthetic reconstituting of her dream signals progress for Alice is unclear. She and Tommy walk away from the camera, seeming rather to lengthen their distance from the viewer than to shorten their distance to "Monterey." Because it is shot with a telephoto lens that exaggerates the distancing effect, the ending captures the tentativeness that Scorsese apparently was after: "The walk represents their future. I wanted it to look diffuse, disjointed, uncertain."[28] So the sign is at once ironic (the only Monterey that Alice is left with) and promising (the reminder that Monterey lives on). However governed by the camera, the act of walking at least converts the implicit stasis of the cafe into the explicit motion of the road. Still, because the movie ends as it began with Alice walking, it is tempting to read the last episode in light of the first: "This scene is, like the opening vignette, a sign of the artificiality of dreams. Both are situated outside the boundaries of the film's narrative, whose extremely realist style evokes an attitude of grim realism toward the world, which seems impermeable to a common woman's dream of success."[29] Yet Alice's future, apparently settled in the cafe, conceivably reopens as she walks. Walking may not equal progress, but it may imagine possibility.

Arguments about Alice's self-realization mostly assume a feminist agenda that Scorsese never intended. He and Burstyn set out to tell the story of a modern woman but not a militant one. Perhaps the not-so-negligible achievement of *Alice Doesn't Live Here Anymore* is to mediate between the rival claims of the cozy home and the open road. The premise of the film, that marriage and career are not necessarily incompatible, is surely as "modern" as the strident feminism that mandates Alice alone. *Alice Doesn't Live Here Anymore* is finally a romantic comedy that manages to update the Doris Day conventions without radically altering them. It is a milder version of Scorsese's far more wrenching genre revisions in such movies as *New York, New York; Raging Bull;* and *Cape Fear.* In any event, *Alice* was easily his greatest popular and commercial success to date. Boosted by Ellen Burstyn's Oscar-winning performance, it scored a box office hit, raising Scorsese's Hollywood profile and winning studio backing for his forthcoming projects. Having struck the gold in California that Alice only dreamed of, Martin Scorsese was poised for his finest achievements.

4

....

Apocalypse and After: God's Lonely Man

"**I** am God's lonely man" Travis Bickle records in the scarifying diary that scripts his voice-over in *Taxi Driver* (1976). Travis is the loneliest of the many lonely protagonists played by Robert De Niro in Scorsese's films of the next two decades. Avatar and apotheosis of the antihero whose pathology Scorsese relentlessly dissects, Travis/De Niro is arguably the central figure—as *Taxi Driver* is arguably the centerpiece—in the cinema of Martin Scorsese. Whether he is making music *(New York, New York);* KOing opponents *(Raging Bull);* or fronting businesses *(Casino),* the De Niro character embodies the dictum of Marlow, the narrator of Joseph Conrad's *Heart of Darkness:* "We live, as we dream—alone." *Taxi Driver* remains, however, Scorsese's most harrowing case study in loneliness: Travis is the loneliest of the lonely, so alone as to be singled out by God. Travis's formulaic conflation of isolation and belief evokes the nearly predestinarian sense of vocation that Scorsese's lone wolf heroes regularly embody. Although the idea of a God-ordained singularity informed by loneliness is pretty self-serving (I am what I am because of God) if not hypocritical, it explains who Travis thinks he is and what he thinks he is doing. He is God's avenging angel, scouring the world—in this case New York, for provincial Americans like Travis (who hails from the Midwest) a very Sodom and Gomorrah of depravity—of evil. Loneliness is thus converted from a debilitating liability—Travis's stabs at bridging the distance between himself and others are as futile as they are misconceived—into a holy calling.

If Scorsese treated loneliness solely as an aberrant condition that feeds the paranoid fantasies of the Travis Bickles of this world, *Taxi Driver* would function primarily as a study in abnormal psychology.

What is truly harrowing about Travis's case, however, is not its apparent singularity but its implicit commonality. Paul Schrader, whose script Scorsese follows with uncommon fidelity, quotes Thomas Wolfe's "belief that loneliness, far from being a rare and curious phenomenon, is the central and inevitable fact of human existence" as the epigraph to *Taxi Driver*. During the summer of 1972, out of work, his marriage on the rocks, Schrader "fell into a period of real isolation. . . . And out of that isolation came *Taxi Driver,* which was written in just ten days. . . . It just jumped out of my head like an animal." Not only his own loneliness but its distinctive pathology seeped into Schrader's portrait of Travis: "I was very enamored of guns, I was very suicidal, I was drinking heavily, I was obsessed with pornography in the way a lonely person is, and all those elements are up front in the script."[1] Add pill-popping, racism, sexism, and a preternatural hatred of filth of all kinds, and the portrait of Travis is nearly complete. All that seems to be missing is the motivation underlying Travis's ever more bizarre actions, unless loneliness itself is motivation enough.

Apparent evidence of what makes Travis tick pops up early in *Taxi Driver*. The anonymity of the title suggests that he may be an over-the-top Everyman designed to probe the limits rather than to prove the typicality of the human condition. De Niro, a sometime New York cabbie in leaner days, researched his role by renewing his taxi license. "I drove with him several nights," recalls Scorsese. "He was totally anonymous. People would say anything, do anything in the back seat—it was like he didn't exist."[2] It's a description that fits Travis as well as his real life counterpart. And if Travis is one of us—"I've had the feelings he has," maintains Scorsese, echoing Schrader—then he likewise carries the diseases of his time and place. Travis is a former marine, a Vietnam vet whose frequent dressing in combat fatigues signals potential or actual violence. Like many disillusioned and disaffected ex-soldiers of the Vietnam era, he is haunted by wartime memories that spill over into civilian life. For Travis, hacking in New York is little different from soldiering in Vietnam. It is war all over again, waged on similarly bloody, filthy, and corrupt terrain. At that, he simply seconds his creator: "Life is one long moral Vietnam, and you can't get out of it," Schrader once told an interviewer. Travis's pathology is unmistakably American, his actions only marginally less so. Dedicated to purgation if not redemption through violence, he is bent on cleaning everything up and wiping everybody out. Like other apocalyptic films of its era, *Taxi Driver* invokes violence as the final solution to personal and societal evil. It is no coincidence that so many movie Vietnam vets are psychos, like Travis deranged by the horrors of war. While his symptoms are not invariably war-related, they resemble those of his movie—and real-life—counterparts: disorientation, alienation, paranoia. Travis subsists on junk food and cheap booze. Because he cannot sleep, not even with the help of the pills he habitually swallows, he drives by night, gradually lengthening his hours to fill the time he cannot obliterate. By day, sleepless still, he watches porno movies and television soaps, complementary distortions of human intercourse that intensify his alienation from actual life. His vision of the excremental city, extrapolated from soldiering in Vietnam and magnified by taxi driving in New York, casts himself as its scourge and redeemer.

"Redemption through Self-Destruction" Schrader titled an American Film Institute seminar he gave in 1989, invoking his overarching personal theme as well. At the time he wrote *Taxi Driver* Schrader was interested in "suicidal glory," that of an uneducated man in the person of Travis Bickle, later that of an educated man in the person of the eponymous hero of *Mishima* (1985), a movie Schrader both cowrote and directed. The ultimate expression of the sacrificial motif—and of its religious wellspring—occurs in *The Last Temptation of Christ*, which Schrader wrote between *Taxi Driver* and *Mishima*, and which Scorsese finally brought to the screen in 1988. No less than Schrader, Scorsese had long been fascinated by the idea of purgation through destruction—witness the endings of *Mean Streets* and *Boxcar Bertha*. From the time he finished reading Nikos Kazantzakis's novel, Scorsese was obsessed with filming *The Last Temptation of Christ*. The triad of Scorsese/Schrader collaborations beginning with *Taxi Driver*, continuing with *Raging Bull*, and culminating in *The Last Temptation of Christ* can arguably be read as variations on the theme of redemption through self-destruction. In an interview with Scorsese for *Cahiers du Cinema*, reprinted as the introduction to the screenplay of *Taxi Driver*, Schrader calls *The Last Temptation* "the final panel of the triptych. No more middleweights [*Raging Bull*'s Jake LaMotta]; this time we'll deal with a heavyweight sufferer" (p. xix). It was the religious aspect of the script, as reflected particularly in the obsessiveness of its protagonist, that initially drew Scorsese to *Taxi Driver*. Schrader had been reared in a Calvinist moral order no less parochial and even more constrictive—not until he was eighteen did he see his first movie—than Scorsese's own Catholicism. Their similar moral backgrounds are reflected in Travis's sexual repression no less than in his self-fashioned role of God's commando. Mirroring the virgin-or-whore concept of women held by Scorsese's alter egos of the *Mean Streets* trilogy, the chronically lonely cabbie fixates on Betsy (Cybill Shepherd), a shimmering blond movie incarnation of the Virgin Mary. Predictably, his offsetting obsession is with Iris (Jodie Foster), a twelve-year-old hooker who must be rescued from her pimp, Sport (Harvey Keitel)—"the worst scum of earth," Travis calls him—removed from the excremental city, and returned home to her parents in pristine Middle America. That his derangement is rooted in muddled religiosity surfaces after Travis is rejected by Betsy and casts the hitherto spotless dream girl into perdition ("You're in Hell"; "You'll burn in Hell"). It would seem that God's lonely man is a product of the ravages of war exacerbated by the distortions of religion.

Schrader, however, dismisses Vietnam as peripheral to his design, no more than a "part of the subtext" of *Taxi Driver:* "I didn't really make him a Vietnam vet. . . . It's assumed that he has some kind of searing memory and that he's had some familiarity with weapons, but it's not meant to be a story about Vietnam and Vietnam is never discussed."[3] Disingenuous as this may seem—Travis claims to be a former marine, honorably discharged, when he applies for his taxi driving job; and he may even be hired because the interviewer was himself a marine—it squares with Schrader's repeated denials of the film's sociological and/or psychological foundations. (The original script refers only to Travis's honorable discharge; neither his own nor his interviewer's marine background is mentioned.) Schrader similarly disclaims the influence of film noir ("Not too much") despite the undeniably *noirish* atmospherics of *Taxi Driver.* Perhaps, like the supplied Marine references, it is a case of the director fleshing out the script in accordance with his own vision. Scorsese does not so much violate the script as re-create it, thereby fashioning it into something more than the sum of its words. Moreover, Schrader's disclaimer is suspect in light of his confession that while writing *Taxi Driver* "the darkness of *film noir* attracted me." And as a film scholar and former critic whose "Notes on *Film Noir*" (1971) remains a classic essay on the genre, Schrader could hardly have swept away every vestige of noir from a film like *Taxi Driver.* Whatever traces of noir—or of the Vietnam syndrome and Calvinist repression, for that matter—appear in *Taxi Driver,* they are viewed by Schrader as incidental to the film's conception: "*Taxi Driver* really comes . . . out of French existentialist fiction. . . . Travis's is not a societally imposed loneliness or rage, it's an existential kind of rage. The book I reread just before sitting down to write the script was Sartre's *Nausea,* and if anything is the model for *Taxi Driver,* that would be it."[4]

Antoine Roquentin, the antihero of *Nausea* (1938), is one of those literary creations like Kafka's Joseph K who slips the confines of his text to embody the sensibility of an age. A writer and intellectual dogged by self-doubt and metaphysical anguish, Roquentin is far more sophisticated than Travis Bickle, but his legitimate precursor nonetheless. "I live alone, entirely alone. I never speak to anyone, never; I receive nothing, I give nothing" reads one of Roquentin's early diary entries. Like Travis, he is a compulsive diarist who defines himself by the condition of loneliness. That Travis writes at all, much less in a diary, testifies to an introspectiveness his character does not figure to possess. As a diarist he is given to flashes of eloquence sorely absent from his habitually taciturn and broken speech. It is as if Schrader is willing to sacrifice Travis's believability on the altar of literary influence. Other attributes of Sartre's existentialism, however, fit Roquentin and Travis equally well. They share a nearly palpable loneliness derived in part from a felt disjunction between themselves and their surroundings. Sartre's title refers to the nausea that symptomizes Roquentin's constant revulsion from the filth and squalor that are similarly evoked in Travis's voice-overs as he cruises the garbage-laden streets of New York. (The New York trash collectors' strike, which coincided with the filming of *Taxi Driver* in the summer of 1975, was a lucky break for the moviemakers if not for the beleaguered citizenry.) Like Roquentin, Travis is living at a high pitch of metaphysical intensity through an identity crisis brought about by the *mauvaise foi* (bad faith) that for Sartre characterizes the guilty actions of modern man. That Travis takes up arms against a sea of troubles while Roquentin simply broods reflects the difference between the European introspection of *Nausea* and the American violence of *Taxi Driver* without denying their common existential foundation. This difference is similarly apparent in the fate of the respective protagonists. Roquentin intuits in a snatch of jazz the creative outlet that might validate his life; if he can create—albeit in words rather than in music—an authentic work of art, then perhaps he will be able to remember his life "without repugnance." Travis, however, takes the more typically American route—violence—to regeneration. Neither *Nausea* nor *Taxi Driver* posits any guarantee: Roquentin could as easily relapse into lassitude as write his book; and Travis could as easily come unhinged again as maintain mental equilibrium.

There is no finality in existential texts, only uneasy closures that reflect the instability of the self.

Nausea may have been Schrader's "model" for *Taxi Driver,* but another existentialist classic, Dostoyevsky's *Notes from Underground* (1864), shares top billing as a literary influence. Schrader said as much when he defined Travis as a "younger, less intelligent, and violent" American counterpart of the European hero created by Sartre and Dostoyevsky. Dostoyevsky was on Scorsese's mind when he first met Schrader in 1974 and prodded him to do a script of *The Gambler.* But Brian De Palma, who had introduced them, spirited Schrader away for a crucial three hours during which the Dostoyevsky novella became the idea for *Obsession* (1976) (Scorsese finally got to make his version of *The Gambler* in 1989 with *New York Stories: Life Lessons.*). Luckily, Scorsese had also wanted to make a film of *Notes from Underground,* and when he read Schrader's script for *Taxi Driver* at DePalma's suggestion he found it "fantastic" and "the closest thing to it *[Notes]* I'd come across."[5] Even more anonymous—he is never named—than Travis Bickle, Dostoyevsky's underground man inhabits one of those vast cities that become hellish symbols of the modern world. Scorsese's New York, like Dostoyevsky's St. Petersburg, is an urban nightmare as harrowing as Balzac's Paris or Dickens's London and apparently as unredeemable. A feeling of resentment constantly exudes from the underground man who is as divided from society as he is divided within himself. *Notes from Underground* distills the extreme mental states—sadomasochism, schizophrenia, paranoia—that the divided psyche invariably exhibits in Dostoyevsky's major novels as well. That Travis enacts the violence that the underground man represses reveals no essential difference in their respective pathologies but simply the chasm separating twentieth century America from nineteenth-century Russia.

"I am a sick man. . . . I am a spiteful man," writes the underground man in the diary entry that opens *Notes from Underground.* "I believe my liver is diseased," he goes on, prefiguring Travis's "I think I've got stomach cancer." Plagued also by recurring and worsening headaches, Travis, like the underground man, lives in a state of permanent dyspepsia that epitomizes his inner turmoil. Pent-up conflict erupts in seesaws of altruism and brutality. Travis's "rescue" of Iris recalls the underground man's attempts to reform Liza, another prostitute. This salvational impulse, whatever its outcome, is as crucial to the cinema of Scorsese as to the fiction of Dostoyevsky. Travis is a "present-day saint," according to

Scorsese, "like Charlie in *Mean Streets*. He's a would-be saint, a Saint Paul. He's going to help people so much he's going to kill them."[6] This rage to kill, like the rarer impulse to save, is a product of the conflicted self. The underground man only dreams of avenging insults both real and fancied; Travis's all-consuming rage, frustrated in political assassination, is finally satisfied in brothel slaughter. The implication that presidential candidate Palantine and whoremonger Sport are interchangeable likens Travis's universal hatred to that of the underground man.

Whether his rage originates in existential angst à la Schrader or in the quagmire of Vietnam as Scorsese would have it—"It was crucial to Travis Bickle's character that he had experienced life and death around him every second he was in South-east Asia"—Travis is a time bomb waiting to explode.[7] Menace—in Travis's voice-over diary, in De Niro's every look and gesture (the twisted smile, the halting speech), in Bernard Herrman's haunting score—marks the rhythm of *Taxi Driver*. Ever the cineaste, rarely the litterateur, Scorsese locates Travis's character in American movies rather then in existential texts. Chief among those movies is John Ford's *The Searchers* (1956), a Western that had fascinated Scorsese since boyhood. As noted earlier, it is the film that is always on the mind of J.R., Scorsese's alter ego in *Who's That Knocking at My Door?* and the one film that Charlie, the slightly older version of J.R., pointedly goes to in *Mean Streets*. (Ethan Edwards [John Wayne], the hero of *The Searchers,* is a confederate veteran, permanently disheartened and disaffected by the losing cause he is still psychologically fighting three years after the end of the Civil War. The title reflects Edwards's unrelenting search for his niece Debbie, the sole survivor of a Comanche raid that massacred his brother's family.) What separates *The Searchers* from similar Westerns is neither its quest motif nor its outcome but the uncertain motives of Edwards. As much as he wants to rescue Debbie, he also wants to get Scar, the Comanche chief who kidnapped her and has surely made her his squaw during the five years of her captivity and of Edwards's obsessive quest. What lends even greater urgency to Edwards's search is the certainty that the kidnapped child would mature into the violated woman irremediably stigmatized as an Indian consort. With each passing year, Edwards's mind grows harder to read: will he take Debbie home when he finds her; or will he put a bullet in her head on the theory that she is better off dead than dishonored? Not until the very instant when he scoops his terrified niece into his arms—"Let's go home, Debbie"—does the suspense lift. After she is safely deposited in the bosom of the frontier community, Edwards turns on his heel and strides away, receding from view in a framing shot that is a studied reversal of the shot that framed his original (re)entry into the community. Not for him are home, family, friends: he strides out of the movie as he strides into it—alone.

The lone hero, the obsessive quest, the murderous intent, the successful rescue, even the racist undercurrent and the confused ideology stamp *Taxi Driver* as an updated, urban version of *The Searchers*. Travis first appears behind the wheel of a taxi—itself a metaphor of loneliness that Schrader once called a "steel coffin"—slicing through the Stygian gloom of noirish New York streets. Glimpsed through a haze of rising smoke that enhances the analogy to Hell, Travis's taxi comes into view like some monster from the deep: horror movies figure in *Taxi Driver* along with Westerns. Emulating Edwards, Travis will drive out of the movie as he drove into it—alone. It is loneliness that Schrader plays up in the opening paragraph of his published script (Faber and Faber, 1990) for *Taxi Driver:* Travis is "the consummate loner" whose "ominous strains" evidence "a life of private fear, emptiness, and loneliness. He seems to have wandered in from a land where it is always cold, a country where the inhabitants seldom speak." Travis shares with Edwards the alienation of a stranger in a strange land, preferring the wilderness of dangerous precincts to the safety of familiar surroundings. Like Edwards, who is more comfortable on horseback stalking Scar through hostile Indian territory than before the hearths of his fellow Texans back home, Travis is most at ease cruising in his taxi and sealed off from the society he invariably regards as loathsome. His evident contempt for blacks parallels Edwards's hatred of Indians; and his attitude toward women recalls the virgin-or-whore mentality that complicated Edwards's response to Debbie. It is in Travis's relationship with Iris, Debbie's counterpart, that *Taxi Driver* most resembles *The Searchers*.

Travis's obsession with Iris rechannels his earlier obsession with Betsy. A similarly repressed Ethan Edwards whose hidden love for Martha is frustrated—she is his brother's wife—spends what remains of his emotional capital on her daughter, Debbie. After Travis's bizarre date with Betsy—he ignorantly takes her to a porno movie, which she exits in disgust—she seems as lost to him as Martha, massacred by the Comanches, was to Edwards. Both men shift their sights to sullied child–women who conveniently provide a raison d'être for their dubious saviors along with a valid excuse for loosing apocalyptic fury against their despoilers. Just as Travis equals Edwards and Iris equals Debbie, Sport the pimp equals Chief Scar and like him is fated to die with his people in a climactic shootout. Although Travis wipes out the brothel crowd single-handedly while Edwards needs the help of the Texas Rangers to dispose of the Comanches, they both see themselves as avenging angels, their victims as subhuman devils. Sport and his crew, like Scar and his tribe, are filth that must be scoured from the earth, exterminated like any vermin. Unlike Edwards's single-minded pursuit of Scar, Travis's vendetta against Sport seems an arbitrary alternative to the botched assassination of Palantine, the target of choice. This inter-changeability of targets suggests that evil, endemic in *The Searchers* where it is confined to the Other (Scar and his Comanches) is pandemic in *Taxi Driver* where it infects all New York. Although evil is everywhere for Travis and mostly elsewhere for Edwards, the similarity of their modi operandi is invoked in Travis's self-conscious appropriation of cowboy-and-Indian motifs. Travis reinvents himself as a gunslinger, becoming a walking arsenal of concealed weapons in preparation for the attempt on Palantine's life. But it is his Mohawk haircut—startlingly emphasized by a panning shot that climbs slowly up Travis's body—that clinches his identification with Western imagery when he shows up at the outdoor rally where he plans to kill Palantine. Travis's subsequent confrontation with Sport, whose long black hair and headband look as Indian as Travis's Mohawk haircut, apparently pits Indian against Indian in a bizarre configuration of Western symbolism. Certainly good and bad Indians sometimes collide in Western movies, but the sequence—called the "Scar scene" by Scorsese and Schrader—jells only after Travis asks "How are things?" and Sport replies, "OK, cowboy." The jostling of cowboy and Indian identities in Travis reflects his schizoid persona. Distanced from Sport as a cowboy, Travis merges with him as an Indian. The effect is similar to the one Edwards produces in *The Searchers* when he scalps the dead Scar. Scourges of evil both, Travis and Edwards come to resemble more than casually the foes they so violently hate.

Taxi Driver shadows *The Searchers* in its external form more than in its internal dynamics. What is missing from *Taxi Driver* that is present—though hardly idealized—in *The Searchers* is any idea of a viable commu-nity. When Edwards decides to return Debbie rather than to kill her, he assigns to "home" a value that is positive if only by contrast to a Comanche wigwam. Not that home is anything like the sanctum sancto-rum of more conventional Westerns including many of Ford's: Debbie's return is mediated by communal attitudes toward miscegenation that are as bigoted as Edwards's own. Nevertheless Ford has already included enough of his habitual symbols of communal harmony—the hearth, the feast, the wedding, and particularly, the dance (Edwards is not above warming himself by the fire or eating and drinking his share, but he pointedly refrains from dancing)—to offset any ironic reading of his "happy" ending. Although the degree of viability *The Searchers* assigns to "home" is debatable, *Taxi Driver* explodes the very concept, most notably in the brief encounter between Iris and Sport (the "Scar" scene). Schrader initially opposed the scene (one of the few additions to the draft script to appear in the screen version), feeling that everything in *Taxi Driver* should reflect Travis's point of view, but Scorsese wanted a meaty scene for Harvey Keitel. (A shot of Travis looking up at a window as if he were watching Iris and Sport was inserted so that no world but Travis's would exist.) What is so crucial about the "Scar" scene, a scene conspicuously "missing" from *The Searchers,* is its evocation—and mediation—of the idea of "home." A love scene between a whore and her pimp, it is not so ironically, the tenderest moment in *Taxi Driver.* As they dance—a sly commentary on Ford's weightiest symbol of community— Sport soothes the distraught Iris with assurances of his undying love: "I wish every man could have what I have now, that every woman could be loved the way I love you." Iris easily believes him, perhaps because, as she told Travis earlier, "Sport never treated me bad, honest. Never beat me up once." That a pimp does not manhandle a whore may be unremarkable, but it is as convincing a proof of love as exists in *Taxi Driver.* By lighting the room where Iris turns tricks with the same softly glowing candles he employed in the devotional scenes of *Who's That Knocking?* and *Mean Streets,* Scorsese blurs the distinction between church and brothel. He has converted "There's no place like home" into "Home is no place." Iris's parental home, like Travis's, exists only as an offscreen cliché as does the "commune in Vermont" that Iris offhandedly suggests when Travis asks her where she wants to go to escape her wretched life in New York. Travis's dismissive reply that a commune he once saw in a magazine picture "didn't look clean" effectively pairs commune with city in their common filth. "In *Taxi Driver* 'home' is reduced to a photograph on a wall and a letter read aloud on a sound track. The function of the 'Scar' scene seems to be, in opposition to this, to call into question any easy assumption we might have that *anything* would be preferable (for a thirteen-year-old girl) to prostitution: with Sport, Iris shares an equivocal tenderness, whereas there is no indication that 'home' offers her anything at all."[8]

Taxi Driver's negation of community exposes the essential loneliness of the human condition. Travis is merely the supreme exemplar of a universal affliction: "I think you're a lonely person; you're not a happy person," he tells Betsy in the course of their first meeting at Palantine headquarters. Of all people, it is Betsy who least figures to be lonely. Yet Travis has struck a common chord: his bit about loneliness is what lures her into meeting him for "some coffee and pie." Betsy's role in *Taxi Driver,* however, is not so much to invoke the common loneliness as to expose the uncommon loneliness of Travis. Travis is the flip side of the comic tabula rasa character played by Peter Sellers a few years later in Hal Ashby's *Being There* (1979). A lifelong recluse thrown suddenly into the world, Sellers can relate to others only via the television images that represent his only contact with "reality." Making love to Shirley MacLaine he cannot go beyond the kissing stage since he has witnessed nothing more on TV. Similarly, Travis learns about love from pornographic movies, about human relationships from TV soap operas. So distorted is his idea of the real world that he takes Betsy to a porno movie on their first date. Her predictably indignant reaction, "This is like saying 'let's fuck,' " bewilders Travis who lamely replies, "I don't know much about movies. . . . Tell me what you want to see." What Betsy takes to be an unbelievably crude sexual ploy is more likely a particularly flagrant instance of Travis's characteristic anomie. While it is possible that the failure to connect with Betsy explains Travis's evolution from passive to aggressive loner, the aborted date is more a symptom of his pathology than a cause. At times his alienation seems congenital, an inborn inability to establish much less to sustain relations with fellow human beings. At other times his failure to communicate seems rather to reflect societal formation than genetic markings. True, the society is viewed only through Travis's eyes and is therefore subject to the interpretation of an increasingly deranged mind. Yet the raw data of filth and violence undeniably exist; Travis's tunnel vision may distort reality but not create it. The nightmare ambience of New York is no figment of a diseased imagination: Travis's voice-over diary entries merely convert quotidian randomness into a unified image of the excremental city.

It may be that Travis refashions the city in his own image, that he is its creation more than its creator. *Taxi Driver* is a title that conjures up images of New York as surely as it supplies metaphors for loneliness.

And it is Travis's vision of New York as Hell that animates his growing sense of mission. The role of "God's lonely man," cast in misery, is recast in heroism as Travis, no longer God's victim, becomes instead His avenging angel. New York did not spawn Travis even if, as Schrader denies but Scorsese affirms, his loneliness and rage are societally imposed. Whether Travis's pathology stems from existential angst (Schrader) on the Vietnam War (Scorsese), however, it is undoubtedly exacerbated by his experience of New York. Insomnia, hysteria, paranoia, homicidal and suicidal impulses—the scary symptoms of Travis's encroaching dementia—flourish in the city he regards as Hell. And though its noxious climate may be exaggerated by Travis's morbid sensibility, his perception of New York eerily reflects Scorsese's: "We shot the film during a very hot summer and there's an atmosphere at night that's like a seeping kind of virus. You can smell it in the air and taste it in your mouth; . . . a strange disease creeps along the streets of the city and, while we were shooting the film, we would slide along after it."[9] In *Taxi Driver,* as in so many of Scorsese's movies, the determinant role of New York cannot be overlooked.

Travis is driven by a twisted rage for order that he equates with cleanliness. More and more he becomes obsessed with the mission of washing away the filth of the city, human refuse included. During a cab ride with Travis, candidate Palantine asks "What is the one thing about this country that bugs you the most?" By way of reply, Travis vents his disgust with the "open sewer" of a city: whoever is elected president should "clean up the whole mess. . . . Just flush it down the fuckin' toilet." That he regards the excremental city as the country's greatest problem testifies more to Travis's obsession with cleanliness than to his faith in a political solution. So all-encompassing is the filth that its scouring may resist human agency and depend ultimately upon divine judgment. Some such solution occurs to Travis as he steers his cab down rain-slicked streets: "Thank God for the rain which has helped wash the garbage and trash off the sidewalks." And again, "Someday a *real* rain'll come and wash all this scum off the streets." Travis's vision of a great cleansing rain conflates apocalyptic and utopian fantasies in a potentially explosive witches' brew that figures recurrently in the American experience as it does in his own. When he finally explodes against Sport, Travis replays the purgation through violence scenario enacted in Vietnam. That his fury is directed initially against Palantine may indicate Travis's rejection of the political process the candidate incarnates. The recourse to (violent) individual action, as American as apple pie, understandably targets Palantine, the exemplar of the establishment politics that condones if it did not create the cesspool of New York. The ensuing brothel shootout implies something more than the cynical likening of pimp to politician, revealing Travis's apocalyptic yearnings even more clearly than did the planned assassination. For he rages against existence itself; if Sport had turned out to be as well-protected as Palantine, Travis would simply have picked a third target. *Taxi Driver* posits no end to his rage because Travis sees no end of the evil he abhors. Asked whether Travis has "purged himself and is now safe and sane" after slaughtering Sport and his cronies, Schrader demurred: "No, I think the syndrome is just going to start all over again."[10]

Rescuing Iris is a corollary to killing Sport and is nearly as crucial to the "syndrome" Schrader identifies. Travis's utopian vision of a New York washed clean by God's great rain is objectified in his obsession with returning Iris to her parents' home. A key component of American utopianism is the notion that, contrary to Thomas Wolfe's dictum, you can go home again. Earlier versions of American utopianism looked to the frontier, imagining not the return home so much as the creation of a new home. A Huck Finn—or an Ethan Edwards, for that matter—soured on "civilization" could always light out for the territory. Travis writes a letter to his parents but shows no inclination to return home: despite his hatred for New York he never invokes home or anyplace else as a viable alternative to the excremental city. Maybe he is too far gone to imagine a different life. Or maybe he is condemned by the force of his cleansing vision to the hell he imagines New York to be. No matter that Travis cannot—or will not—go home again; Iris must, even though she might prefer a brothel in New York or a commune in Vermont.

Travis's insistence that Iris return home reflects the nostalgia of latter-day American utopianism that shares his aversion to the modern world, as incarnated most famously in New York. His desire to deliver Iris back to her parents is part and parcel of his compulsion to clean up the city. In each instance he wants not to begin a new order but to restore an old one. Travis's simplistic response to the complexities of contemporary city life reflects provincial and conservative America's anxieties about modernity in general, and about urbanization in particular. His rescue of Iris recapitulates American captivity narratives dating from the Puritan experience of the New World. *Taxi Driver* follows *The Searchers,* the classic cinematic expression of the captivity narrative, in demonizing the stolen woman's captors and in symbolizing the wilderness they remove her to as Hell. In New York, the wilderness Hell of *Taxi Driver,* the captivity narrative intersects with epic accounts of the hero's descent into the underworld. A stopover in Hell is essential for Odysseus, Theseus, and Aeneas, the ultimate test of their heroic stature. Heracles makes off with Cerberus, the watchdog of Hell; and Orpheus almost rescues his wife Eurydice from the kingdom of the dead. Travis, already in Hell, must brave its nether regions to rescue Iris. Like any epic or Western movie hero, he signals his fitness for the task ahead: "I'll work anywhere, anytime," he tells the personnel officer who interviews him for a taxi-driving job. "I go all over," he says later, cruising anonymous streets in his taxi. "I take people to the Bronx, Brooklyn, I take 'em to Harlem. . . . I don't care, don't make no difference to me."

What so often distinguishes the American male hero from his ancient and/or foreign counterpart is his instinctive recourse to violence. Travis, like Edwards, exemplifies the American macho tradition that takes no prisoners. In *The Searchers,* Edwards's public mission—finding Debbie—is arguably a smokescreen for his private obsession—killing Indians. A grotesque scene in which he shoots as many buffalo as he can in order to deprive the Comanches of food illustrates Edwards's top priority and prefigures the climactic slaughter of the tribe. Logically, he should lay off the buffalo since starving Debbie's captors means starving her as well. Edwards's vendetta against the Comanches is, however, justified by their massacre of his brother's family. No such justification sanctions the bloodbath Travis perpetrates against Sport and his "tribe." In fact, by diluting the motivation for the carnage, Scorsese distances Travis from such macho forebears as Edwards. The brothel shootout thus parodies and rejects the myth of resolution/regeneration through violence so dear to American hearts. There is a faint whiff of parody even in *The Searchers* (e.g., the buffalo slaughter), but, at least from the settlers' standpoint, some good comes from Edwards's wipeout of the Comanches: a safer world for white expansion and exploitation. In the wake of Travis's massacre, however, New York remains unchanged. Whatever its social implications—is New York too far gone to salvage?—the ending of *Taxi Driver* points to the futility of violence. And because it springs from madness, violence is not only futile but insane.

To establish the linkage between violence and madness is not to assert that the mad are inevitably violent. Until he is rejected by Betsy, Travis is more passive than aggressive. When his awkward attempts at conversation are rebuffed by a concessions girl at the porno movie house, he immediately backs off. Hanging out with his fellow cabbies at the all-night Belmore Cafeteria, Travis is habitually reticent, rarely speaking until he is spoken to and hardly ever venturing an opinion. Despite his screenplay characterization as a time bomb waiting to explode, in the film's opening sequences he seems likelier to implode. Popping pills, gobbling junk food, swigging cheap booze, watching porno movies by night and TV soaps by day, Travis reveals little in his early behavior to predict his later violence. Only in his voice-over soliloquies does his pent-up rage boil over. Still, to talk violence is not to act violently: at this point the voice-overs may be a mode of suppression rather than a means of aggression. Only connect, the movie seems to be hinting, and the violence within may be contained. Some such idea occurs to Travis: "All my life needed was a sense of direction, a sense of someplace to go. I do not believe one should devote his life to morbid self-attention, but should become a person like other people." No sooner does he utter this voice-over than the possibility of salvation appears before him. Although it is late afternoon of another day when Travis spots Betsy emerging from the congested human mass, her appearance follows hard on the heels of his wish to become a real person. A first-time viewer of *Taxi Driver* might be excused for likening the sight of Betsy to the death of Alice's husband in *Alice Doesn't Live Here Anymore* as a deus ex machina granting of a wish that changes the protagonist's life. It is instantaneous wish-fulfillment as much as anything else that conventionally symbolizes a new life. Thus Betsy appears under the same heading (Further Thoughts) and on the same page (13) of Schrader's script as Travis's voice-over. "She appeared like an angel out of this open sewer," he marvels. "Out of this filthy mass. She is alone: They cannot touch her." It is a magic moment made more so for Travis by his identification of Betsy with the cleanliness he values above all else.

Of course romance with Betsy is not meant to be. After the fiasco of the porno movie date, the humiliated Travis tries desperately to see her again, but to no avail. In a compelling sequence that perfectly captures the agony of his rejection, Travis calls Betsy from a wall pay phone in a dingy building. As he holds the receiver—Betsy has apparently hung up—the camera slides away from the forlorn Travis, panning the long, empty corridor. It is as though Travis were stretched further still on the rack of his loneliness, a loneliness rendered now so painful that, led by the pitying camera, the viewer too flinches from the sight/site. Equally pitiful and pitiless is the tracking shot across the interior lower wall of Travis's room which reveals the several wilted bouquets of flowers that Betsy has refused. The symbolism of the rotting flowers is not lost on Travis: "The smell of the flowers only made me sicker. The headaches got worse, I think I've got stomach cancer," he records in his diary. This premonition of death shrivels him even more into himself. Keeping to his room, curling into a fetal position, subsisting on crazy combinations of food such as stale bread soaked in apricot brandy, he seems to be preparing for death. As his already flimsy identity buckles under stress, Travis's decline recalls the last days of Gregor Samsa who, transformed into a bug in Kafka's harrowing story "The Metamorphosis," gradually loses the will to live. Like Gregor, Travis seems to be relaxing his hold on life, not exactly willing his own death but not doing much that looks like living either. He is an implosion waiting to happen.

Yet just as implosion seems imminent, intimations of explosion multiply. Travis's turn toward violence commences with his rejection by Betsy. Scorsese and Schrader have programmed their hero for mayhem all along: the failure of love may be the proximate cause of his eventual explosion, but the explosion itself is inevitable. More than once Scorsese has sited Travis "somewhere between Charles Manson and St. Paul," evoking a personality so deranged as to span the entirety of the moral spectrum. Actually the saint label sticks less well to Travis than it did to J.R. and Charlie whose religious impulses reflected spiritual conflict rather than psychotic derangement. Like Travis, J.R. and Charlie are dichotomous characters, only less so; occupying a narrower band on the moral spectrum, they are incapable of the enormities of a Charles Manson. By the time he made *Taxi Driver,* Scorsese had abandoned the Catholic Church that had both sustained and inhibited his earlier alter egos. This is not to imply that mass murder originates in religious abeyance but only to suggest that a component of the loneliness that flares into rage is a dearth of affiliation, religious or otherwise. Travis, a man of no affiliations, either personal or institutional, makes a stab at connecting which, frustrated, drives him back into the dark confines of the individual psyche. His longer and longer hours behind the wheel reflect his steady retreat from the external world into an internal one increasingly of his own making. Dostoyevsky's underground man reports from the precinct of the isolate self whose suburb is death—the fate of the still more isolate Gregor-turned-bug in Kafka's haunting study of the ultimate loss of affiliation. A "steel coffin" (Schrader) in which

Travis is enclosed and immured, the taxi becomes the surpassing emblem of his loneliness and alienation. What is striking about *Taxi Driver* is its assumption that loneliness and violence go hand in hand. While it is true that Travis's violence is in one sense purely an expression of individual madness, in another it is a conceivable expression of the national identity. His makeup perfectly reflects D. H. Lawrence's view of the American as "hard, isolate, stoic, and a killer." Hardly a universal American trait, this fatal symbiosis of loneliness and violence is nonetheless a recognizable American phenomenon. Individualism, arguably *the* badge of American identity, devolves into loneliness, thence into madness and violence. *Taxi Driver* thus deconstructs a key component of the master narrative of American history, namely the myth of the lone hero who rescues/regenerates society through violence. "To the extent that this myth had also provided the basis of Classic Hollywood's thematic paradigm, and the traditional American ideology itself, *Taxi Driver* undertook to challenge the whole of American culture," maintains Robert B. Roy. And apropos of its putdown of simplistic responses to complex problems, Roy goes on to argue, "*Taxi Driver* allegorized the American experience in Vietnam: detached isolationism followed by violent, and ultimately ineffective, intervention."[11]

Because it is *Taxi Driver*'s contention that violence is as native to the American character as it is to Travis's, intimations if not actual incidents of violence fill nearly every frame. *The Texas Chainsaw Massacre* (1973), itself a response to rabid American violence, plays at a movie house Travis drives by early in *Taxi Driver*. Scorsese's camera lingers on the marquee title just as it does on Travis's glass of Alka Seltzer in a scene with the other cabbies at the Belmore Cafeteria. The Alka Seltzer shot, lifted from Godard's *2 or 3 Things I Know about Her* (1967), zooms in to saturate the screen with an enormous close-up of bubbling seltzer, its seething carbonation apparently representing the turmoil of Travis's mind. Another Belmore scene, this one a faux existential exchange between Travis and Wizard (Peter Boyle), the resident philosopher of the cabbie hangout, is as "absurd" as anything cooked up by the French. A classic failure of communication, their dialogue consists mainly of Wizard spouting soothing platitudes—"Relax, Killer, you're gonna' be all right"—and Travis's anguished confessions—"I just wannago out and really . . . really do something. . . . I really got some bad ideas in my head." Wizard's calling Travis "Killer," Travis's "bad ideas," a black cabbie meanwhile pointing his finger at Travis as if it were a gun (the Scorsese trademark gesture that Sport later directs at Travis and that Travis repeats, at his own head, after the brothel massacre) similarly foreshadow violence. Travis's mat-ter-of-fact remark that "sometimes I clean the blood off" the back seat of his taxi attributes violence to business as usual. A man zigzags through the streets inexplicably yelling, "I'll kill her, I'll kill her, I'll kill her." Two old men fight on a street corner, one apparently trying to rob the other. Eggs hurled by marauding youths splatter against Travis's windshield. Blacks loom threateningly, at least in Travis's sick imagina-tion. (So intent was Schrader on raising every indicator of violence to the boiling point that the draft of the script he sold depicted Travis as a virulent racist and all the people he kills at the end as blacks.)

Although the telltale signifiers of violence are everywhere, Travis subsumes his own violent impulses in his fantasy of God's cleansing rain. Only when he fails with Betsy does he conflate divine justice with per-sonal violence. The flowers she refuses to accept catalyze his transforma-tion from victim to victimizer. Initially overcome by the death-dealing ("I think I've got cancer") properties of the desiccating flowers, Travis suddenly burns them. Another offending object—the television set, pro-jector of phony soap opera characters as remote from him as Betsy—explodes when he kicks it over. Moreover, Travis incarnates American racism as well as American violence. Racist fantasies underlie the Mohawk haircut he adopts for assassinating Palantine; and his final con-frontation with Sport invokes a clash between Indian rivals. In appropri-ating the narrative of *The Searchers, Taxi Driver* retains and embellishes its ambient racism. Native Americans are most often debased and demo-nized in Western movies despite the token appearance of the Noble Savage (a term that demeans even as it apparently exalts). True, *The Searchers* largely contains its racist rhetoric in Ethan Edwards and the Noble Savage is fleetingly invoked in Chief Scar's dignified lament for his lost sons. Yet racism is depicted as alive and well in the white com-munity at large, albeit in less violent form than it rages in Edwards. By adding to *Taxi Driver* the "Scar" scene *The Searchers* so conspicuously omitted, Scorsese deepens the Iris/Sport relationship of his own film and arguably challenges racist and sexist stereotypes. But the implied equa-tion of Sport with Scar hardly flatters American Indians and the climac-tic scene that casts Travis and Sport as good and bad Indians respectively reduces "the image of the Noble Savage . . . to the rhetorical gesture of a psychopath, the revolutionary rage of the Ignoble Savage to the self-vindication of a pimp."[12] In fact, by retaining the racist elements of *The Searchers* and intensifying them immeasurably by invoking the sickness of black/white relations, *Taxi Driver* becomes as scathing a comment on American racism as it is on American violence. Schrader wanted all the people Travis kills in the brothel shootout to be black because "it was true to the character." Even without Schrader's incendiary climax, Travis's racism—and that of others—figures prominently in *Taxi Driver*. In one of the key scenes that prefigure Travis's turn to violence Scorsese himself plays a betrayed husband whose murderous fantasy is voiced in racist—and sexist—rhetoric. "A nigger lives there," this passenger reveals from the back seat of Travis's cab as they watch a woman's silhouette framed in a second-story apartment window. Miscegenation worsens the sin of infidelity to the nth power, "ruining" the (white) woman and rendering her unredeemable. It was, of course, Ethan Edwards's similar theory about the ruinous effects of miscegenation that added urgency to his pursuit of Debbie and that nearly led to her death at his hands after the passing years had guaranteed that Scar had made her his squaw. Scorsese had not cast himself as the crazed husband: he took over the role as an eleventh hour replacement for the indisposed George Memmoli (Fat Joey, the poolroom manager in *Mean Streets*). But because the interchange between passenger and driver is equally and inevitably a transaction between Scorsese and De Niro, this already crucial scene becomes even more so. After he *directs* Travis's gaze to the tell-tale silhouette in tandem with his own, the passenger raves on: "Did you ever see what a forty-four magnum can do to a woman's pussy? That you should see. . . . I know you must think I'm pretty sick." Surely one of the most misogynistic outbursts in screen history, the passenger's words reflect the same hostility to women that he obviously feels toward blacks. Of course, he is "sick," but again, so is Travis whose own "gaze" at the world is "validated" in this conflation of racism and sexism. That it is Scorsese, both in and out of character, who is directing the gaze, further empowers the scene as a defining moment in Travis's life—perhaps *the* moment that turns him into a killer. By "identifying" the filth (e.g., women, blacks) that Travis abhors and its means of elimination (violence), the passenger/Scorsese has "directed" the remaining action of the narrative. It comes as no surprise, then, that the passenger's juxtaposition of the gaze with power in general and with the devastating power of the .44 Magnum in particular determines

Travis's future course. "An extension of the gaze's power, the .44 Magnum is the first gun Travis buys from Easy Andy," observes Christopher Sharrett after explaining that the taxi driver's "voyeuristic 'gaze' at everything in his experience signifies his unsuccessful integration in the object–world."[13] Thus the passenger does not so much alter the fundamental nature of Travis's gaze as (re)direct it, sharpening its focus as a precondition of homicidal intent.

The change in Travis from (im)passive observer to lethal force is ritually enacted in the seriocomic gun-buying scene. The taxi—Schrader's primary metaphor of loneliness—not only isolates Travis behind the wheel but interposes its bulk between him and the urban life he observes but rarely engages. Not directly but only through its windshield and windows does Travis experience the external world. Insulated by glass and steel he mediates reality still further by watching it habitually through his rearview mirror, a mechanism of inversion and distortion if there ever was one. He never looks at his passengers directly, not even at the demented husband played by Scorsese who virtually seizes his gaze. (Im)passively Travis reduces the world and the people in it to meaningless objects, alike in their numbing sameness. He regards Scorsese's homicidal misogynist through the rearview mirror, apparently no more excited by the passenger's impassioned ravings than he was by the eggs that spattered against his windshield. Yet, Travis is affected as he has not been before—perhaps by the passenger's repeated invocation of the annihilating power of the .44 Magnum—and propelled out of his taxi and into the meeting with Andy, the accommodating gun salesman. In the voice-over diary entry that immediately precedes the meeting, Travis notes the all-important moment of transition: "The days move along with regularity, over and over, one day indistinguishable from the next, a long, continuous chain. Then suddenly, there is change." Henceforth, he will more frequently relinquish the (relative) safety of his cab for the riskier environment of the streets. The linkage of Easy Andy, the purveyor of death, with Iris—Easy is her name, she initially tells Travis—the purveyor of sex, confirms the similar identification,.44 Magnum with unfaithful wife, which Travis's vengeful passenger had previously invoked. No sooner does Andy open his suitcase to reveal row upon row of gleaming new handguns than Travis asks, "You got a .44 Magnum?" Schrader's script again conflates sex and death, the gun becoming a potent stand-in for Travis's impotent penis: "Andy . . . cradles the long eight-inch barrel in his palm. The .44 is . . . huge, oversized, inhuman," a gun that "belongs in the hand of a marble god, not a slight taxidriver." As noted, De Niro lost fifteen pounds to play the gaunt taxidriver and improvised a scuttling walk to approximate the crab he saw in Travis. The analogy likewise invokes confinement: encased in its shell the crab reflects Travis's isolation. It is paradoxically the very weapon he is (symbolically) unfit to handle that empowers him to handle it. Inspired by the look and feel of the .44 Magnum—perhaps more than he would have been by any woman, Betsy included—Travis will henceforth forego the booze and pills, kick the junk-food habit, perfect his shooting ability, and begin a strict body-building regimen, all designed to ready him for the combat ahead. Meanwhile, however, the transaction with Easy Andy evolves into a devastating parody of the action heroes Travis hopes to emulate:

> The gun-buying scene has many intertextual aspects, presenting a kind of condensed repository of the popular culture that has been a contributing force in Travis's delusions. Travis buys a Walther PPK (James Bond), a snub-nose Smith and Wesson .38 (Mike Hammer), a pocket-sized .25 automatic (also Bond ordnance) and the .44 Magnum (the most popular handgun in America following the success of *Dirty Harry* (1971). Travis mounts the .25 automatic on a retractable spring he wears up his sleeve, the trick of riverboat gamblers and Robert Conrad in "The Wild, Wild West." He tapes a huge knife to his boot and pulls it free as he tumbles onto a cot, mimicking the death of Jim Bowie at the Alamo.[14]

The Bowie imitation symptomizes a facet of Travis's pathology that snowballs in importance in the wake of the gun-buying scene. Travis's namesake, like Bowie a martyred defender of the Alamo, achieved mythic status via suicidal bravado. That Travis regards his planned assassination of Palantine as a suicide mission is evident in the closing words of the note he leaves Iris along with her getaway money: "By the time you read this I will be dead." And even after he miraculously survives the brothel shootout, "his blood-soaked body blending" with the red velvet sofa on which he has collapsed, Travis "forms his bloody hand into a pistol, raises it to his forehead and, his voice croaking in pain, makes the sound of a pistol discharging." Schrader's description makes it clear that Travis's purifying zeal extends even to himself and that catharsis consists of exorcizing the demons within as well as eliminating the demons without. Since only in death can he be free of his own personal demons, Travis embraces the assured closure of suicide though he is out of bullets and can only pantomime the act. In this reading, the apocalyptic shootout is the penultimate action of a purgative ritual, the finale of which is suicide. "*Taxi Driver* was suicidal glory in the person of an uneducated man," according to Schrader whose interest in suicidal glory would peak in the ritual *seppuku* of the educated eponymous hero of *Mishima*. In any event, Travis repeatedly telegraphs his suicidal impulses in the interval between the gun-buying scene and the "farewell" note to Iris.

"Travis Gets Organized" Schrader titles the episode that immediately follows the gun-buying scene but that occurs several weeks later. From his apartment where he is doing pushups to "get in shape" the scene shifts to a firing range where "with each blasting discharge from the Magnum, Travis's body shudders and shakes" in an imitation orgasm that again likens the .44 Magnum to the penis. What is more, continues Schrader's script, relentlessly pressing the sex/violence analogy, "each recoil from the giant gun was a direct attack on his masculinity." As if it were not enough to equate the action of gun and penis, he goes on to cement a cause-and-effect relationship between repressed sex and violent action in "Foreplay to Gunplay," an episode whose title says it all. As Travis watches a porno film, the feigned ecstasy of a female movie voice fades into Travis's voice-over back in his apartment where a tracking shot inches along a "wall covered with Charles Palantine political paraphernalia." At the end of the track stands Travis, .44 Magnum in hand. A series of follow-up shots shows him preparing for action: practicing fastdraws, concealing his weapons, dumdumming the .44 bullets. "Here is a man," proclaims Travis's voice-over diary entry, "who wouldn't take it any more, a man who stood up against the scum, the cunts, the dogs, the filth." Not only in the diary entry that expresses the paranoid hatred and the coiled violence of the lone avenger but in the preceding exposure of the psychosexual roots of his malaise, "Foreplay to Gunplay" extends *Taxi Driver*'s parody of the American action hero.

Travis's bizarre preparatory rituals pay off in the next scene when he guns down a strung-out junkie attempting to rob an all-night delicatessen in Spanish Harlem. That the would-be robber is black is hardly accidental casting. What is most striking about the "Incident in a Deli" scene, however, is neither the shooting nor the racist overtones but the overkill at the conclusion. In Schrader's original script, Travis's single shot kills the black stickup man. But on the screen, Melio the counterman finishes off the wounded youth who lies helplessly on the floor by beating him to a pulp with a baseball bat. Perhaps Scorsese escalates the violence to show that rage (and racism?) are not confined to Travis. If so, it seems redundant in a film that has repeatedly made the same point before. More likely Scorsese is setting the stage for the apocalyptic violence unleashed by Travis in the brothel massacre. According to Schrader, who dubs the climactic bloodbath "The Slaughter," *everything* in *Taxi Driver* set the stage for this moment. What Schrader is after, however, is not narrative closure but transcendence. An asterisk at the end of "The Slaughter" in the original script refers the reader to a "Screen writer's note" that explains Schrader's intentions:

> The screenplay has been moving at a reasonably realistic level until this prolonged slaughter. The slaughter itself is a gory extension of violence, more surreal than real. The slaughter is the moment Travis has been heading for all his life, and where this screenplay has been heading for over 85 pages. It is the release of all that cumulative pressure; it is a reality unto itself. It is the psychopath's Second Coming.

Although Scorsese's stated ideas about catharsis in self-sacrifice and purgation in fountains of blood mesh with Schrader's own, he puts a slightly different spin on "The Slaughter":

> I wanted the violence at the end to be as if Travis had to keep killing all these people in order to stop them once and for all. Paul saw it as a kind of Samurai 'death with honor'—that's why De Niro attempts suicide—and he felt that if he'd directed the scene, there would have been tons of blood all over the walls, a more surrealistic effect. What I wanted was a *Daily News* situation, the sort you read about every day: 'Three men killed by lone man who saves young girl from them.'[15]

The mind boggles at Scorsese's suggestion that Schrader favored an even bloodier mise-en-scène. And such effects as the impressionistic lighting and acute camera angles, as well as the sound of trickling blood, the slow motion close-up of fingers blasted off an old man's hand, the bloody finger Travis presses to his head, and so forth, could hardly be more surrealistic.

If "The Slaughter" is the stuff of tabloid headlines, then it functions primarily as a critique of American popular culture. Travis's showdown at the brothel replicates and parodies famous last stands ranging from the conventional—Custer's at the Little Big Horn, Doc Holiday's at the OK Corral—to the revisionist—Pike's in Sam Peckinpah's *The Wild Bunch* (1969), McCabe's in Robert Altman's *McCabe and Mrs. Miller* (1971). Travis's own last stand stubbornly resists the closure that the term implies. What he envisions as a personal Armageddon is nothing of the kind, if only because Armageddon is a final and conclusive battle between good and evil, and while Sport and the brothel crew qualify as evildoers, Travis is badly—and deliberately—miscast as the knight in shining armor. That Travis survives the bloodbath he creates is as likely to guarantee the persistence of evil as its elimination since it is even money, as Scorsese and Schrader agree, that Travis will kill again. Like the famous "You talkin' to me?" sequence that prefigures it, the brothel shootout is the imitation of an action. Travis's confrontation with his mirror image in the earlier scene rehearses his showdown with Sport, another mirror (Indian vs. Indian) confrontation. What is common to the mediated last stand, the phony Armageddon, and the self-reflexive confrontations is their subversion of the master narrative of the action hero. Travis's "heroism" is as spurious as it is derivative, the end product of a series of gestures drained of their nominal value(s). And Travis himself is a pastiche of the movie clichés that he evokes and enacts, an empty reflector of the equally empty popular culture that created him. Travis's makeup reflects his cinematic no less than his philosophical (existentialism) and his sociocultural (Vietnam era) antecedents. And despite Schrader's affinities with Bresson and Scorsese's homage to Godard, Travis's—and *Taxi Driver*'s—precursors are mostly American. *Taxi Driver* and its protagonist amalgamate three of the most prominent American film genres—the Western, film noir, and the horror film. It is even possible to schematize the contribution of these genres in the formation of *Taxi Driver.* The Western, notably *The Searchers,* structures the narrative; film noir determines the mise-en-scène; the horror film spawns the protagonist. Naturally, genre influences wax and wane as well as overlap. Travis's pastiche personality, for example, accommodates all three genres, often coterminously. And the sovereign position of *The Searchers* makes the domination of the Western practically inevitable. Still, the powerful contributions of the noir and horror genres to the formation of *Taxi Driver* are hard to ignore.

In "Notes on *Film Noir,*" written only a year before the script for *Taxi Driver* "jumped out of my head like an animal" during ten days in the summer of 1972, Schrader characterized what he called the "third and final phase of *film noir,* from 1949—53," as "the period of psychotic action and suicidal impulse." This final phase witnessed the transformation of the noir hero who started to go bananas. The psychotic killer . . . now became the active protagonist; . . . *film noir*'s final phase was the most aesthetically and sociologically piercing. After ten years of steadily shedding romantic conventions, the later *noir* films finally got down to the root causes of the period: the loss of public honor, heroic conventions, personal integrity, and, finally, psychic stability. The third-phase films were painfully self-aware; they seemed to know they stood at the end of a long tradition based on despair and disintegration and did not shy away from that fact. The best and most characteristically noir films . . . stand at the end of the period and are the results of self-knowledge. The third phase is rife with end-of-the-line heroes.[16]

Nearly all of this is apposite, but what is particularly striking is not so much Schrader's anatomizing of the noir hero—Travis's psychic lineage can be traced as firmly back to horror films as to "third-phase" film noir—as his sense of loss. *Taxi Driver* too is animated by a sense of loss as palpable as that in "third-phase" noir and as culturally determined. As much as Schrader downplays the noir connection in favor of French existential texts and Bresson films, he can hardly disclaim what he, at least in part, has wrought. Scorsese, of course, has invariably invoked the Vietnam War as *the* key to Travis's pathology and by extension to America's social malaise as well. *Taxi Driver*'s ending clarifies and deepens the sociocultural critique that infiltrates the film from its beginning and that should come as no surprise from the director of *The Big Shave* and *Street Scenes*.

The last two scenes of *Taxi Driver* have been variously reviled and/or misinterpreted as a gratuitous coda that weakens if not spoils the film. In "Letter from Pittsburgh" the camera tracks the wall formerly plastered with Palantine material but now sporting new clippings whose headlines—"Cabbie Battles Gangster," "Taxi Driver Hero to Recover"—valorize Travis, the heroic rescuer. Accompanying the tracking shot, a voice-over of Iris's father reads a thank-you letter to Travis who, by returning their daughter—now "back in school and working hard"—has made the lives of her parents "full again." *Taxi Driver* concludes with "Old Friends": a fully recovered Travis picks up Betsy, a fare whose voice he recognizes but whom he continues to regard solely through his rearview mirror. The effect is to reduce her to a disembodied presence and though after he drops her off she hints at seeing him again, he drives away non-committingly, his taxi slowly disappearing from view. Far from being an anticlimactic addendum to a film that should have ended with the brothel shootout, the postapocalyptic denouement indicts a society that is arguably as psychotic as its new-found hero: "the admiration Travis now enjoys is born out of a superficial and misleading image of him perpetrated by the media (the news clippings on the wall) and by the political structure afraid to examine its own bankruptcy. Travis is thus fed into the media to become the type of apparition that constructed him." The film's deliberately cynical ending makes it "apparent that general alienation is profound, pervasive, and resistant to any interpretation or cure."[17] The construction of celebrity and its sociocultural implications, a phenomenon that Scorsese invokes and investigates first in *Taxi Driver,* will subsequently become a crucial motif in such apparently diverse films as *New York, New York; Raging Bull; The King of Comedy;* perhaps even in *The Last Temptation of Christ.*

Travis's media-made celebrity would be funny if it were not so scary. There is an element of black comedy after all in the tabloids and in the banality of the letter that confer heroism on Travis as well as in the reversal of positions in his final encounter with Betsy. But valorizing the psychotic Travis has sinister implications that the equally absurd adulation of the recessive couch potato of *Being There* and the talentless comic of *The King of Comedy* (another Scorsese/De Niro collaboration) do not. Unlike the harmless celebrity of the others, which simply reflects the gullibility and vulgarity of the shapers and consumers of American public opinion, Travis's additionally reflects the glorification of violence. When Pauline Kael called *Taxi Driver* "one of the few truly modern horror films" she cited as evidence its symbolic equation of blood-spattering release and sexual consummation. What is truly horrifying, however, is that the media grant public sanction to Travis's private fantasies. It is akin to glorifying Norman Bates, the similarly psychotic killer in that quintessential modern horror movie, *Psycho.* There is no stronger cinematic correlation between sex and violence than *Psycho*'s famous shower scene. But unlike *Taxi Driver, Psycho* ends with its crazed killer locked in a cell not loosed on the streets. The humor of Betsy's last scene with Travis dissolves in the realization that what attracts her to him is the celebrity achieved by violence. And he is still "God's lonely man," a killer threatening to kill again, absolved from judgment and glorified beyond it. Five years after *Taxi Driver,* the copycat violence of John Hinckley's attack on President Reagan recalled Travis's attempt to assassinate presidential candidate Palantine. Like Travis's, Hinckley's real target was sexual, not political: the six shots fired at Ronald Reagan were meant to catch the sympathetic eye of Jodie Foster, Hinckley later explained, adding that his fifteen (!) viewings of *Taxi Driver* had made him do it. If life imitates art in Hinckley's emulation of Travis, then art imitated life in Travis's emulation of Arthur Bremer, the would-be assassin of presidential candidate George Wallace. It was Bremer's diary, one of Schrader's sources for *Taxi Driver,* that inspired the compulsive diary-keeping of Travis. These bizarre transactions are freighted with political implications, not the least of which is the suspicion that American life is no more than the game of images evoked in *Taxi Driver*'s conclusion. Hinckley follows Travis in making his private fantasy into a public event, imagining perhaps that the media will grant him the identical cultural and political seal of approval it conferred on Travis. Yet it is Ronald Reagan himself, the icon of an age in which media spin displaces political substance, who ironically benefits from his own near-assassination. The attack created a wave of sympathy for Reagan and replenished his dwindling political stock at a crucial moment in his presidency.

All this is not to argue that *Taxi Driver*'s aim is chiefly political, only to indicate the range of its importance. A triumph of personal filmmaking if there ever was one, *Taxi Driver* was Scorsese's finest achievement to date and one of the seminal American films of the 1970s. The movie marked the end of the golden age of postwar American film that began in the late 1960s. Scorsese once called 1971 to 1976 "the best time," the years in which he and other brilliant young auteurs revolutionized Hollywood, revitalizing moribund genres and questioning the cozy assumptions of American life. In art if not always in politics, the counterculture prevailed, though by 1976 it had already begun to disintegrate. A year after *Taxi Driver,* George Lucas's *Star Wars* heralded the advent of the age of the blockbuster and the end of an era of personal and critical moviemaking. Winner of the *Palme d'or* at the 1976 Cannes Film Festival, *Taxi Driver* is one of those rare movies that alters its initial reception and transgresses its chronological and cultural boundaries. "When I talk to younger film-makers," said Schrader in 1990, "they tell me that it was really the film that informed them, that it was their seminal film, and listening to them talk I really can see it as a kind of social watermark." The day *Taxi Driver* opened, Schrader arrived at the theater for the noon show to discover a huge line for the two o'clock show already snaking around the block. "So I ran inside and watched the film and everyone was standing at the back and there was a sense of exhilaration about what we had done. We knew we'd never repeat it."[18]

The Sound(s) of Music:
From the Bands to The Band

Conventional wisdom has it that Martin Scorsese's directing career orbited with *Taxi Driver* but nosedived with *New York, New York* (1977). True, the cost overruns and so-so box office of *New York, New York* rattled the Hollywood moguls whose backing Scorsese would need for future projects. After making the critically and financially successful *Taxi Driver* for a piddling $1.9 million and in the process establishing himself as one of America's premier filmmakers, Scorsese was given nearly $7 million, by far his biggest budget to date, for *New York, New York*. When it ran $2 million over budget and an unplayable four and a half hours in its initial cut, *New York, New York* had all the earmarks of not only a costly but an indulgent bomb. And though it was pared down to a commercially viable 153 minutes for its American release and still further to 136 minutes in its European version, the film's very malleability seemed to signal its muddled intentions. Scorsese attributed *New York, New York*'s problems to a runaway script—an unwonted tribute to *Taxi Driver*'s success: "We started to get cocky. So throw away the script! We improvised a lot of it. And so we shot a lot of film." Yet despite its apparent catch-as-catch-can assemblage, *New York, New York* emerged as an artifact so unified as to resist alteration/mutilation: "We tried to cut the film down, and it didn't want to cut . . . . It was like a monster. It was impossible." What Scorsese strongly implies is that a film widely regarded as a failure in its compromised version was anything but in its original form. Admitting that "while each scene might work, the whole suffered," he nonetheless defends the finished product even in its variously truncated shapes. It is a "better picture than the original script . . . . But if I had gone about the reconstruction of that script and that story, and known what I wanted from the beginning, it would have been much stronger."[1] Maybe. But it may equally be argued that even so apparently intractable a film might have been cut more proficiently. Exhibit A is the all-but-interminable opening nightclub scene when Jimmy Doyle (Robert De Niro) first encounters Francine Evans (Liza Minnelli). A brilliantly filmed sequence, it is too long by half. On the other hand, an equally brilliant sequence—the twelve-minute "Happy Endings" production number showcasing Liza Minnelli— wound up on the cutting room floor, only to be restored when *New York, New York* was rereleased in 1981 to a host of favorable critical reappraisals. Running two hours and forty-four minutes, the 1981 rerelease, preserved in a 1989 digital video transfer in the letter-box format and billed as "the original uncut version," has since become *the New York, New York.* Unlike the bloated *Casino* (1995), which all but cries out for judicious cutting, *New York, New York* is a Scorsese film in which less is *not* more. Scorsese himself attributes *New York, New York*'s chilly 1977 reception not so much to what was missing as to what was misunderstood. By 1981, he maintains, audiences finally figured out that the film was about personal relationships. Four years earlier, led by reams of nostalgia publicity to welcome the return of the big Hollywood musical, audiences were turned off when they got the fractious relationship between Jimmy Doyle and Francine Evans instead. *New York, New York is* a big Hollywood musical of sorts; it is just that the narrative arc transcribed by Jimmy and Francine is not of the standard sort.

Music infuses the cinema of Martin Scorsese from the beginning: whether it is the classic rock of *Who's That Knocking?* and *Mean Streets,* the twanging bluegrass of *Boxcar Bertha;* the mishmash of pop styles in *Alice Doesn't Live Here Anymore;* or the slinky Bernard Herrmann soundtrack of *Taxi Driver,* music powerfully evokes time, place, even character and action. Music is everything in *Woodstock* and in *The Last Waltz* (1978), the documentary celebrating The Band's farewell concert that Scorsese shot only a month after wrapping up *New York, New York.* And Paul Schrader's Gershwin script, written for Scorsese in the mid-eighties, may never get made, but Scorsese, who loves the ending of Woody Allen's *Manhattan* (1979) with its swelling Gershwin soundtrack, still talks wistfully of making it. The idea of doing homage to the Hollywood musicals of the late forties and early fifties was itself a sort of homage to another defunct tradition, that of the classic Hollywood director who, à la Howard Hawks, could make a film noir as easily as a screwball comedy, a gangster picture as easily as a love story. *New York, New York* is Scorsese's anachronistic bid for industry status, a valentine to a long dead studio system that the movie reflects. Yet it is more than a self-aggrandizing display of virtuoso filmmaking. The big band music celebrated in *New York, New York* was the music Scorsese grew up with, the music of his parents' generation. He fell in love with their swing records and with songs like "Deed I Do" and "Love Letter" and was taken by his father to the Paramount and Capitol and Strand Theaters to hear the big bands of Paul Whiteman and Eddy Duchin and Ted Lewis. As fascinated by photographs of his uncles in World War II uniforms as by the music of their era, Scorsese conceived *New York, New York* as a salute to his family as much as to a style and a system. Yet in evoking the people and music he loved, Scorsese cannot help evoking himself. "My light frothy musical turned out to be my most personal film," he claimed in a *Newsweek* (May 16, 1977) interview. Although this seems debatable in light of a *Who's That Knocking?* or a *Mean Streets,* characters and events in *New York, New York* gradually slip out of the predictable confines of the forties and fifties and into the messier arena of the seventies. Jimmy Doyle, unable to cope with Francine's pregnancy, subsequently deserts her and their newborn child. Julia Cameron, Scorsese's second wife, was expecting even as their marriage was unraveling; and Diahnne Abbott whose sultry "Honeysuckle Rose" steals a nightclub scene in *New York, New York* had recently married De Niro and was also pregnant. Rumors of Scorsese's not-so-secret affair with Liza Minnelli and of his recurring bouts with drugs raised the pressure on a production whose shooting schedule and budget were spiraling out of control. Andy Warhol alludes to both rumors in a couple of diary entries from the 1977—78 period during and just after the filming of *New York, New York.* On July 10, 1977, Warhol reports Julia Scorsese's reaction to the Liza Minnelli affair—"She went on about that a lot and she was walking sort of drunkenly on high heels and her pupils were dilated"—and her revelation "that Marty has coke problems and he got blood poisoning and now he takes medicine to clean himself out." And on May 11, 1978, at lunch with Scorsese, Warhol cannot help noting that "Marty was shaking like crazy. I guess from coke."[2] In any event, Scorsese's high living came to a crashing halt, at least temporarily, on Labor Day, 1978, when he landed in the hospital with internal bleeding. Whatever its genesis, pain was crucial to the making of *New York, New York:* "If we hadn't gone through that pain we never would have gotten that story—the story of the marriage in the film. In the final analysis, it's a very honest film about marriage and, in some ways, it's a beautiful film."[3]

Scorsese is referring to the pain of reconstructing the script scene by scene, mostly by improvisation. Still, it is the personal pain that dictates what each painstakingly constructed scene would become. Thus Scorsese subverts the original design of *New York, New York* not because he set out to revise a genre but because the genre became revised under the pressure of invoking it. And while it is true that he attributes his rejection of Earl MacRauch's first version of the script to his own swelled head after *Taxi Driver*'s success, he expressed no reservation initially. Even before he began *Taxi Driver,* Scorsese had read in *The Hollywood Reporter* that producer Irwin Winkler had bought the script rights to *New York, New York* but had not yet signed up a director. When Scorsese and Winkler got together they thought it would be a commercial project, a potential hit. MacRauch's script was classic Hollywood material: boy meets girl, boy loses girl, boy gets girl, all to the big band era tunes that he plays and she sings. Endless rewrites later, during the course of which MacRauch finally bailed out and Scorsese's wife, Julia Cameron, and old NYU buddy and former collaborator Mardik Martin were brought in, the recast script became a pretext for improvisation rather than a text for performance. Martin recalls that "everything got out of hand. . . . I came up with a dozen endings and none of them worked." Since nobody knew where the film was heading, "there was a resolution to this story, but never a dramatic ending." *New York, New York* was "painful" to Martin who "did a lot of work on that film . . . the kind of work that would drive you nuts, writing the night before you shoot, trying to save the picture."[4] As a glossy, old-fashioned confection became an edgy postmodern construct the music stayed sweet but the romance turned sour.

In its simultaneous awareness of two eras *New York, New York* effects their transformation into a more complex "reality" than either might reflect alone. This restructured view is self-reflexive, calling attention to its imitativeness because *New York, New York* is as much about film itself as anything else. Whereas *Taxi Driver*'s pastiche invokes multiple genres via single pictures, *New York, New York* employs many pictures to invoke a single genre—the big-band musical. It is hardly a fail-safe formula: more than one film noir contributes to the mise-en-scène of *Taxi Driver;* and noirish elements infiltrate the sound-stage fabrications of *New York, New York.* Beyond revising the master narrative of Hollywood musicals, *New York, New York* provides a running commentary on the genre itself and on the era when it flourished. The "Happy Endings" number recalls the kitschy dream sequences of *Lady in the Dark* (1944). Francine's travails owe something to those of the long-suffering heroine of *The Glenn Miller Story* (1954); the rocky relationship between Jimmy and Francine stems from the similar out-of-sync careers of the showbiz couple in *A Star is Born* (1954); and the nightclub sequences are patterned on those of *Pal Joey* (1957). *New York, New York's* opening credits are foregrounded against a stylized Manhattan skyline, its color painted(!) on a strip of film from Raoul Walsh's *The Man I Love* (1946). According to Scorsese, the style, the color, and the decor of *New York, New York* are copied from *The Man I Love* and *My Dream Is Yours* (1949), both musical film noirs about nightclub singers. That he invokes such relatively dark musicals as these side-by-side with sunnier ones—*Meet Me in St. Louis* (1944), *Singin' in the Rain* (1952)—indicates the scope of Scorsese's genre critique. Among the remembrances of films past, however, *New York, New York* relies most on the big-band musicals of Vincente Minnelli.

It is Vincente Minnelli's world—idealized, stylized, and fabricated on a Hollywood soundstage—that Scorsese compulsively reconstructs in *New York, New York*. As pointedly as any director of his day, Minnelli paid meticulous attention to details of color and light, costume and decor. "Now I wanted to re-create that mythical city, as well as the feeling of the old three-step Technicolor with lipstick that was too bright and make-up even on the men," Scorsese recalls.[5] This obsession with fabricating an entire world à la Vincente Minnelli led Roger Copeland in a September 25, 1977, *New York Times* article written shortly after the film's release to voice what later became the popular critical view of *New York, New York:* "Scorsese goes out of his way to call our attention to the blatantly fabricated nature of this cinematic world" that the big-band musicals of the studio era "encouraged us to accept . . . as the real thing." As unexceptionable as Copeland's account of Scorsese's intentions seems to be, it may slight Minnelli et al. The creators of the big-band musicals of the forties and fifties were anything but naive artificers bent on convincing gullible moviegoers that fabricated sets equaled real locales. Many of the musicals produced by Arthur Freed for MGM—the studio most famously associated with the genre—were as sophisticated in their integration of music, color, dance, decor, costume, editing, and camera movement as any revisionist clone of a later era, *New York, New York* included. Scorsese credits not only what he films but how he films it to Minnelli:

I tried to follow the example of Vincente Minnelli's films in moving the camera and then took it further. First the camera would track in on the band for a few bars of music before the first cut, with no master shot, which would run for 24 bars. Next the camera would track at one angle for 12 bars, then another for 12, and so on back and forth until this became a style. I applied it to the studio sequences in *The Last Waltz* and to the boxing scenes in *Raging Bull*, where every fifteen or twenty punches there was a different angle with no coverage, and even to the pool games in *The Color of Money*.[6]

This abandonment of the traditional master shot, all but de rigueur in establishing mise-en-scène, and the consequent greater reliance on a moving camera, mark Scorsese's shift to a more rhythmically fluid editing style. Far from being confined to dream-factory images, Minnelli's influence invokes a way of seeing crucial not only to *New York, New York* but to the subsequent cinema of Martin Scorsese. What's more, revisionism—a postmodern buzzword for what Scorsese's generation of filmmakers was up to—was already apparent in the very genres they set out to reviv(s)e. The title of Minnelli's *The Band Wagon* (1953), for example, refers back to an old Broadway musical starring Fred Astaire who in the movie version plays a veteran hoofer whose songs are lifted from the 1931 show. And Gene Kelly's *Singin' in the Rain* (1952), arguably the greatest Freed musical of all, is as fully aware of its generic lineage and as reflexive in treating it as *New York, New York:* "In addition to its parodic historical representation of Hollywood's conversion to synchronized sound, the technology that made musicals possible, *Singin' in the Rain* contains its own reflexive history of MGM musicals, from their 1929 beginning to the 1952 present. The film's score . . . is a virtual compilation of hit tunes from MGM musicals . . . of the 1930s and 1940s. All but two of the songs in *Singin' in the Rain* come directly from earlier MGM musicals, for which they were written by the same man who now produced MGM musicals."[7] Even Kelly's tap dance through rain puddles in his famous staging of the title song as well as his surrealistic pas de deux in the balletic "Broadway Melody," both of which Scorsese quotes, are as stylized as anything in *New York, New York*.

New York, New York is, of course, a revisionist musical. But what it revises is not a naive faith in artificial "reality." Minnelli's world was as knowingly fabricated as Scorsese's and for many of the same reasons. Without belaboring the question of intention—whether *New York, New York,* was born revisionist or began life as a straightforward nostalgia homage to the big- band musical only to wind up subverting the genre—

it is clear that the film is revisionist not so much in its attitude toward artifice as in its characters, in its action, ultimately in its closure. In the blatantly fabricated 1940s world of *New York, New York* songstress Francine Evans's meteoric rise to success threatens to leave jazzman Jimmy Doyle, the lover she later marries, in the lurch. Liza Minnelli, daughter of director Vincente Minnelli and legendary singer Judy Garland, and a contemporary superstar in her own right, embodies the recaptured past of *New York, New York*. As if her name and fame and the painstakingly created studio sets she foregrounds were not enough to evoke her mother's era, Liza Minnelli reflects the Garland look and mannerisms to a nearly campy degree. Maybe a campy Minnelli figures to be right at home in the over-the-top mise-en-scène of *New York, New York*. In any event, Scorsese highlights the Garland resemblance more and more as the movie rolls on: in Minnelli's final numbers, her close-cropped hair and mascaraed hazel eyes, skintight black pants and flaring red top startlingly invoke her mother. Yet Minnelli's Garland turn transcends details of appearance to become an integral component of *New York, New York*'s reconstruction of the past. For her changing look reflects her changing fortunes much as Garland's did in real life. By reprising via Minnelli's performance the fame-and-fortune-at-a-price scenario of *A Star Is Born*, the ultimate Judy Garland film, Scorsese invokes *the* privileged narrative of the Hollywood musical that, not so incidentally, is also the Judy Garland story. That Liza Minnelli draws top billing despite the presence of De Niro, whose Oscar-winning performance in *The Godfather, Part II* (1974) and electrifying Travis Bickle in *Taxi Driver* had catapulted him into the top echelon of screen actors, suggests the focus of *New York, New York*. True, Jimmy Doyle shares nearly every frame with Francine Evans in accordance with Scorsese's theory that they are stuck together and with his stated intention of making a picture with two central characters rather than the one of *Alice* and *Taxi Driver*. But *New York, New York* is, after all, a musical—Liza Minnelli's kind of movie even if she were not essentially playing her mother. And while De Niro's screen time approaches Minnelli's, until Jimmy Doyle gains belated success as leader of his own sextet and prosperous nightclub owner his sputtering career is eclipsed by the skyrocketing of Francine Evans's. The status he finally achieves cannot approximate Francine's; his hard-won success seems tenuous and fragile, her stardom inevitable and indestructible. De Niro's relationship to Minnelli in *New York, New York* is reminiscent of James Mason's to Judy Garland in *A Star Is Born*. Like De Niro,

Mason is eclipsed by the woman he loves and though he manages to contain the violence that De Niro unleashes, Mason is no less haunted by the specter of failure. Mason's Norman Main has known glory only to have it snatched away while De Niro's Jimmy Doyle snatches at glory only to have it elude him until the film is nearly over. Both male costars are essentially second bananas, shadowed by failure and overshadowed by their women. Liza Minnelli was drawn to *New York, New York* by what she considered an honest representation of a woman. Francine gets angry and swears, unlike her 1940s celluloid counterparts whose offstage lives are relatively unexamined interludes between musical numbers: "It's a story I can relate to. When the man leaves, it's not her undoing. She has fulfillment in her work."[8] *New York, New York* may actually be the women's picture Scorsese thought he had made with *Alice Doesn't Live Here Anymore.*

What she says about fulfillment and implies about its cost incorporates the Garland myth and empowers Minnelli's Garland impersonation. Inhabiting her daughter's looks and clothes and mannerisms, Garland likewise haunts the master narrative of *New York, New York.* Memories of Garland linger about Soundstage 29 at MGM, site of so many big-band musicals and Scorsese's chosen set for *New York, New York.* Liza Minnelli, ensconced in her mother's former dressing room, surrounded by flowers and attended by a personal entourage that would have done Garland proud, was already playing the triumphant backstage finale of *New York, New York* even before the cameras rolled. George Cukor, who directed Judy Garland in *A Star Is Born,* put in an appearance on the set as did Vincente Minnelli who tearfully remarked on his daughter's uncanny resemblance to her mother. So intent was Scorsese on recapturing the 1940s that he briefly toyed with the idea of shooting *New York, New York* in the 1:1.33 ratio of the big band era that had long since given way to the 1:1.66 of the wide screen. Only a director as obsessive as Scorsese would even dream of risking his audience to make a historical point. Realizing it would be economic suicide to shoot in 1:1.33 he nonetheless elected to frame within that ratio. The fanatical attention to detail—from reprinting and repainting the Manhattan skyline of *The Man I Love* to framing within a 1:1.33 ratio—is the base of a narrative superstructure that only begins with outward show. In calling up movie history in the form of the Hollywood musical and in the person of Judy Garland, Scorsese evokes cultural icons not merely for their own sake. Though *New York, New York* apparently incarnates the "nostalgia film" that American directors were popularizing in the 1970s, it recaptures the look and feel of an era not primarily to relive it but to reinvent it. The same thing is evident in George Lucas's *American Graffiti* (1973), a film that memorializes the way we were in the 1950s. A far "purer" nostalgia film than *New York, New York, American Graffiti* evokes the past as an end whereas *New York, New York* employs the past as a means. And the end of *New York, New York* is not confined to its ending. True, the idea of an eleventh hour genre reversal may have figured in the decision to exhume the genre in the first place. Yet Scorsese aims not only to manipulate a sector of film history but to illuminate it.

When Francine Evans and Jimmy Doyle ultimately fail to reconnect it is the end of an era as well as the end of an affair(e). And it is not just loss of the belief that once mandated happy endings that mediates the indeterminate closure of *New York, New York*. Undoubtedly, Scorsese *is* saying that happy endings reflect the reel world of the 1940s more than the real world of the 1970s. But he is also saying that the reel world was coming to an end in the real world long before *New York, New York* set it up for a fall. For the MGM musicals of the early 1950s masked beneath all their happy hoopla a sad suspicion that they were the last of their kind. Well before nostalgia infiltrated American cinema in the 1970s, reflexive and retrospective films like *Singin' in the Rain* and *The Band Wagon* mourn the demise of the very tradition they so exuberantly celebrate.

> By the mid-1950s, MGM had already begun deserting original musical ideas, assigning Vincente Minnelli to adapt stage shows like *Brigadoon* and *Kismet*. The original screen musical died with the original screenplay. It also died with the studio system that produced a certain number of musicals each year and kept a stable of musical talent stocked expressly for that purpose. With the death of the studios that developed such musical talent, the world was condemned to a future with no new Kellys, Garlands, and Astaires, who no longer had a school for study nor a showcase for displaying their wares.[9]

Judy Garland, whose singing rivals the dancing of Kelly and Astaire in mythologizing the Hollywood musical, perfectly embodies the demise of a genre and the end of an era. More even than Kelly and Astaire who were still going strong long after her death at forty-seven in 1969, Garland occupies the delimited historical zone of the Hollywood musical, its rise and fall roughly corresponding to her own. From 1935 when the thirteen-year-old Garland first signed on with MGM until 1950 when the studio canceled her contract, she spanned and personified the golden age of the Hollywood musical. Within those fifteen years she appeared in twenty-three lead roles. Although she came back stronger than ever for Warner Brothers in *A Star Is Born,* the picture capped something old rather than started something new. Her last—and definitive—backstager, *A Star Is Born* simultaneously celebrates and elegizes personal gain and loss. While Garland's Vicki Lester is the winner and James Mason's Norman Main the loser, the entire you're-in-and-you're-out of the money scenario prefigures the dramatic highs and lows of Garland's remaining years. The concertizing Garland was far from washed up, but she no longer incarnated the musical's equation of stardom and self-fulfillment. Ironically, *New York, New York* preserves this equation as a by-product of the very lost innocence that is conventionally invoked as *the* trope of Garland's career in its final stage. In *New York, New York* stardom is not only self-fulfilling but self-sufficient: once lost, the innocence that might naively have sacrificed all for love no longer interferes with being a star. What is truly radical about Scorsese's ending is not merely that lovers go their separate ways but that they are probably better off doing so. Stardom was no more Garland's salvation than it was the salvation of the ballerina heroine of *The Red Shoes,* one of Scorsese's favorite movies. A dancer whose overnight rise to prima ballerina matches the meteoric ascent to stardom enacted by Garland in so many MGM musicals, the young heroine of *The Red Shoes,* unable to resolve the conflict between "art" and "life," finally kills herself. Scorsese resolves the conflict by eliminating it: in *New York, New York* art and life are ultimately one. Not so for Garland whose life began to unravel even as she remained a star and became a legend.

The sense of an ending that mediates *A Star Is Born* haunts *New York, New York* as well. One reason why Jimmy Doyle, a purist who is more at home jamming with black jazzmen after hours in Harlem than fronting a conventional white dance band, is so fiercely protective of his music is that he fears for its survival. Not that the hard-driving jazz he favors is dying in the 1950s, but it is gradually being relegated to clubs like the one Jimmy moonlights in uptown. Earl MacRauch's early scripts characterize Jimmy's jazz as too sophisticated for an American public in search of simpler and less challenging musical pleasures. Even the big bands that once filled ballrooms where middle-class white couples flocked to dance were growing sclerotic. *"New York, New York* is about the decline of the big bands," Scorsese said in 1975 shortly after reading MacRauch's original screenplay. After the symbolic apogee of the big band era is invoked in the opening nightclub sequence featuring the Tommy Dorsey band celebrating V-J Day, it is all downhill. Playing saxophone in the touring band he subsequently leads, Jimmy watches his audiences growing smaller and older. While the band's decline coincides with the departure of the pregnant Francine, there is also a sense of inevitability about it. Less apparent than the end of the big band era is the beginning of the end of the traditional show biz that Judy Garland incarnated and that Liza Minnelli recalls in *New York, New York. A Star Is Born* was at once the last gasp of the traditional backstage musical and the herald of the innovative antimusical (e.g., Bob Fosse's 1972 *Cabaret,* starring Liza Minnelli) of a later era. By the end of Garland's career, studios were no longer making her kind of movie and rock was blowing away her kind of music. At the end of *New York, New York,* Francine's superstar status seems graven in stone. Yet Liza Minnelli's multiplication of Garland signifiers and Scorsese's reminder that the film's music is his parents' generation's suggest that in the not so distant future Francine's voice will be no more popular than Jimmy's sax.

Within the frame of the movie, however, it is not the comparable fate of their music in the future but the contrasting reception of their music in the present that is crucial. Because in the genre Scorsese revives and revises music is destiny, it figures that Jimmy Doyle is shaped by the uncompromising jazz he plays and by his equally uncompromising attitude toward it. Whether Jimmy the Harlem cultist ever yearns for the mass appeal of Francine the Broadway showstopper is unclear. What *is* clear is that the tension between them stems as often as not from clashing musical values reflected in his disdain for her music and resentment at its success. And it is this matrix of tensions produced by Jimmy's non-stop anxiety that infects *New York, New York* and effects many of its genre subversions. A relentless antihero from the future, Jimmy Doyle is an alien in the tinsel-and-moonlight world of the 1940s. Foregrounded against Scorsese's meticulously reconstituted version of the past, Jimmy's latter-day complexes are thrown into high relief. It is this deliberate mismatch of character and context that energizes *New York, New York.* Time past is conjured up immediately in the opening ballroom sequence where uniformed men and women dance to the music of the Dorsey band. Outside in Times Square newspaper headlines proclaim the end of the war: it is V-J Day, 1945. Back inside, the plush furnishings, the golden glow of the brass instruments, the spiffy musicians and the swirling dancers are lovingly and lingeringly caressed by the camera. Equally stylized are such later scenes as Jimmy's audition for a small-time club date, which goes poorly until Francine joins in and which then takes off in time-honored Hollywood musical fashion, and the couple's impulsive midnight marriage before a sleepy justice-of-the-peace clad in bathrobe and slippers. The marriage scene is staged against a studio-fabricated snowscape whose glaring artificiality trumpets the bogus romanticism that inspired the ceremony. By re-creating the world of the Hollywood soundstage in the 1970s, Scorsese piles artifice upon artifice, flagrantly displaying what older movies sought to conceal.

In first revealing the tricks of the trade, then making that revelation an essential element of the mise-en-scène, Scorsese examines not only the psychological and emotional assumptions of the 1940s but the ways in which those assumptions were transcribed into film. The myth of romantic love that sustained countless studio-era musicals is equally crucial to *New York, New York.* Scorsese exploits it to invoke the narrative predictability he will ultimately revoke. Aspiring songstress Francine meets ambitious saxophonist Jimmy, who first glimpses her across a crowded ballroom. Despite his transparently predatory intentions, sleazy self-confidence, and synthetic sincerity, a long history of similar movie meetings sanctions this one as love's first glimmer. No doubt sweet Francine will transform smarmy Jimmy into the usual American romantic ideal, and the pair will find married bliss in the last reel: it is 1945, after all. Their relatively early marriage may be the first hint of narrative instability in *New York, New York.* If boy gets girl so fast, what do they do for an encore in the anticipated happy ending? But predictability seems restored when Francine leaves Jimmy and the band to go back to New York to have her baby. The band (again predictably) fails without her and Jimmy, increasingly self-centered and mean-spirited, takes out his frustrations on his long-suffering wife. They split, each to find success alone, she as Judy Garland incarnate, he as jazz purist and prosperous nightclub owner. Six years after they parted and sitting on top of their respective worlds, Jimmy and Francine meet again in the sort of climactic dressing-room scene that conventionally prefaces a happy ending. Their prospective reconciliation is promisingly staged at the Starlight Terrace—they first met at the Moonlight Terrace—where Francine has just triumphed in her latest show. When in the same scene Jimmy confronts their handsome son whom Francine has bravely reared alone, the restoration of the family and the consequent happy ending seem inevitable.

As if all the usual signals were not enough, the reinstated "Happy Endings" number that showcases Francine for twelve minutes and that Jimmy watches in a movie theater a few scenes prior to their climatic backstage reunion blares great expectations. Not only the title but the action of "Happy Endings" seem to promise that Francine and Jimmy will get back together. In Francine's movie-within-a-movie, she plays an usherette in a movie theater—nowhere in *New York, New York* is its movie-made world so lavishly invoked—whose dream of stardom comes wondrously true. Looking very much like Judy Garland in an usherette's red pillbox hat and sounding very like her in dramatically belting out "Happy Endings" while clad in a sexy red dress slit practically to the waist during the dream sequence, Francine cavorts in the best *A Star Is Born* tradition. When it turns out that the producer who made her a star in her dream is for real—he appears in the theater when she reverts back to usherette—she becomes a star in reality. And back in the "real" theater Jimmy watches a newsreel showing Francine, now a superstar, triumphantly returning to New York where she is welcomed by a mob of adoring fans. In light of *New York, New York*'s actual closure, the "Happy Endings" number can be read as a parody of overnight success stories and thus of the Hollywood musicals that contained them. Indeed, the velocity and magnitude of Francine's success recalls *A Star Is Born*, casting her as Garland's Vicky Lester and provisionally casting Jimmy as James Mason's Norman Main. Though Vicky plays the martyr till the end when, after her washed-up husband's suicide, she valiantly preserves the illusion of a happy ending by introducing herself to a crowd as "Mrs. Norman Main," her success is yoked to his failure. Scorsese alludes to the rise-and-fall scenario of *A Star Is Born* in the producer's fear that "I'd only be Mr. Peggy Smith" to Francine's usherette-cum-star in the "Happy Endings" sequence. No sooner does the newsreel Jimmy is watching conclude, however, than *New York, New York* seems to regain its narrative predictability. Newspaper headlines and record charts chronicle his success as a songwriter and nightclub owner. By employing for Jimmy the identical montage technique that, via a cascade of fan magazines and movie studio scenes, recorded Francine's rise to stardom, Scorsese deflects the rise-and-fall pattern associated with *A Star Is Born*. True, Jimmy's fame can never match Francine's just as his music can never be as popular as hers. The point is not, however, that one person's success is purchased with another's failure but that success is mutual. "New York, New York," the song Jimmy wrote and Francine sings as the grand finale of the Starlight Terrace sequence reflects this mutuality. A complex symbol, the song evokes concord and discord simultaneously: Francine's singing popularizes Jimmy's music, but he disdains her version of his song. Only after the backstage meeting comes to nothing does the title song privilege discord; and only then does "New York, New York" belie the promise of "Happy Endings." When Jimmy's status finally approximates Francine's, *New York, New York* abandons the scenario of *A Star Is Born*. The skidding husband, the sacrificing wife, the consolatory ending of *A Star Is Born*—all are invoked in *New York, New York* expressly to be revoked in the final analysis. Because they are equals, Francine need not sacrifice her career—or herself—for Jimmy. Nor need she echo her mother's plaintive cry ("I'm Mrs. Norman Main") that lends tear-jerker pathos to the ending of *A Star Is Born*. Alive and prospering, Jimmy needs Francine no more than she needs him. Their mutual recognition of their mutual independence mediates the backstage scene and determines its aftermath.

A conceivable reading of their failure to (re)connect—and of the revisionist agenda of *New York, New York*—lies in the character of Jimmy Doyle. He is a refugee from a *Mean Streets* or a *Taxi Driver* stranded in a facsimile of a Hollywood musical. Via Jimmy, Scorsese fast-forwards *New York, New York* into the 1970s by which time romantic reconciliations had lost their old-time movie-made inevitability. *New York, New York* thus subverts the mythology of the big-band musical by denying its basic assumption—the efficacy of romantic love. Yet Scorsese recalls the love-conquers-all scenario even as he denies it. *New York, New York* restructures "reality" by fashioning its competing versions into a new order. Something akin to T. S. Eliot's historical sense, which "involves a conception not only of the pastness of the past, but of its presence," animates *New York, New York*. It is a cinematic restatement of the lesson of *The Waste Land*—that art renews itself not merely by feeding on the past, including its own, but by shaping a "simultaneous order." In reviving and transforming an apparently lifeless genre, *New York, New York* is as much about time present as time past.

Whatever the reading of its complex interplay of past and present, *New York, New York* is ultimately about breaking up. Given the many rewrites and improvisations, even Scorsese had trouble figuring out the meaning of the film: "Eventually I understood the picture. Jean-Luc Godard . . . in talking about how much he liked *New York, New York* . . . said it was basically about the impossibility of two creative people in a relationship—the jealousies, the envy, the temperament. I began to realize that it was so close to home that I wasn't able to articulate it while I was making the film."[10] No doubt Godard cuts to the heart of the matter. Yet the backstage scene and its aftermath play out somewhat differently on screen. Jealousy, envy, and temperament indisputably led to the breakdown of the relationship and prolonged the six-year separation. But the conclusion that two creative people cannot make it together is misleading. In the first place, the emotional symptoms that Godard spots are exclusively Jimmy's. Francine's outbursts are rare and are largely confined to her pregnancy, and they are triggered not by jealousy or envy but by Jimmy's implied then actual rejection of their child. That he does not want the baby and leaves the hospital without ever seeing it perverts the myth of proud fatherhood. Seldom denied in any movie genre, much less in the Hollywood musical, fatherhood traditionally cements marriage— not destroys it. Jimmy's copout reflects his resentment at Francine no less than it valorizes career above family. Not only had she brought about what little success he has enjoyed, but the decline of the band in her absence suggests that without her he is nothing. All the jealousy and envy in *New York, New York* are Jimmy's. It is true that the birth of the baby signals Francine's commitment to her career no less than Jimmy's to his. But her total ambition results from his desertion, a desertion that reflects his total ambition. Until the baby is born, Francine seemed set to reprise the sacrificing role of Vicky, Norman's long-suffering wife in *A Star Is Born*. Vestiges of that role persist till the end when even as a superstar Francine remains a single parent. Ever ready to forgive and forget, she exhibits no trace of justifiable outrage when an unapologetic Jimmy shows up at the Starlight Terrace. Though for the past six years he has apparently acknowledged their son only by the odd present, neither Francine nor the boy expresses any resentment throughout the backstage sequence. And because success has mellowed Jimmy and dissolved his former bitterness, the time seems ripe for reconciliation. Exiting the dressing room, he pauses to exchange affectionate words with his son and even to kiss the boy good-bye. Once outside, Jimmy runs for a phone booth where he calls Francine who agrees to meet him at the stage door, a promise that, combined with the dressing room byplay, fairly shouts HAPPY ENDING. Scorsese cuts back and forth between Francine approaching the Exit sign and Jimmy waiting by the phone booth. At the sight of the sign she hesitates, drawing back. Another outside shot of Jimmy waiting, an inside shot of Francine pushing the elevator button, then back outside to Jimmy who walks out of the frame as inside Francine disappears into the elevator. A final shot from overhead trails down Jimmy's body to his shoes and umbrella before dissolving into a track of deserted and rain-slicked streets whose patent artificiality provides a last reminder of the studio era that inspired *New York, New York*. It is a parting shot that fittingly summarizes Scorsese's strategy of invoking the look of the past by way of revoking its assumptions. When Jimmy departs alone, he walks away from the persona he never really was. An outcast from a Scorsese movie of a different kind, he is no fitter for happy endings than Travis Bickle or Jake LaMotta.

What is as remarkable as the couple's failure is its cause. Despite Scorsese's second of Godard's view that relationships between two creative people are destroyed by jealousy, envy, and temperament, the ending of *New York New York* says otherwise. A mellower Jimmy and a receptive Francine, poised for togetherness, spontaneously and simultaneously opt out. For the usual emotional fireworks of the happy ending they substitute the shrug of denial. *New York, New York* ends not with a bang but a whimper—getting back together is not worth the hassle, the prospect of emotional risk is not worth the potential gain. The failure of their relationship belies the promise of their successful collaboration on "New York, New York" just as the dark and empty rain-slicked streets of the last shot belie the song's celebration of the city. A tinny piano rendition of the title song accompanies the last shot, in flagrant contrast to the swelling orchestral arrangement of Francine's rendition at the Starlight Terrace. True to form, music mediates the emotional climate of *New York, New York* to the end. Jimmy once defined his goals as a "major chord": "The woman you want, the music you want, and enough money to live comfortably." Ironically, he is fighting with Francine in a cab—cars are often the site of emotional trauma, à la *Taxi Driver*—when he bids thus for her sympathy and eventual love. Even as she yields to Jimmy, rushing with him to an audition in the cab she wanted for herself, the dynamics of the scene militate against his major chord. True, Jimmy prioritizes romance in pursuing Francine to Roanoke: "Didn't you understand that when I said major chord—I meant it about you?" But even in Roanoke he is arguably as anxious to get into the Frankie Harte band she is singing with as to get back together with her. Still, the major chord lingers on, if not in fact—the marriage ends for practical purposes with the birth of their child—then at least in theory throughout *New York, New York*. "I'm going to sing a song now by a friend of mine who is a big believer in major chords," announces Francine, launching into "New York, New York" as Jimmy looks on from a ringside table at the Starlight Terrace. Richard Lippe spots how the movie expresses itself in music: "Indeed, the 'New York, New York' number is the film's true climax, drawing together a whole complex of emotional threads: Francine's acknowledgment of the past relationship, the unfulfilled possibilities it suggested; the sublimation of that relationship into art (the 'Major Chord'), its tensions resolved in joint expression (his name, her lyrics, her performance); Francine's declaration of independence, the creation of the star."[11] That the now successful Jimmy opens a nightclub called The Major Chord is hardly surprising. The aptly named club (re)states his priorities—as if they were not pretty clear all along. Never has he been willing and/or able to compromise his music much less sublimate it in marriage.

Whereas the Starlight Terrace sequence most strikingly counter-points music and meaning, nearly everything that goes on in *New York, New York* finds musical expression. Francine's songs—"You Brought a New Kind of Love to Me," "You Are My Lucky Star," "The Man I Love"—evoke her love for Jimmy and trace the progress of their rela-tionship. After Jimmy takes over the Frankie Harte band he takes out his professional frustration on Francine in the "Taking a Chance on Love" rehearsal scene. No doubt angered as much by her crucial role in the band's success as by her attempt to set the beat, Jimmy turns on Francine, berating and even slapping her in front of the embarrassed musicians. Meantime, the song's title foretells the growing uncertainty of their relationship: "The implications of the "Taking a Chance on Love" rehearsal scene are fully acknowledged later in the film when the now pregnant Francine is rebuffed when she attempts to join Jimmy on stage at the Harlem Club."[12] Jimmy expresses his aggression musically, accel-erating the tempo and turning up the volume as sax and horns combine to drive her back. Maybe he is afraid that she will outshine him on his own turf as she had when first they performed together in the audition scene that set the stage for their subsequent relationship. Jimmy's play-ing left the auditioner unmoved until Francine came to the rescue, tai-loring his musical style to her singing and getting them both hired in the process. This early suspicion that without Francine he is going nowhere grows after he takes over the Harte band only to watch it decline after she leaves. Jimmy's resentment boils over in a violent physical brawl. Precipitated immediately by the Harlem Club rejection though predicted by the rehearsal scene slap, the fight follows a key sequence where a close-up of Francine's eyes as she studies herself in a mirror reveals the pent-up pressures she feels. To dramatize the depth of Jimmy's hostility toward Francine's pregnancy and its potential impact on their careers together, Scorsese stages a fight scene worthy of *Mean Streets* or *Taxi Driver* in the close confines of a car. Getting into the car with Minnelli and De Niro, Scorsese propelled them into a knockabout sequence so violent that they all landed in the hospital. Like many another sequence in *New York, New York,* it is an over-the-top evocation of the thematic and stylistic tensions that the film embodies and refuses to resolve.

Neat resolution, the staple of Hollywood musicals, has no place in *New York, New York.* It is not only the happy ending that is missing. Even in a 1940s or 1950s musical, happy endings are not de rigeuer—witness the triumph tempered by tragedy of *A Star Is Born.* What is missing from *New York, New York* is the *sense* of an ending, happy or not. Postmodern art thrives on contingency, not certainty. Though the "unsatisfactory" closure may be nothing more than a revisionist statement vis à vis the big band musical, in a larger sense it conforms to Scorsese's usual practice. A typical final shot depicts a lone male protagonist unwilling or unable to initiate, renew, or to sustain relationships. Aside from *Boxcar Bertha* and *Alice Doesn't Live Here Anymore* Scorsese's is a male-centered cinema. Liza Minnelli's top billing and musical dominance may suggest that *New York, New York* is a woman's film. Yet it is De Niro's Jimmy who determines what happens; Francine mostly follows his lead, at least until he walks out on her and the baby. And Jimmy's smug assumption that jazz is superior to pop valorizes his playing above her singing, his career above hers. Francine remains a bit cowed even at the end, her chastened air and nervous giggle anticipating his disdain for her arrangement of "New York, New York." If there is such a thing as a distinctly male sociology, it is clearly evident in Jimmy's negation of the family unit. Far from being the idealized construct of Hollywood musicals—witness Judy Garland's insisting that she is Mrs. Norman Main at the end of *A Star Is Born*—the family is reduced to a disposable item in *New York, New York.* Jimmy's callous disregard for and abandonment of his wife and child is the direct antithesis of Garland's desperate need to reinstate a family shattered by death. *New York, New York* reverses the dynamics of the time-honored hospital scene where worshipful fathers coo over valorous mothers and precious newborns. Turning his back on the recumbent Francine and walking out of the hospital without bothering to see his son, Jimmy deconsecrates perhaps the most sacred real-life as well as reel-life family tableau. A depiction of maleness at its worst, what happens in the hospital is nonetheless consistent with the masculine agenda Jimmy lives by. Not that he was ever the ideal husband. No sooner does Francine leave the band than Jimmy takes up with the singer who replaces her. And in the same Harlem Club scene where he musically rebuffs his still-pregnant wife, Jimmy's byplay with the sexy black singer of "Honeysuckle Rose" suggests that for him casual infidelity is the rule rather than the exception. Like the heroes of *Taxi Driver* and *Raging Bull,* the Scorsese films that bracket *New York, New York,* Jimmy Doyle is a case study in distorted masculinity.

Although Jimmy resembles Travis Bickle and Jake LaMotta more than the conventional Hollywood musical hero, the rampant machismo of *Taxi Driver* and *Raging Bull* is effectively mediated in *New York, New York.* In the "Taking a Chance on Love" rehearsal scene shortly after their marriage, Francine counters Jimmy's unwarranted slap by deliberately knocking over the microphone after finishing the number. Trivial at first glance, the upended microphone is an early declaration of Francine's ensuing independence. After the romantic exultation of "You Brought a New Kind of Love to Me," "You Are My Lucky Star," and "The Man I Love," the songs Francine sings as their love crests, "Taking a Chance on Love" exposes the fault lines in the relationship and forecasts trouble ahead. The end of the affair is likewise expressed vocally when Francine sings "And the World Goes Round" alone in a recording studio. Scorsese shoots the scene in a single long take, spotlighting Francine against a dark background. Thus isolated by the camera, she is (re)born as a star in her own right. Henceforth, she will go her own way, independent of Jimmy and singing her own songs in her own manner. The lyrics of "And the World Goes Round" imply what her highly emotive rendition expresses: resignation, detachment, most of all independence. No less than the song, the recording studio is itself an objective correlative of independence achieved. A key component of a mise-en-scène designed to evoke self-reliance, the studio embraces Francine and her music in a new relationship that seals off and detonates the old one with Jimmy. It is the moment when *New York, New York* achieves equilibrium and fulfills what its title promises: parity between male and female, jazz and pop, uptown and downtown. Tempered by Francine's musical declaration of independence, Jimmy's machismo, privileged earlier in the movie, must now coexist with her feminism.

That the New Yorks separated by the comma of the title should conflate in a recording studio is one of the ironies of *New York, New York*. A
big-band musical, the film resolves its key relationship not in the public
venue of the bandstand but in the private confines of the studio.
Moreover, the career arc invoked in the studio and embodied in Liza
Minnelli's Francine has affinities with Judy Garland's. Garland sings the
take-charge "Here Is What I'm Here For" in a recording scene of *A Star
Is Born* that, given Scorsese's penchant for Garlandizing Minnelli, may
well have inspired the similar message and setting of "And the World
Goes Round." Francine's song announces her transition from big-band
songstress to recording star, from relative dependence to complete independence. After *A Star Is Born* Garland switched from making movies to
concertizing—a star is *re*born scenario that may have suggested
Francine's blossoming forth in *New York, New York*. When Francine and
Jimmy break their stage-door date, the victory of individual over collab-
orative expression—in life as well as in music—is sealed. *New York, New
York*'s ideology of individualism, likewise incarnated in Garland's con-
certs, similarly challenges the master narrative of the movies. In *Meet Me
in St. Louis* (1944), one of Vincente Minnelli's most famous MGM musicals, Garland embodies the traditional American values of the generical-
ly named Smith family. Smith père ultimately decides to forego a job
transfer to New York and the career and financial advancement it represents in order to remain in St. Louis. The antithesis of cold and loveless
and fearsome New York, St. Louis is the locus of traditional home life
and family values. In *New York, New York,* success in New York is all-
important. "If I can make it there, I'd make it anywhere," Francine belts
out triumphantly in the title song. In *Meet Me in St. Louis* Esther
(Garland) falls in love with the boy next door; her prospective marriage,
like the Smith's safe and tranquil home life, would be jeopardized by a
move to New York. Actually, any departure from the home is regarded
as a threat. The Smith home is self-sufficient and all the action of *Meet Me
in St. Louis* takes place in or near it. Like the great majority of Hollywood
musicals, the movie relies upon and valorizes the dominant American
ideology. And like the great majority of Scorsese movies, *New York, New
York* ultimately rejects it.

Like *New York, New York,* Scorsese's next feature-length film—the
rock documentary *The Last Waltz* (1978)— is about endings. *The Last
Waltz* preserves the Thanksgiving 1976 farewell concert of The Band,
one of the sixties' top rock'n'roll groups. In celebrating The Band's last

hurrah, the movie also memorializes an entire era of rock that was fast disappearing. Being asked during the last week of shooting *New York, New York* to direct *The Last Waltz* struck Scorsese as serendipitous. To celebrate his own generation's music even as he was recalling his parents' would comprise a nearly seamless "history" of the music in his life. Moreover, *The Last Waltz* came as a welcome relief from the mounting artistic—and personal—pressures of *New York, New York*. Jonathan Taplin, who had produced *Mean Streets* and had later managed The Band for four years, "recalls the day when 150 fully dressed extras stood around while Scorsese spoke to his therapist from his trailer" as a typically tense moment on the set of *New York, New York*. When Taplin, at the behest of The Band's Robbie Robertson, asked him to shoot *The Last Waltz,* Scorsese was "overjoyed."[13] Robertson wanted the concert, set for San Francisco's five-thousand-seat Winterland, a former skating rink where The Band had first achieved national recognition in 1969, to be preserved on film.

The idea of merely recording the event for archival purposes, which could be done in 16 mm or on videotape for that matter, soon evolved into an ambitious plan to shoot it in 35 mm with full sync sound and seven cameras. Scorsese got so carried away with the project that he began thinking of it in grandiose terms, borrowing the *La Traviata* set from the San Francisco Opera Festival, bringing in Boris Leven, the set designer on *New York, New York,* even appropriating Winterland's only two chandeliers. He prepared meticulously beforehand, creating a two-hundred page script from the sheets Robertson gave him. A single sheet for each song listed the title, the vocals, the verses, the instrumentalists, and the lead performer at every stage of the number, enabling Scorsese to map out his camera movements, design his lighting effects, and coordinate both. A veritable who's who of cameramen including director of photography Michael Chapman *(Taxi Driver, Raging Bull)*, Laszlo Kovacs *(New York, New York),* and Vilmos Zsigmund collaborated on *The Last Waltz,* the first concert film to be shot entirely in 35 mm and the first to employ a twenty-four-track recording system. As usual, Scorsese wound up with reams of film, the seven hours of concert footage supplemented by material shot at The Band's recording studio and on an MGM sound stage. Combined with the highly complex recording system, the superfluity of footage created an editing nightmare. Meanwhile *New York, New York* demanded Scorsese's attention: "So now I had two features to cut and that is why

The Last Waltz took two years to come out. During this time, Robbie Robertson would keep coming back with new ideas, saying we should have a 'Last Waltz Suite' comprising 'Evangeline,' 'The Last Waltz,' and 'The Weight,' because the footage of the stage version of 'The Weight' was incomplete."[14] Robertson also wanted Scorsese, who once called himself "the world's worst interviewer," to conduct interviews with The Band's members. Intercut with the concert footage, the interview segments are mawkish and superficial as often as they are illuminating. Along with a final instrumental number played by The Band on a bare studio stage that tries too hard to turn *The Last Waltz* into a rock era elegy, the majority of the interviews are superfluous. So brilliant are the concert sequences, however, that talking heads and a lame finale hardly diminish *The Last Waltz,* arguably the finest of all rock-concert movies.

What excited Scorsese was the notion of breaking the mold of the conventional concert film:

> And in *The Last Waltz,* the main thing to consider was that we were sick and tired of all these shots of the people in the audience in most concert films. So . . . we stayed on the stage. You see the intensity of the interrelationship of the performers, and you see how they work as a group. . . . Each song became like a rounded person. It is amazingly physical. . . . What I discovered in *The Last Waltz* was to stay on the stage, stay with the people.[15]

The Last Waltz captures the uncommon richness of The Band's mix of American musical styles ranging from jazz and soul to folk and country. Though the group became legendary in its own right, it first gained fame backing Bob Dylan. It is this galaxy of invited stars—Eric Clapton, Neil Young, Van Morrison, Joni Mitchell, Muddy Waters, Ringo Starr, and Dylan, among others—reflecting and magnifying The Band's own eclecticism, that lends elegiac status to the concert. In *The Last Waltz,* The Band—four Canadians, including lead guitarist Robbie Robertson, bassist Rick Danko, pianist Richard Manuel, electric keyboardist Garth Hudson, and a lone American, drummer Levon Helm—plays most of its own famous songs like "Up on Cripple Creek" and "The Night They Drove Old Dixie Down." Yet the concert is as communal as it is personal, evoking the music of an entire generation no less than that of a single group. So The Band accompanies Joni Mitchell on "Coyote" and Emmy Lou Harris on "Evangeline"; Robertson trades guitar riffs with Clapton on "Further on up the Road"; and everyone joins in on the exultantly climactic "I Shall Be Released." These and equally affecting numbers—Neil Young's "Helpless," Ronnie Hawkins's "Who Do You Love?," Van Morrison's "Caravan," and Dylan's "Forever Young"—virtually summarize the history of sixties' rock. None of this detracts from The Band. Indeed, the interaction between the featured group and its famous guests reflects the scope and artistry of The Band's own music.

"We wanted it to be more than a concert—a celebration—of the beginning of the end of the end of the beginning," Robertson says of *The Last Waltz*. Despite this cryptic conflation of beginnings and ends, the concert is a valediction of the past, not a blueprint for the future. Nearly all the songs in *The Last Waltz* were recorded originally eight years or so before the concert, at the beginning of The Band's success as Bob Dylan's backup. Not that they are resting on their past laurels. Still, a feeling that their best work is behind them and it is time to call it a day may account for a certain world weariness that emerges in the interviews. Robertson explains The Band's decision to retire by recalling their sixteen years on the road, particularly the grueling early years of touring the boondocks. Too much time on the road is life threatening, he claims, citing Janis Joplin, Jimi Hendrix, and Elvis Presley among the "great ones" the "road has taken." Though the "road was our school" and "taught us all we know . . . you can press your luck." It is pretty fanciful to blame the road for these rock greats' deaths— and outright silly in Presley's case—but Robertson seems bent on mythologizing the decision not to play along with the playing itself. For him, *The Last Waltz* turned out to be nothing less than a "spiritual experience." Yet in the interviews Robertson's inflated aspirations are all too frequently deflated by the banality of the chitchat. Colorful and poignant memories of The Band's early days—like the time they backed a one-armed go-go dancer in a Texas dive that had no roof and belonged to Jack Ruby—are typically undercut by a sniggering admission that the easy availability of rock groupies is a (if not *the*) stellar attraction of life on the road. That the interviews are invariably set in nondescript and dimly lit spaces—a kitchen, a poolroom—adds to their desultory effect. And Robertson, articulate and sporadically charming but also calculating and self-dramatizing, talks too much, monopolizing the interviews no matter who else is present. Yet the music is the message of *The Last Waltz*, not the talk. As Robertson puts it, "The music took us everywhere . . . physically, spiritually. . . . It wasn't always on the stage though we were on the stage." A bit incoherent and hyperbolical as usual, he still manages to evoke the same transcendent experience of music that he assigns to *The Last Waltz*. For Scorsese, too, *The Last Waltz* "was something very special, something very close to my heart. It was the most perfect thing I had made."[16] Robertson's hyperbole must have been contagious: *The Last Waltz* is hardly Scorsese's "most perfect" film. But it is as good as nearly anything else of its kind and a fitting climax to the major phase of Scorsese's involvement with music. Never again will music play so critical a role as it had played in his movies from *Who's That Knocking?* through *The Last Waltz*.

The physical and emotional toll exacted on Scorsese by working on *New York, New York* and *The Last Waltz* simultaneously is manifest in his ensuing relationships with Liza Minnelli and Robbie Robertson. Prolonging the professional—and amorous—liaison with Minnelli that began on the set of *New York, New York*, Scorsese agreed to direct her in *The Act*. A stage play that continues the Francine Evans story, *The Act* thrust him out of his element. Though he soon disliked the project and realized his shortcomings as a theatrical director, Scorsese stuck with the play through its August 1977 Los Angeles premiere under the title *Shine It On*. By the time it opened on Broadway two months later, the original title had been restored and Scorsese had been replaced by former star dancer Gower Champion. Either Champion's three-week salvage job failed or the show was unsalvageable: *The Act*'s New York reviews were poor and Scorsese, still listed as director in the October 29, 1977, opening night *Playbill*, was blamed for the debacle. Meanwhile Julia Cameron sued for divorce, citing his infatuation with cocaine and with Liza Minnelli. At about the same time Robertson, whose wife had also had enough, moved into Scorsese's Mulholland Drive house with him. Fast buddies by now, the director and the rock star shared a bizarre lifestyle, watching four or five films a night with friends in Robertson's bedroom which doubled as a projection room. To offset problems with light and birds, Scorsese blacked out the house with shades and installed a soundproof air system so that people could breathe with the windows shut. "We were like vampires," recalls Mardik Martin, who must have sensed déjà vu in a situation eerily reminiscent of the period when he and Scorsese locked themselves away from their wives in Martin's Valiant writing *Mean Streets*. For the Mulholland Drive film freaks, "It was like, 'Oh, no, the sun is coming up.' We never got to sleep before 7, 8 A.M. for six months. We did all kinds of crazy things in those days," according to Martin.[17]

Nocturnal movie madness was only one component of a go-go lifestyle that shuttled Scorsese in and out of the hospital with asthma attacks. Another was cocaine, if Julia Cameron, Andy Warhol, and persistent tabloid rumors are to be trusted. In any event, drugs figure prominently in *American Boy*, Scorsese's fifty-minute low-budget documentary about his twenty-something friend and sometime junkie, Steven Prince. Prince, who played gun dealer Handy Andy in *Taxi Driver*, talks mainly about his acts of violence, his fascination with guns, and his addiction to drugs. *American Boy* is the second of Scorsese's projected six-film cycle on American ethnics begun with *Italianamerican*. Prince reveals less about the Jews he is supposed to represent than he does about his generation as envisioned by Scorsese. Still, he does tell Scorsese and friends about his middle-class Jewish upbringing and his relationship with his dying father. *Italianamerican* focuses on the fathers and the America they built, *American Boy* on the sons and the America they are demolishing. Maybe Scorsese envisioned the two documentaries as companion pieces, but *American Boy* may reflect *Taxi Driver* and *The Last Waltz* more than *Italianamerican*. Steven Prince comes over as a real-life clone of insouciant Andy who is as eager to supply Travis with drugs as with guns. And his stories about working as a road manager for Neil Diamond, who guest stars in *The Last Waltz*, plug Prince into the rock scene and thus contribute to his emblematic status. An avatar of the sixties generation, he is also an alter ego for Scorsese at one of the bleakest periods of his life. On Labor Day 1978, Scorsese, his always fragile constitution ravaged by a self-destructive lifestyle, was hospitalized with internal bleeding. Physically, psychically, and professionally on the ropes, frazzled by a jumble of projects but ready for none, he would, incredibly, bounce back with his chef d'oeuvre—*Raging Bull.*

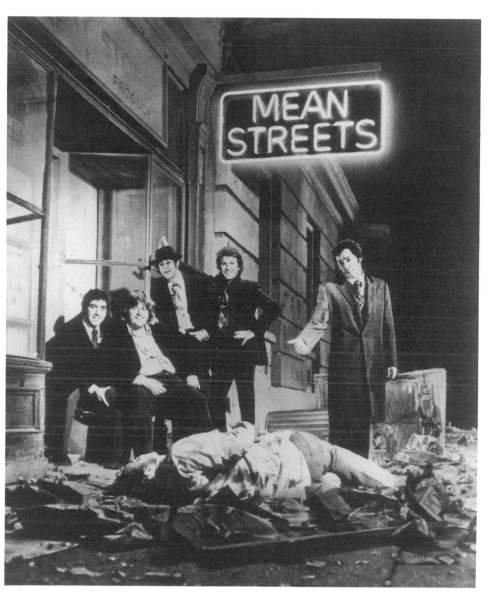

Time out from *Mean Streets* (1973)

Robert De Niro as Travis Bickle in *Taxi Driver* (1976)

Below:
Liza Minnelli as Francine Evans performs the "Happy Endings" musical production number in *New York, New York* (1977)

Robert De Niro as Jake LaMotta knocks out Tony Janiro
(Kevin Mahon) in *Raging Bull* (1980)

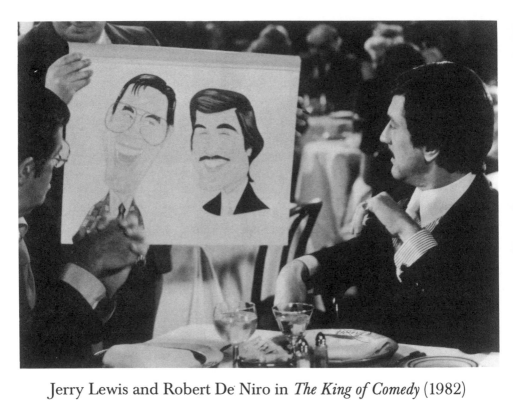

Jerry Lewis and Robert De Niro in *The King of Comedy* (1982)

Griffin Dunne and Rosanna Arquette in *After Hours* (1985)

Tom Cruise and Paul Newman in *The Color of Money* (1986)

Willem Dafoe as Jesus
in *The Last Temptation
of Christ* (1988)

Robert De Niro in *Goodfellas* (1990)

Robert De Niro and Martin Scorsese as fellow filmmakers in
director Irwin Winkler's *Guilty By Suspicion* (1990)

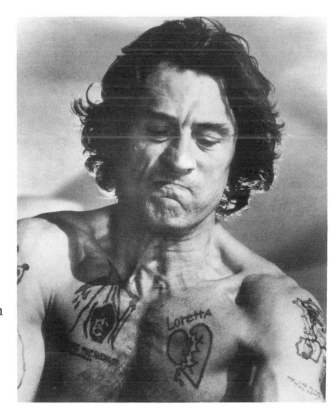

Robert De Niro in
Cape Fear (1991)

Michelle Pfeiffer and Daniel Day-Lewis in
The Age of Innocence (1993)

6

That's Entertainment:
Performance as Destiny

"**Y**ou don't make up for your sins in church," goes Charlie's opening soliloquy in *Mean Streets*. "You do it in the streets. You do it at home." Or you do it in the ring if you are Jake LaMotta, boxing's middleweight king from June 1949 to February 1951. *Raging Bull*, LaMotta's autobiography and "the true story of a champ," is a saga of crime and punishment. Ghostwriters Joseph Carter and Peter Savage portray a guilt-ridden LaMotta who, believing he once killed a bookie, atones for his sin by absorbing vicious punishment in the ring. In Scorsese's vestigially Catholic moral calculus, however, the presence of sin evokes the possibility of redemption: "The Jake LaMotta film. It's called *Raging Bull*. It's really a straight, simple story, almost linear, of a guy attaining something and losing everything, and then redeeming himself. Spiritually."[1] Spiritual (re)awakening is the point of the film's Final Title which quotes John 9:24–26:

> So, for the second time [the Pharisees] summoned the man who had been blind and said: "Speak the truth before God. We know this fellow is a sinner." "Whether or not he is a sinner, I do not know," the man replied. "All I know is this: once I was blind and now I can see."

It is the "sinner," of course, who gave the blind man sight: "The man called Jesus made a paste and smeared my eyes with it, and told me to go to Siloam and wash. I went and washed and gained my sight" (John 9:10–12). More remarkable even than the gift of sight is the power of the giver. By prefacing the punch line of the Final Title with the preceding byplay between the Pharisees and the man who had been blind, Scorsese grants LaMotta the same divine grace that Jesus granted the blind man. That this final touch reflects Scorsese's obsession more than LaMotta's insight was not lost on Paul Schrader whose script had not included the biblical quotation: "That's purely Marty. I had no idea it was going to be there, and when I saw it I was absolutely baffled. I don't think it's true of LaMotta either in real life or in the movie; I think he's the same dumb lug at the end as he is at the beginning, and I think Marty is just imposing salvation on his subject by fiat."[2] Certainly Schrader's bafflement is understandable if redemption is a corollary of wising up. Yet the message of John 9 is not about the blind man's deserts. To the disciples who attribute the blind man's sightlessness to sin, Jesus replies, "It is not that this man or his parents sinned . . . he was born blind so that God's power might be displayed in curing him" (John 9:3–4). Neither the gravity of LaMotta's sins nor the credibility of his illumination is at issue in *Raging Bull*. In fact, the graver his sins and the dimmer his illumination, the greater the miracle of God's grace. Scorsese, who talks endlessly about the movies in his life but rarely about the books, made a point of recalling Graham Greene's *The Heart of the Matter* (1948) in an April 1991 *Playboy* interview. What struck Scorsese most about the novel was the fate of its hero, Scobie, who elects to commit suicide because he cannot go on offending God. Although the perverse pride that keeps LaMotta on his feet plowing ever forward under avalanches of blows verges on the suicidal, the analogy between *Raging Bull* and *The Heart of the Matter* has less to do with the impulses of their heroes than with the workings of God. A Catholic, Scobie had knowingly damned himself by committing suicide. When his widow voices the conventional Catholic wisdom about suicides in the closing scene of *The Heart of the Matter*, Father Rank demurs: "For goodness' sake, Mrs. Scobie, don't imagine you—or I—know a thing about God's mercy." What the priest implies about the persistence of grace and the inscrutability of God in Scobie's case applies equally to LaMotta's. For if in His infinite mercy God may forgive the one, He may as readily forgive the other. The conspicuously placed crucifixes and holy pictures of *Raging Bull* invoke a Catholicism as palpable as it was in *Who's That Knocking?* and *Mean Streets*, Scorsese's seminal essays in guilt and redemption.

If the Jake LaMotta story is an exemplum of God's grace, then the graver LaMotta's sins the greater God's power. Like the blind man of John 9, LaMotta seems to be a hopeless case. Yet a God who can redeem the blind man's sight can surely redeem LaMotta's soul. Jesus chooses the blind man to demonstrate God's power; another man with another affliction might serve as well. Scorsese chooses LaMotta, who just happens to be a fighter, for the role of Everyman: "You could take anyone, you see; the ring becomes an allegory of whatever you do in life." And "anyone," in his most intensely personal films like *Raging Bull*, is likely to be Scorsese himself: "You make movies, you're in the ring each time."[3] It was this perception of himself in LaMotta that drew Scorsese to *Raging Bull*. The idea of filming the boxer's autobiography was Robert De Niro's; Scorsese took on the project reluctantly and only after he "had found the hook—the self-destructiveness, the destruction of people around you, just for the sake of it. I was Jake LaMotta."[4] Because it was self-destructiveness that landed him in the hospital in late 1978 when De Niro dropped by to find out once and for all whether they were doing the movie, Scorsese was ripe for the epiphany that bound himself to LaMotta. Redeeming LaMotta at the end could be Scorsese's way of redeeming himself. After the commercial if not artistic debacle of *New York, New York*, Scorsese saw *Raging Bull* as a chance to rehabilitate his career. By the time of its release in 1980, however, he feared that *Raging Bull* would be his Hollywood swan song and that he would wind up living in New York or Rome and making documentaries and educational films for television. "I put everything I knew and felt into [*Raging Bull*] and I thought it would be the end of my career. It was what I call a kamikaze way of making movies: pour everything in, then forget all about it and go find another way of life."[5]

Jake LaMotta, the Bronx Bull, is a throwback to primeval man. A barely civilized human beast, he is the least articulate of Scorsese's protagonists, none of whom would make a debate team. Because LaMotta can express himself and be expressed only in action, *Raging Bull* is a nonstop assault on the senses, what Scorsese calls a cinematic "punch in the face." Whatever he feels—rage, guilt, even lust—LaMotta puts into body language. He responds to crises at home as he disposes of challenges in the ring, slugging wives and opponents alike. When Vickie (Cathy Moriarty), his second wife, casually alludes to Tony Janiro's good looks, LaMotta destroys the handsome fighter in a fit of paranoid jealousy. "He ain't pretty no more," quips a ringsider after LaMotta's relentless attack has reduced Janiro's face to bloody pulp. "I'm gonna make him suffer," LaMotta swore before the bout, unconsciously revealing the sexual motivation behind his vendetta against Janiro: "He's a pretty kid . . . . I gotta problem if I should fuck him or fight him." If LaMotta vents his sadism on Janiro, he enacts his masochism in the title defense against Sugar Ray Robinson. Enduring and even inviting a fearsome pummeling by the man regarded as one of the greatest boxers of all time, his face raw meat and his blood spattered about the ring and sprayed over the ringsiders, LaMotta nonetheless taunts Robinson: "You never got me down, Ray." Though the result was a foregone conclusion several rounds before the thirteenth when the Bronx Bull, still on his feet, was stopped by Robinson and lost the title, LaMotta "sacrificed" his body on the altar of his guilt and of his corresponding need of self-esteem. Years earlier, coerced to play ball with mobster Tommy Como (Nicholas Colasanto) and take a dive against Billy Fox in order to get a long-sought title shot, LaMotta follows orders but cannot bring himself to fall. Though Fox duly wins the sham bout, LaMotta's refusal to go down makes the fix so obvious that the Board suspends him and withholds his purse. Inarticulate as ever, LaMotta weeps in his dressing room after the loss, shattered not by the guilt of throwing a fight but by the shame of betraying his own body. For the compulsively macho LaMotta, the psychic wounds of the Fox fiasco fester longer than the bodily wounds of the Robinson battle. Immolating himself against Robinson, may, in fact, be LaMotta's way of atoning for disgracing himself against Fox.

On the surface, LaMotta is all macho posturing, Ur-man at his most sadomasochistic. Yet the joke about fucking or fighting the "pretty" Tony Janiro may be one of those all-too-revealing Freudian slips. Paul Schrader refers to the "hidden sexual bond between brothers" in explaining Jake's conviction that Joey (Joe Pesci) is Vicki's lover. "Did you fuck my brother?" Jake shrills at Vickie, striking her. Incredibly, the three principals disagreed about their characters' sexual moves: De Niro told an interviewer that Joey *was* with Vickie, while Cathy Moriarty denied it as did Joe Pesci who called De Niro's theory "Bobby's paranoia as Jake."[6] And Scorsese "clarifies" Schrader's notion of a "hidden sexual bond" that links Jake to Joey and (implicitly) to Janiro. According to Robin Wood, Scorsese revealed "in a conversation that, though he was not aware of it while making the film, he now saw that *Raging Bull* has a 'homosexual subtext.'"[7] For Joyce Carol Oates, the sexual dynamic lurks in the heart of boxing itself:

> No sport appears more powerfully homoerotic: The confrontation in the ring—the disrobing—the sweaty heated combat that is part dance, courtship, coupling—the frequent urgent pursuit by one boxer of the other in the fight's natural and violent movement

toward the "knockout": Surely boxing derives much of its appeal from this mimicry of a species of erotic love in which one man overcomes the other in an exhibition of superior strength and will. The heralded celibacy of the fighter-in-training is very much a part of boxing lore: instead of focusing his energies and fantasies upon a woman the boxer focuses them upon an opponent. Where Woman has been, Opponent must be.[8]

Boxing and sex conflate in the Janiro fight where LaMotta imprints his homoerotic desires on his opponent's body. Whether he thereby purges the "homosexual subtext" from his own body is debatable: perhaps purgation, if it comes at all, awaits the title-losing slaughter by Robinson when LaMotta absorbs a beating every bit as fearsome as the one he gave Janiro. In any event, the erotic equation of boxing and sex is evident not only in the fight scenes per se but in their juxtaposition with scenes from domestic life. By intercutting LaMotta's home movies with action footage of his fights, Scorsese converts the apparent polarities—marital and pugilistic—of LaMotta's life into a symbiosis. A montage sequence of The Bronx Bull on a three-year roll commencing in early 1944 clarifies the relationship between fighting and loving. Two stills from the Basora fight (August 10, 1945), then home movie footage of Jake and Vickie marrying; alternating step-motion and freeze frames of the Kochan fight (September 17, 1945), then home movie footage of Jake and Vickie horsing around at poolside; three nine-frame action stills from the Satterfield fight (September 12, 1946), then home movie footage of Jake carrying Vickie into their house highlight the conjunction of boxing and domestic success during what is arguably the happiest period of LaMotta's life. Wood argues that the home movie intercuts represent an "intrusion" of color and therefore of "illusion" into the "established" black and white "reality" of *Raging Bull.* LaMotta's preservation on film of the heterosexually charged episodes with Vickie may be an unconscious defense against his unacknowledged homosexual instincts. "Directed" by LaMotta himself, the home movies "construct" a necessary illusion of domestic bliss that is as fragile as it is short-lived. Immediately following the montage sequence is a more typical (i.e., black and white, discordant) domestic scene climaxing in Jake's jealous reaction to Vickie's remark about Tony Janiro's good looks. Whether the ensuing massacre of Janiro signals the return of LaMotta's repressed homosexuality or not, it may reflect fears about his own masculinity triggered by Vickie's casual observation. Whatever its roots, jealousy

increasingly poisons his relationship with Vickie, destroying the symbiosis between pugilistic and marital success evoked in the montage
sequence and exposing its fleeting and/or illusory nature. Similarly, his
greatest triumph—defeating Marcel Cerdan for the middleweight title—
is soured by the next sequence, which portrays an already pudgy (larded
with some of the nearly sixty pounds De Niro famously gained) LaMotta
accusing even Joey of sleeping with Vickie. Joey's rejoinder—"That's a
sick question; you're a sick fuck, and I'm not gonna answer it"—and his
advice—"Try a little more fucking and a little less eating."—expose both
Jake's outward symptoms and his inward fears. The intimation of heterosexual failure raises the suspicion of homosexual repression. And
while abstinence was previously justified by the hoary boxing maxim
that sex saps a fighter's strength, LaMotta, no longer in training and
relaxing between fights, seems to prefer eating to lovemaking. Viewed
retrospectively, the scene that culminates in LaMotta's pouring ice water
down his shorts, thereby aborting his most passionate scene with Vickie
in apparent compliance with boxing's conventional wisdom, becomes
an early example of the sexual evasion that Joey remarks on years later.

The homosexual subtext of *Raging Bull* is written in Jake's recurring
anxiety about his masculinity. Because he equates masculinity with violence, the atavistic Bronx Bull responds to real and fancied slights the
only way he knows how—with his fists. The alternating boxing and
domestic sequences blur the distinction between fighting in the ring and
fighting in the home. Although boxing is a singularly masculine profession that effectively distinguishes men from women, its practice fails to
allay Jake's hidden fears: "My hands. . . . I got these small hands. I got a
little girl's hands," he tells Joey. "Come on, don't be a little faggot. . . . Hit
me," Jake taunts, until Joey complies and opens the still-fresh cuts from
the Reeves fight. "Fuckin' queer. Faggot," Jake's first wife screams after
him a few shots later as he and Joey depart for a nightclub, leaving her
behind. Once established, this homosexual subtext lurks barely beneath
the surface of *Raging Bull.* When Jake embraces and kisses Joey, begging
for his brother's kisses in return near the end of the film, the "moment
can be read as an ironic inversion of the notion of the kiss as a privileged
climactic moment of classical cinema, epitomizing the construction of
the heterosexual couple."9 While Joey's response is cool, his promise at
least to call reflects the dominant masculine ethos of *Raging Bull.* A two-
time loser at marriage and separated from his children, Jake intuits—he
sends Emma the stripper off in a cab when he spots Joey—that the only

viable human relationship open to him is that with his brother, another man. That he plays kiss-and-make-up not with Vickie but with Joey means that Jake instinctively opts for the male bonding he has implicitly privileged all along.

Jake's craving for self-punishment outstrips the punches elicited from Joey and the beating inflicted by Robinson. Projecting his feelings of inadequacy onto the women in his life, he alternately shouts down and beats up both of his wives. His pathological jealousy of Vickie, fed by recurring fantasies of her infidelity, is directed as much against himself as it is against her. So unremitting is his need to punish himself that Jake "progresses" from asking Joey "Did Salvy fuck Vickie?" to "Did you fuck my wife?" After Joey indignantly leaves, Jake asks Vickie the same questions, pulling her hair and slapping her when she refuses to answer until she bursts out, "I fucked all of them. What do you want me to say? I fucked all of them—Tommy, Salvy, your brother!" His worst fears thus "confirmed," Jake rushes to Joey's house where he beats his brother until he is pulled off by Vickie and Joey's wife. Further enraged by the "unfaithful" Vickie's interference, he then turns against her, decking his wife with a vicious blow. The end of the relationship between the brothers, it is also the beginning of the end of the relationship between husband and wife. A product of Jake's obsessional need simultaneously to protect and display his fragile masculinity, the attack on Vickie and Joey is ultimately an attack on himself. Alone in a prison cell near the end and bereft of surrogates to strike or be struck by, LaMotta punishes himself most explicitly, repeatedly banging his head against the wall of his cell and crying, "I'm not an animal."

Jake's disclaimer, rendered doubtful by its head-banging accompaniment, recalls his heated argument with first wife Irma at the beginning of *Raging Bull* that prompted Larry the neighbor to holler, "What's the matter with you out there, you animals?" True to his characterization, LaMotta rages back, threatening to eat Larry's dog for lunch. Less than human yet more, being an animal has its advantages despite its obvious drawbacks. LaMotta enters and exits the ring in a leopard-skin robe; and he liked being called the Bronx Bull so well that *Raging Bull* became the title of his autobiography. Unlike Sugar Ray Robinson who dazzled opponents with footwork and finesse and finished most fights virtually unscathed, LaMotta waded into his opponents, taking their best shots on the way to bludgeoning them into submission. "I ain't never liked violence," Robinson once said. But LaMotta thrived on it, attributing his success in the ring to utter disdain for his own survival and half wishing he might atone with his life for the life he (mistakenly) believed he had taken in a robbery. Wanting overtly to be punished for suspected murder and covertly to be chastised for suspected homosexuality, he fought as much to hurt himself as to hurt others. It is no accident that Joyce Carol Oates invokes LaMotta as her prime example of boxers who

> invite injury as a means of assuaging guilt, in a Dostoyevskian exchange of physical well being for peace of mind. Boxing is about being hit rather more that it is about hitting, just as it is about feeling pain, if not devastating psychological paralysis, more than it is about winning . . . .The boxer prefers physical pain in the ring to the absence of pain that is ideally the condition of ordinary life. If one cannot hit, one can yet be hit, and know that one is alive.[10]

Nobody in *Raging Bull* ever accuses LaMotta of being overly smart, and it is probably the intimation of subhuman intelligence that sparks his rage at Larry's animal reference and accounts for his head banging in prison. More often than not, however, Jake the animal is indistinguishable from Jake the male. In and out of the ring, he is the primal brute, savaging everybody indiscriminately in the apparent if subconscious belief that being a man means acting the animal. And because acting the animal in the ring is the only way he knows how to fight—unlike the slick Robinson—LaMotta's style and disposition reflect one another. When he ceases to rage against Robinson and, arms lowered in surrender rather than raised in defense, accepts his brutal punishment, LaMotta may be at his least animalistic and most human. It may be that his simultaneous attraction and aversion to animality reflects an anxiety about his basic humanity that parallels his concerns about his masculinity. Along with other Scorsese/De Niro protagonists, notably Travis Bickle (*Taxi Driver*) and Rupert Pupkin (*The King of Comedy*), LaMotta seems lacking in those affiliations—class, culture, religion—that conventionally define the human condition. The same working class neighborhoods, Italian mobsters, and Catholic icons that conferred identity on Charlie in *Mean Streets* leave no discernible imprint on LaMotta. Nothing of the camaraderie and commonality that, however tenuously, sustain Charlie is available to Jake, not because they do not exist but because he is unable or unwilling to accept them. Next to LaMotta, even the taciturn Bickle comes off as gregarious in his desultory and dispirited human contacts. Dysfunctional in those roles—husband, father, brother—that might ordinarily add up to an identity, LaMotta effectively exists in a state of isolation and alienation approaching Bickle's. At least Bickle makes sporadic stabs at being human, jawing with Wizard, seeking out Betsy, caring for Iris. And unlike Jake, who slugs friends—wives and brother included—and foes indiscriminately, Travis erupts in violence only against his (perceived) enemies. Even Travis consents to share a table with his fellow cabbies; Jake sullenly resists joining Como and the boys until he is practically dragged over to their table. Bickle cannot form relationships with people; LaMotta destroys what relationships he does form. The Bronx Bull charges from one violent and/or abusive episode to another, sh(r)edding human attributes in the process until an uncomprehending body is all that remains of his identity.

This process of erasing LaMotta's identity quickens with the title-losing Robinson fight and culminates in its wake. Because boxing inscribed whatever sense of himself he possessed, LaMotta's decision to retire figures to deflate if not puncture his self-image. As usual, a fight scene is closely followed by a domestic scene, this one revealing the by now grossly overweight LaMotta lounging poolside at his Miami house. He tells a reporter that he was tired of keeping his weight down; he has a beautiful wife and three children and wants no more from life. Then he poses for family photographs as if to authenticate and preserve the happy domestic tableau he has just invoked. What the photos apparently record is LaMotta's smooth (d)evolution from pugilist to paterfamilias. They imply that the deflation of an identity conceived in the ring is more than offset by the inflation of an identity achieved in the home. Moreover, this primary role change from fighter to family man promises to burnish his heterosexual credentials and thus to banish his homosexual affinities. But the photo session also recalls LaMotta's home-movie footage of an earlier poolside sequence, one of several attempted valorizations of the Jake and Vickie relationship. Like those former "proofs" of heterosexual harmony and stability, the Miami photos conceal more than they reveal. Again, the apparent concord of reel life dissolves into the actual discord of real life. No sooner does Jake in his new capacity as nightclub owner and lounge comic announce one night that he and Vickie will soon celebrate their eleventh anniversary than early the next morning when he finally exits the club Vickie announces that she is leaving him. This time she will not be talked out of a divorce, she is taking the children, and she will call the cops if Jake comes around. As she pulls away in their Cadillac, LaMotta, neither paterfamilias nor prizefighter, is left in the dust alone.

In a rapid procession of scenes—his arrest for pandering, his doomed attempt to raise $10,000 in bribes to get the case dropped, and his subsequent imprisonment and head banging against the wall of his cell—he hits rockbottom. LaMotta's money-raising tactic of hammering the jewels from his championship belt is as definitive of the man as it is pathetic in the result. Without the belt—i.e., without the identity it confers on jewels and man alike—the jewels are worth a mere $1,500, a sum LaMotta indignantly refuses. As broken as the belt, the jailed LaMotta first rages, then weeps, "You're so stupid. . . I am *not* an animal." Perhaps the admission of the first phrase justifies the denial of the second. If so, it may be the necessary preface to the redemptory text.

According to Paul Schrader, Scorsese imposes "salvation on his subject by fiat" and then only in the final title. Yet even Schrader, who "never really got from him [Scorsese] a terribly credible reason for why he did it," qualifies but does not dismiss Scorsese's claim that *Raging Bull* is a film about redemption: "Yes, but redemption through physical pain, like the Stations of the Cross, one torment after another. Not redemption by having a view of salvation or by grace, but just redemption by death and suffering which is the darker side of the Christian message."[11] Read thus, LaMotta's head banging in his cell is the climactic "torment" of a redemptive action dependent on the pain and suffering he absorbs from others and inflicts upon himself. And he is not disqualified for redemption by the seeming implausibility of his insistence that he is not an animal. As originally scripted, the prison scene began with Jake trying unsuccessfully to masturbate but unable to sustain an erection because every time he imagines a woman he remembers how badly he treated her. Blaming his hands, he smashes them against the wall. Instead of shooting the scene as written, Scorsese substituted "I am not an animal," which, coming from a man who can articulate his feelings only through violence, is open to doubt. Anyway, being an animal is not all bad in light of Mary Pat Kelly's claim that Scorsese sees Jake "as almost another order of being. He [Scorsese] cites St. Thomas Aquinas, who said that perhaps animals serve God better than men because they have no choice but to live their natures purely. Jake, for Scorsese, has that primal quality." Yet Jake *is* conscious of his wrongs and sees the defeats that culminate in his jailing as punishment in kind. And it is this consciousness that he articulates in prison, first, predictably, in violence but then, at last, in the words that humanize him: "He faces himself and, somehow, redemption begins," argues Kelly. "The sign of salvation is small—he embraces his brother—but the moment is unforgettable. A man recognizes his own soul."[12] So whether Jake is Schrader's "same dumb lug at the end as he is at the beginning"—nearly an animal—or Kelly's saved soul—fully a man—redemption is possible. It is this either/or interpretation of *Raging Bull* that the Final Credit embodies: whatever his nature, man may be saved by the grace of God.

An aspect of its hero's redemption figures in the narrative arc of *Raging Bull.* The movie ends as it began with a middle-aged and flabby LaMotta rehearsing his patter in a dressing room at New York's Barbizon-Plaza. Outside, the sandwich-board sign reads: "An Evening with Jake LaMotta." Preceded only by an over-the-credits opening shot of a young and sinewy Jake shadowboxing in the ring before a fight, the initial Barbizon-Plaza sequence sets up the extended flashback that runs the length of *Raging Bull* and concludes back in the same dressing room. The framing device obviously exploits the physical contrast between two versions of LaMotta; less obviously, it invokes a comparison between two modes of performance. "That's Entertainment," the last words Jake voices in the first dressing-room scene, still echo as he takes a vicious shot to the face more than two decades earlier. And "That's Entertainment," equally valid for what Jake is doing outside the ring in 1964 as for what he did in it in 1941, suggests that for him performance is destiny. LaMotta's dressing room spiel is a warm-up ritual analogous to his slow-motion shadowboxing over the opening credits. The footage culminating in the Reeves fight thus establishes linkages between past and present, youth and age, boxing and stand-up comedy. Because Reeves's 1941 punch cuts short Jake's 1964 dressing room warm-up, the full implications of the Barbizon-Plaza scene must await its more extended replay. Between Jake's attempted reconciliation with Joey and the Final Title, the second Barbizon-Plaza scene signals redemption as much in its context as in its content. Jake embraces his brother with a tenderness he has never shown Joey before. In his salad days, the Bronx Bull's terms of endearment were as violent as the tremors of his rage. Brotherly love/hate took the form of blows given and received, mute signifiers of what Jake could not or would not speak. That he is at last actually able to voice his love may be the verbal equivalent of "once I was blind and now I can see." Because the central relationship of Jake's life is not with Vickie—or with any woman for that matter—but with Joey, it figures that this final scene between the brothers should be the first glimmer of redemption. The scene may even clarify the "homosexual subtext" of *Raging Bull*. Paul Schrader, whose "main contribution" to the film "was the character of Joey LaMotta," greatly expanded the relationship between the brothers. "Jake didn't like his brother much, so he wasn't in the first draft and there was no drama there," says Schrader. Only after meeting the real Joey and finding him "much more interesting" did Schrader decide to build up his role, focusing on the "hidden sexual bond between brothers."[13] When instead of slugging Joey he kisses him, Jake arguably comes to terms with the latent homosexuality he hitherto repressed with his fists. Wood's reading of the moment, "as an ironic inversion of the notion of the kiss as a privileged climactic moment of classical cinema, epitomizing the construction of the heterosexual couple," might be the last word on *Raging Bull* had the film ended with his "climactic moment." By following it with the second dressing-room scene, however, Scorsese privileges Jake's concluding monologue. Not that the kiss is not a crucial factor in Jake's animal-to-human evolution, itself a necessary precondition of redemption. Without the kiss there is no redemption; but the redemptive premise (and promise) of the kiss is fulfilled only in what follows.

The movie-ending second dressing-room scene apparently picks up where the first left off. *Apparently*, because while the place is the same, the title—New York City 1964—that fixed the time of the first scene is missing from the second. In the first scene Jake is a bumbling clown who jokes about a fight night when "I took off my robe/And what'd I do?/I forgot to wear shorts." In the second he is a more than passable monologist who feelingly and flawlessly recites Marlon Brando's famous "I coulda' been a contender" speech from *On the Waterfront*. Either Jake has miraculously pulled himself together during the course of a single evening or the two scenes take place on different evenings. The one-shot theory makes less sense but emits the same signals. And because it is inconceivable that the scene of his aptitude should precede the scene of his ineptitude, the man who recites from *On the Waterfront* is the man LaMotta has finally become. Like Brando's Terry Malloy, LaMotta was a boxer who relied on his brother for professional advice and emotional sustenance. Both Malloy and LaMotta are persuaded by their brothers to throw a fight. But whereas Malloy, who "coulda' been a contender," instead gets a "one-way ticket to Palookaville," LaMotta goes on to win the title. So Jake quotes Malloy to liken not their careers but their relationships with their brothers. Like Malloy, Jake confronts his brother in a crucial moment of emotional and intellectual honesty. The opening lines [in] the scene from *On the Waterfront*– "it was you, Charlie. You was my brother!"–are "bookended" by the closing lines: "Let's face it. It was you, Charley [sic]. It was you." Given that Jake is speaking these lines to his own reflected image in the dressing-room mirror, it becomes clear that the words signify his revelation about the crucial role that Joey has played in his life. It was Jake's own unresolved sexual conflicts that contributed to the formation of his obsessively jealous, violent, and self-destructive nature.[14]

This resolution of his sexual conflicts—prefigured in the kiss he gave Joey in the previous scene—promises an end to Jake's raging, a putative precursor of redemption.

If what he resolves is crucial to LaMotta's redemption, then how he resolves it is crucial as well. As contender and champ, even as has-been and jailbird, LaMotta led an entirely sentient life. All but incapable of introspection, he defined himself as others defined him, strictly in physical terms. The most inarticulate of Scorsese's protagonists, LaMotta expresses himself solely in "body language" both inside and outside the ring. What verbal language he attempted spewed out in the form of the limited store of obscenities that passed for an entire vocabulary. Possessed of few words, LaMotta instinctively recoils from prolonged conversation, letting his fists do the talking when talk he must. When he suspects Vickie of infidelity, for example, no sooner does he confront her than he slugs her: the words that "normally" intervene between accusation and action are conspicuous in their absence. Jake's killer instinct, sanctioned and applauded in the ring, brands him as an animal outside it. Because he is unable to make the transition from war to peace, from blows to words, he rages unabated against friend and foe alike. If he is to be sprung from the cage of his body to achieve anything like the fuller humanity necessary to redemption, LaMotta must first learn how to speak.

It is therefore significant, if not ironic, that in retirement LaMotta, of all people, should resort to words for his livelihood. At the microphone in "Jake LaMotta's," the Miami nightclub he opens after quitting the ring, the former Bronx Bull plays the lounge comic. "So gimme a stage/where this bull here can rage/ and though I can fight/I'd much rather hear myself recite," Jake versifies and then leads the crowd in the rousing finish: "that's entertainment." It's the spiel he rehearses practically verbatim in the first dressing-room scene. Banal as it is, the patter nonetheless represents Jake's first groping attempt at articulating *anything* beyond his usual grunts and curses. Grasping the microphone—a mechanism of communication—he works the crowd rather than working it over: the "that's entertainment" sing-along is a form of mutual verbal discourse that, no matter how rudimentary, is more than LaMotta managed before. Learning to talk is, however, a glacially slow process: Jake is still rehearsing eight years later in New York the identical words he recited in Miami back in 1956. And even the clearly more articulate monologist who delivers the "I coulda' been a contender" speech with considerable aplomb is merely repeating another's words. Still, the passage he chooses to recite reflects Jake's own struggle no less than Malloy's. As heartfelt as they are personal, the words soar above the empty versifying of the earlier routine(s) to reveal a man in the act of redeeming himself.

LaMotta's transformation from man of action to man of words has about it a certain logic despite its apparent incongruity. Boxing and acting—whether as stand-up comic or serious monologist—are both performance arts. "That's entertainment," reverberating between the initial dressing-room and boxing scenes, links the two activities by their primary function. Ringside tables at a nightclub evoke boxing's ringside seats in tacit acknowledgment of the affinity between two forms of show biz. Boxing itself takes up only ten to fifteen minutes of a film that is just as much about acting. From LaMotta's "That's entertainment" at the beginning to his "I coulda' been a contender" at the end, boxing and acting maintain a symbiotic relationship. It is not too much to suggest that Jake is redeemed via his hard-won ability to translate the body language of the boxer into the verbal language of the actor. And because LaMotta quoting Malloy is really De Niro emulating Brando, the "I coulda' been a contender" speech anatomizes the very performance skills that Jake is struggling to acquire. A master of the self-transformation that Jake assays, De Niro became a formidable boxer for *Raging Bull* just as he had become a proficient sax man for *New York, New York.* "I'd rank Bobby in the first Top 20 middleweights," the real LaMotta marveled after suffering everything from blackened eyes and loosened teeth to jaw and rib fractures in training sessions with De Niro. Whether fine-tuning his body to portray LaMotta in his prime or ballooning sixty pounds to resemble LaMotta obese and dissolute, De Niro lived the role so completely that he came even to side with Jake in suspecting Vickie of cheating on him. In De Niro's performance, then, boxing becomes a metaphor for acting, most visibly and most decisively in the climactic evocation of Marlon Brando's Terry Malloy.

"Robert De Niro's Rupert Pupkin"—the born loser who emerges as the big winner in *The King of Comedy* (1983)—"is Jake LaMotta without his fists," asserts Pauline Kael. What Kael is talking about, however, is not so much the roles per se as the way the actor plays them: "De Niro in disguise denies his characters a soul. It is not merely that he hollows himself out and becomes Jake LaMotta . . . or Rupert Pupkin—he makes them hollow, too, and merges with the character's emptiness." De Niro's "bravura" acting in *Mean Streets, Taxi Driver,* and *New York, New York* collapsed into "anti-acting" after "he started turning himself into repugnant, flesh effigies of soulless characters . . . . Pupkin is a nothing."[15] Kael's was not the only hostile verdict on De Niro's Pupkin: "People were confused by *The King of Comedy* and saw Bob as some kind of mannequin," opines Scorsese, admitting that he and De Niro were trying to see how far they could push the character. So close to the "edge" did they come that they could go no further in their collaboration at that time and did not work together again until *GoodFellas* (1990). De Niro won a Best Actor Oscar for *Raging Bull,* but he gave his "best performance ever" in *The King of Comedy,* according to Scorsese.[16] Kael and Scorsese see eye to eye on Pupkin's character; where they diverge is in their estimates of De Niro's performance. And performance—by Pupkin and by De Niro playing Pupkin—is what *The King of Comedy* is all about.

Rupert Pupkin shares the Scorsese hero's habitual need to be somebody that De Niro previously incarnated in those other warped personalities—Travis Bickle and Jake LaMotta. Kael's complaint that De Niro "hollows out" his character is apposite, but her contention that this constitutes "anti-acting" is questionable. Like Bickle, Pupkin is a pathetic nonentity whose eventual success exposes the disparity between private persona and public image. A montage of tabloid headlines constitutes instant fame and confers celebrity status on the dubious heroes of *Taxi Driver* and *The King of Comedy.* Travis murders his way to fame; Rupert merely kidnaps talk-show host Jerry Langford (Jerry Lewis) in order to get on television. Still, in both cases public adulation rewards criminal action. And both antiheroes graft a media-made persona—Bickle the gallant savior; Pupkin the new king of comedy—on a hitherto featureless identity. Although Kael applauds De Niro's Bickle and lambasts his Pupkin, the defacement of the central character is already apparent in *Taxi Driver* and simply reaches its (il)logical culmination (Scorsese's point that he and De Niro could go no further) in *The King of Comedy.* Both films ask how performance and identity are related in the era of mass media. Both answer that the relationship is tenuous at best, absurd at worst, and what is more, that it reflects and fulfills the fantasies of a vapid public. "*The King of Comedy* is a film about the desperate need to exist publicly, which is so American," and is for Pupkin, "a matter of life or death," says screenwriter Paul Zimmerman. Zimmerman got the idea for his script from a 1970 David Suskind television show (what else?) about autograph hounds. "I realized that autograph hounds are just like assassins except that one carries a pen instead of a gun."[17] Basking in the reflected glow of a celebrity's signature, the autograph hound achieves his own status of sorts. When Pupkin wants to impress his dream girl Rita (Diahanne Abbott) he shows her an outsized album, riffling its many pages to reveal his prized autographs. The darker implications of Zimmerman's script were apparent to Scorsese who made Pupkin and his equally fanatical female accomplice Masha (Sandra Bernhard) into autograph hounds who would do nearly anything for a precious signature. Although *The King of Comedy* lacks the mayhem of *Taxi Driver* and *Raging Bull*, there is latent violence in Pupkin's taping the kidnapped Langford to a chair, even in Masha's shattering glasses and plates during her staged candlelight dinner with the nearly mummified talk-show host.

It is not the zeal of the autograph hound but the obsession of the would-be comedian that certifies Pupkin as potentially dangerous if not actually demented. Pupkin, a thirty-four-year-old messenger boy living at home with his mother, equates self-esteem with celebrity. "Better to be king for a night than schmuck for a lifetime," he exults in the course of his monologue on the Langford show. An echo of Andy Warhol's classic prediction about everybody being famous for fifteen minutes, Pupkin's quip also implies that no price is too great to pay for those few cherished moments in the spotlight. That a fleeting television appearance hardly justifies the progressive violations of Langford's privacy—crowding into his limo, invading his office, barging into his house, finally kidnaping him and threatening his life—never occurs to Pupkin. In fact, the very concept of privacy is meaningless for a nobody who can become somebody only via media grace. As omnipotent in the media age as God was once upon a time, television displaces the church as the bestower of grace. In one of the more elaborate of Pupkin's many fantasies of stardom, he weds Rita in a surprise ceremony staged by the guests on his own talk show. Arranged by one father figure (Langford) and performed by another (Rupert's high school principal, now a Justice of the Peace) on television, the fantasy wedding trivializes and parodies the sacrament and its site. The imaginary audience applauds the vulgar ceremony—an all too typical television conversion of private celebration into public spectacle—just as the "real" audience will later anoint Pupkin as the new king of comedy after his equally vulgar comic routine. Television *can* turn a schmuck into a king, at least in the eyes of its beholders who, *The King of Comedy* suggests, are even greater schmucks themselves.

Pupkin's conviction that if he can only get on television his identity will be validated and his success assured, apparently the delusion of a deranged narcissist, turns out to be justified. The medium is indeed the message, not because it discriminates between stars and stooges but because it rewards them indiscriminately. When Rupert finally delivers his five-minute monologue on late-night TV it comes off without a hitch. He neither has a script nor needs one he tells the show's anxious producer, who wants to see his material before it is aired on national TV. After all, Pupkin has rehearsed the monologue and relished the moment endlessly in his fantasies. Perhaps most crucially, he has got all the gestures of the typical talk-show host down pat. Whether his monologue is funny or not is beside the point: the studio audience, cued by Tony Randall's lavish introduction, by Rupert's "professional" shtick, and by the clichés governing TV performer–audience transactions cheers his every joke. After a series of grotesque family gags capped by an account of vomiting all over his father's new shoes (a putdown of the "real" father corresponding symbolically to what Rupert, the newly crowned King of Comedy, is doing to his adoptive father and former King of Comedy, Jerry Langford?) Pupkin gets his biggest laugh when he confesses that he kidnapped Langford to get on the show. That the audience reserves its wildest applause for this unfunny truth is the sickest story of the entire monologue sequence. In television's brave new world actions and the words that describe them are equally meaningless.

Rupert Pupkin's TV apotheosis makes his fondest dreams of celebrity come true. All along he has fantasized this magic moment, converting his basement into a make-believe TV studio peopled by life-sized cardboard cutouts of Liza Minnelli and his personal deity, Jerry Langford. On "stage," Pupkin seats himself comfortably between "Liza" and "Jerry" in prescribed talk-show host fashion, kissing her photo and glad-handing Jerry's. The aspiring comedian has the Langford shtick down pat: De Niro's gestures, accent, and expression shadow Lewis without actually mimicking him. And because Langford is not the zany Jerry Lewis who partnered Dean Martin but the "cool" latter-day Lewis who is no longer particularly funny, the gap between his talent and Pupkin's may be more apparent than real. Celebrity has nothing to do with talent: it is not Pupkin's unfunny monologue but his crime that makes him a celebrity. A newscaster announces that Rupert's escapade has made his name a household word. *Time, Newsweek, Life, Rolling Stone,* and *People* magazines feature his picture on their covers. While serving less than half of his six-year prison sentence Pupkin writes a best-selling autobiography that earns him millions. That Pupkin the superstar is created by print/words no less than by TV/images broadens the satire of mass media and of their audience(s). Introduced as "the legendary, the inspirational, the one and only King of Comedy, Rupert Pupkin," he is spotlighted on the bare stage of his own TV show in the film's final sequence. As the audience wildly applauds, Pupkin receives their homage augustly as if it were no more than his due.

Rupert's triumph could be another of his fantasies—just as Travis Bickle's heroic renown at the end of *Taxi Driver* could be the fantasy of a man dying from gunshot wounds. But where would the fantasy sequence(s) begin? With the respective montages that signal celebrity? Or even earlier, perhaps as far back as the key actions—the Langford kidnapping by Rupert and Masha; the brothel massacre by Travis—that make celebrity possible? To beg the question(s) of where reality ends and fantasy begins and vice versa in the case of the endings is risky business: they achieve their full meaning(s) only if they represent reality. For *Taxi Driver* and *The King of Comedy* anatomize private obsession not as an end in itself but as a means of exposing public complicity in the creation of false idols. It is not poor schmucks like Travis and Rupert who are skewered so much as the media-driven and socially accepted process by which nobodies are translated into somebodies. What is scary, in other words, is that fantasy spills over into reality: Travis and Rupert become celebrities not just in theory but in fact.

Unlike Travis's, Rupert's celebrity depends on displacement. To become the new king of comedy, Rupert must dispose of Langford, the current wearer of the crown. This is akin to the son's Oedipal fantasy of deposing the father: Langford is the only begetter of Pupkin's comedic ambition. Watching Langford the night he replaced Jack Paar "convinced me I wanted to be a comedian," Pupkin recalls. Although he is thirty-four, Rupert still lives at home with his mother but apparently without a father. At work as messenger boy and at home playing talk-show host with cardboard cutouts, he is little more than a child, and his mother (played by Scorsese's own mother, Catherine, who periodically scolds Rupert from upstairs though she is never seen) treats him as one. Jerry Langford is the missing father in his physical presence and the symbolic father by virtue of his celebrity. When at the end of the movie Rupert appropriates both roles, he becomes a grown up man as well as the King of Comedy. This double transformation is implicitly acknowledged by Rita, who, viewing Rupert's apotheosis on television, finally takes him seriously. Masha, who also "misses" a father, plays Langford's daughter much as Rupert plays the son. What Robin Wood calls the "Oedipal projects of the children" converge when Rupert and Masha join forces to kidnap Langford. Rupert tapes Langford to his chair, "virtually mummifying him, so that he can barely even turn his head. . . . It is the ultimate denial of Langford-as-person: he becomes an inanimate object who can then be supplanted by the son and made love to by the daughter."[18] Although Masha fails to appropriate Langford's body as Rupert appropriates his fame, her hilariously botched seduction attempt likewise points to the groundless worship of celebrity in the age of mass media. No matter that Jerry Lewis plays Langford as a singularly unattractive figure, cold, empty, and isolated. To his "children," he is a famous celebrity whose reflected glory makes them somebodies. And Masha's hopeful/hopeless tête-a-tête with the helplessly bound Langford, even more than Rupert's basement repartee with Langford's cardboard effigy, suggests the basis of celebrity worship. After Rupert leaves for the studio to negotiate his appearance on the Langford show, Masha stages the candlelight dinner seduction scene. Acting out her fantasy of a close encounter with Jerry, whereas Rupert's was largely confined to his own imagination, Masha arguably raises the stakes of the idolizing game. Undressing before Langford, she confesses to the immobile and impassive "father" that she loves him, something she has never told her own parents who, she claims, never loved her. "You're gonna love me like nobody's loved me, come rain or come shine," she croons to him. It is a later verse of "Come Rain or Come Shine," first sung by Ray Charles over the opening credits. "I'm gonna love you like nobody's loved you" goes the song's opening verse, which, taken together with Masha's follow-up, invokes the reciprocal love that she yearns for. Under the spell of her own fantasy she ungags and untapes Langford, releasing him for the lovemaking she is convinced they both desire. He responds by smacking her in the face and stalking out of the building, Masha, clad only in bra and panties, in hot pursuit. In its single-minded obsession, its total exposure of body and soul, its imperviousness to embarrassment and indifference to consequences, Masha's foredoomed seduction scenario says as much about what Zimmerman calls "the need to exist publicly" as nearly anything that even Rupert can dream up.

It is this desperate need to go public that informs American life and that Rupert and Masha embody. The restaurant waiter who proudly announces his name to the uncaring diner, the groupie who stalks media/sports/political bigshots—they are all performers manqué. Rupert lives life as a continuous stand-up performance, utterly failing to distinguish between private and public space:

> In this performative take-over of the public sphere by the individual, the notion of the individual here is paradoxically redefined by complete incapacity to differentiate an internal and external reality, or to put it another way, by a total evacuation of an internal subjectivity and a reconstitution of it as absolute narcissism. Instead, the surface of a mass-media logic and images fully replace any more traditional figures of psychological crisis (family, parents).[19]

At the same time that he appropriates public space for his own stage, Pupkin stages his performance(s) in the private space(s) of others, notably Langford. A one-man occupation force, Rupert successively colonizes the car, the office, the house, even the person of his idol by way of taking over Langford's show and the King of Comedy title that comes with it. Vampirelike, he has bled Langford of identity (read "celebrity," since the deposed king of comedy is as hollow a media confection as his successor) and transfused it into himself.

Pupkin's (mis)appropriation of Langford's estate is a particularly egregious invasion of private life and personal space. Brushing past a bewildered manservant with a phony claim that he and Rita have been invited for the weekend, Pupkin makes himself at home. So familiar is he with the contents of the house he has never before entered that he points out to Rita the significance of the various Langford memorabilia displayed in the living room. Just as he did with his own basement, Pupkin has converted Langford's house into a stage, even leading Rita on a tour of the premises as if he were hosting a television show. Even when Langford arrives in response to his servant's call (Rupert's intrusion has disrupted Langford's golf game in still another invasion of privacy) to expose the "performance," Rupert remains unflappable. Impervious to Langford's insults, which he tries to turn into jokes, Pupkin is beyond embarrassment. Not so Rita who visibly suffers through Rupert's lame attempt to placate the furious Langford. Yet even in her discomfiture Rita retains enough presence of mind to steal a souvenir from a table before she and Rupert are ejected from the house. "She willingly engages," notes Timothy Corrigan, "in the same appropriative violence that just humiliated her as a spectator."[20] In Rita's petty thievery is a distillation of the studio audience's reaction to Rupert's emergence as the new king of comedy. Action and reaction reflect alike the guilty pleasure(s) of blind celebrity worship that *The King of Comedy* repeatedly invokes. Because Rita is not a fanatic on the order of a Rupert or a Masha, her seduction by the trappings of fame is even more revealing than theirs. When she is obviously wowed by his television image despite her knowledge of the real Rupert, it becomes clear, as the final sequence implies, that celebrity worship is not confined to the crazies.

The King of Comedy opened the 1983 Cannes Film Festival and was chosen by the British Critics Circle as the best film of the year, but bombed in the U.S. A persistently underrated movie despite a respectable critical reception in 1983 and largely favorable reappraisals thereafter, it is probably the Scorsese feature film that is most difficult to find on video. "I think maybe the reason *The King of Comedy* wasn't well received," says De Niro, "was that it gave off an aura of something that people didn't want to look at or know."[21] What they did not want to confront is the Rupert Pupkin in themselves. Although society at large comes off little better in *Taxi Driver* or *Raging Bull,* its darkest attributes are mostly contained within the recognizably aberrant figures of Travis Bickle and Jake LaMotta. But in *The King of Comedy* Pupkin is an Everyman whose aberrancies are recognizably ours, whose need for us is no greater than our need for him, and whose rage to live publicly answers and fulfills our own.

Staying Alive:
Other People's Projects

artin Scorsese "spoke in the first person as if he were Paul, when he directed me," recalled Griffin Dunne who played word-processor Paul Hackett in *After Hours* (1985). Hackett's story is like an "amusing version of Scorsese's tribulations" in trying to make *The Last Temptation of Christ*, the project that had obsessed him for more than a decade.[1] By 1982, Paul Schrader had distilled Nikos Kazantzakis's 600-page novel into a 90-page script, and in early 1983 Paramount agreed to finance the movie. But with the cast already assembled—Aidan Quinn had crash-dieted to play Christ, and Harvey Keitel had dyed his hair red for Judas—Paramount yanked the rug out from under *The Last Temptation*, aborting the film four days before shooting was scheduled to begin. For Scorsese, "The trick was to survive" the cancellation: "It was devastating. . . . So the trick was to find *something*, anything, to work on."[2] The something that turned up was *Lies*, a script owned by Amy Robinson (Charlie's girlfriend in *Mean Streets*) and Griffin Dunne. Written by Joe Minion for Dusan Makavejev's film class at Columbia University, *Lies* became *A Night in SoHo* and finally *After Hours*. So Scorsese was back doing the sort of low budget (under $4 million) independent film he always did so well but which he had not attempted since *Taxi Driver* a decade earlier. Although the Geffen Company eventually took over the financing, allowing four extra shooting days and escalating the film's final cost to $4.5 million, *After Hours* remained a small-scale, hands-on project that "was like a rebirth" for Scorsese.

Paul Hackett, easily the most "normal" of Scorsese's male protagonists, sets out on a nighttime odyssey of close encounters with abnormal, even paranormal planes of experience. Via a dizzying cab ride that approximates Alice's falling down the rabbit hole into Wonderland or Dorothy's flying through the air to Oz, Paul is deposited downtown. There he encounters the various denizens of the night in a series of bizarre adventures that figure to occur rarely during, but regularly after, hours. Paul, a computer drone who lives uptown and works midtown, ventures downtown in pursuit of Marcy (Rosanna Arquette), another of Scorsese's blond temptresses. Early scenes—at the office gazing wistfully at the family portraits on coworkers' desks and coming home to a mono-chromatically sterile apartment—posit his loneliness and imply his sus-ceptibility to romance. Dining solo in a café and reading Henry Miller's *Tropic of Cancer*, Paul meets Marcy and gets the phone number of her friend Kiki (Linda Fiorentino), a sculptress who specializes in plaster-of-paris bagels-and-cream-cheese paperweights. (What is in store for Paul may be foreshadowed by Kiki's offbeat sculptures—and by the sudden pirouettes of the café cashier, apparently a frustrated dancer.) Later the same evening, Paul calls the number and is invited by Marcy to the SoHo loft she shares with Kiki. Careening downtown in a cab ride sequence right out of a Keystone Kops comedy, Paul loses his last $20 bill out the window and cannot pay the cabbie, who irately pulls away. Like the bagel-and-cream-cheese paperweights and the pirouetting cashier, the frenetic cab ride and the lost $20 are comic previews of coming attractions. A far more ominous harbinger awaits Paul when he arrives at the loft to find only Kiki at home. She flings the keys which, filmed from Paul's point of view, barrel down on him like a missile. For Scorsese, the key drop was a "crucial" representation of the ominousness of the movie. For Paul, it is the first of many disturbing episodes involv-ing keys, his own as well as those of others.

Kiki's keys promise access (in) to a realm of experience as alluring to Paul as it is foreign. The taxi sets him down in a matrix of rain-slicked and dimly lighted streets evocative of film noir. As seen through Paul's eyes, SoHo by night resembles the Manhattan nightscape as seen by Travis Bickle in *Taxi Driver*. What is actually or potentially dangerous in *Taxi Driver*, however, becomes mainly symptomatic of Paul's paranoia and anxiety in *After Hours*. It is not that his trepidation is unwarranted, only that it is exaggerated. Exacerbating his natural anxiety is fear of the unknown—he is an alien in SoHo, a tourist from a very different Manhattan. For Scorsese, the challenge was to find a style that reflected Paul's psychology:

I thought it would be a parody of *film noir* and also a parody of a thriller. The angles themselves are parodies—the angles, the cuts, and the Fritz Lang-type shots, the Hitchcock parodies. . . . There was constant cutting to extreme close-ups for no reason, just to build up paranoia and anxiety—total anxiety. . . . There was also Michael Ballhaus's lighting, which was a takeoff on German Expressionism—the shadow of the walls in the staircase, a shadow against the wall. But nothing of *film noir* or psychological horror really occurs. It is all in his [Paul's] head.[3]

Granted Paul's "total anxiety," the menace of the mise-en-scène may not be entirely in his fevered imagination. Moments of genuine "psychological horror" occur in *After Hours* even as they are subsumed in an overall parodic design. Massaging Kiki at her request, Paul praises her "great body." "Yes," she agrees, "Not a lotta' scars." An apparently innocuous non sequitur, Kiki's reply triggers Paul's harrowing story about a childhood experience in the hospital where he went for a tonsillectomy. Afterward, pediatrics was full, so he was sent to the burns ward. There he was given a blindfold by a nurse who warned him that if he removed it he would have to go through the operation again. Before he can tell Kiki what he saw when he *did* take the blindfold off, she falls asleep. Marcy then returns and, leading Paul into her room, excuses herself to take a shower. Anticipating delights to come, he spies a tube of ointment for second degree burns, and his ardor cools visibly despite Marcy's assurance that it is really skin moisturizer. Later, back in her room after they go out for coffee, he discovers a thick book called *Reconstruction and Rehabilitation of the Burned Patient.* No doubt associating the book with what looked to be burn scars on Marcy's thigh and with what he saw in the burns ward as a child, Paul flinches from the hideously graphic photographs of burn victims.

Of course it is conceivable that Paul hallucinates the book just (as it turns out later) as he has hallucinated Marcy's scars. *After Hours* is another of those Scorsese movies that, like *Taxi Driver* and *The King of Comedy*, blurs the boundary between illusion and reality. And because the action of all three films is seen chiefly through the eyes of their disturbed heroes, it is easy to read illusion into nearly anything. In any event there is no reason to dismiss either the implicit horrors of what Paul saw in the burns ward or the explicit horror of what he sees in Marcy's book. That Scorsese elects to invoke the trauma of his own childhood tonsillectomy in Paul's story testifies to its importance as "the source of the symbolic wound in his films," according to Les Keyser who attaches cosmic significance to the lie about "going to a wonderful circus" that Catherine Scorsese told young Martin to prepare her son for surgery: "Even after decades of therapy, Scorsese cannot forgive her; her deceit marked his first encounter with human duplicity and feminine wiles, and provided him a terrifying glimpse into the heart of darkness."[4] Actually Scorsese soft pedals the burn imagery he found in Minion's script where matches, candles, ointments, scars, and the graphic medical textbook all but define Marcy. Quite enough burn imagery remains in *After Hours*, however, to account for Paul's frantic stripping of Marcy's body after her suicide in search of nonexistent scars. And it is her suicide, for which he feels partly responsible—he had fled the apartment shortly after discovering the book—that feeds his paranoia, that subverts his subsequent confrontations with women, and that tinges *After Hours* with a horror that is more than a figment of Paul's overwrought imagination.

Even before she kills herself Marcy has become an icon of suffering. Although her seriocomic account of being raped (*Who's That Knocking?* revisited) for six hours turns out to be more farcical than traumatic— "Actually it was a boyfriend of mine. . . . I slept through most of it."—the story, like the burn imagery, identifies her body as a site of violation. Another violation of sorts is the subject of a second Marcy story, this one about Franklin, her movie-freak husband, who "screamed SURRENDER, DOROTHY every time he came." Confided to Paul over coffee in a diner whose proprietor explains that "different rules apply this late, it is after hours," Marcy's bit about Franklin, like the one about rape, invokes a sexual climate that both excites and repels Paul. He is hot to exploit Marcy's sexual possibilities, to add to the sum of her violations. But nothing pans out: back at the apartment she accepts his kiss passively and breaks into tears. Thus cooled, what remains of his ardor is dispelled by the pictures of burn victims and translated into panicked flight. Henceforth, Paul's SoHo odyssey follows the turn-on, turn-off pattern established with Marcy. A succession of apparently receptive women will incarnate the sexual promise that Marcy exuded and that lured him downtown. But in the wake of her suicide, Paul's odyssey turns from a casual quest for sexual satisfaction into a desperate desire simply to return home. Unfortunately for Paul, the suffering associated with Marcy and culminating in her suicide fastens after her death on him. So completely does the would-be "violator" turn into the may-be violated that he finally laments, "All I wanted to do was go out with a girl and have a nice time. Do I have to die for it?" As it happens, he does not.

Although Minion's script highlights the guilt—"Maybe I deserve to die"—that Paul's question merely implies, *After Hours* ultimately parodies not punishes the sexual adventurer.

SURRENDER, DOROTHY, the orgasmic cry of Marcy's sometime husband, prefigures Paul's change from hunter to hunted and his consequent obsession with going home. By invoking *The Wizard of Oz,* that quintessentially American statement that there is no place like home, the cry may echo Paul's subconscious wish to return uptown even before downtown became threatening. The glitter of Oz and the drabness of Kansas (nicely captured in the contrast between a Technicolor Oz and a black and white Kansas in the Judy Garland movie) notwithstanding, Dorothy can only repeat, "I want to go home." Paul's overt desire to go home begins with his flight from Marcy and the burn imagery he associates with her. "And did you know that Margaret Hamilton's hand was badly burned during the filming of the scene in which the Witch writes SURRENDER, DOROTHY in the sky above the Emerald City, and that her stunt double, Betty Danko, was even more badly burned during the reshoot of the scene?"[5] SURRENDER, DOROTHY, then, evokes not Paul's soon-to-be yearning for home but its proximate cause. This conflation of cause and effect in *After Hours* reverses the homeward bound scenario of *The Wizard of Oz.* "There is no place like home," Dorothy's famously banal mantra delivered when she is safely back in Kansas, is credible only in the narrowest sense. Once her initial fear of the unknown dissolves, Oz poses little threat to Dorothy; it is a pleasant enough place, surely more so than Kansas. Moreover, she can leave Oz anytime she likes: the ruby slippers she wears are a magic carpet to anywhere. Finally, the homeward thrust of *The Wizard of Oz* reflects little more than the narrative predisposition of similar works that evoke the contradictory yet complementary worlds of illusion and reality. In *A Midsummer Night's Dream,* for example, the real world of Athens is not superior to the unreal world of the enchanted forest, only different. The return to Athens is simply an admission that people must live in the real world albeit with the consciousness-raising experience of the enchanted world intact. But the SoHo Paul Hackett stumbles into is neither as benign nor as easy to escape as the land of Oz or the Shakespearian forest.

Actually, *After Hours* resembles *Alice in Wonderland* more than *The Wizard of Oz*. What you see is generally what you get in Oz whereas in SoHo and Wonderland appearances deceive, and Paul and Alice fall into notoriously unstable worlds of fluid identities and arbitrary events.

Marcy's actions are as weird as the Mad Hatter's or the March Hare's and no more predictable. "I feel like something incredible is really going to happen here," she promises Paul from the door of her bedroom. I feel so excited! I don't know why, I feel it." Why she then kills herself instead of making love is no more explicable than why she was excited or why she invited Paul downtown in the first place. Where *The Wizard of Oz* flattens out the distance between home and away, *Alice in Wonderland* and *After Hours* flaunt it. Paul's two scenes at the punk Club Berlin—a sendup of Expressionist "decadence"—are forays into a surreal netherworld light years removed from the "real" world he left behind. The first time he shows up at the club it is "Mohawk day" and, lacking a Mohawk cut, he is refused admittance by a baleful giant of a bouncer. When he finally gets in, Paul is grabbed by several punks who chop away at his hair before he escapes screaming into the night. That it just happens to be "Mohawk day"; that the club's male habitués recall Travis Bickle; and that Scorsese himself, mounted on a platform like God on high, "directs" his floodlight over the crowd objectify Paul's anxiety and paranoia. It is as though the Club Berlin had been constructed solely to confound and persecute him. Later, chased by a rabid vigilante mob, he hides in the now mysteriously abandoned club. As slippery a venue as any in *Alice in Wonderland*, the Club Berlin similarly resists definition: gone are the frenzied punks, the earsplitting music and the roving spotlight, replaced by an idle bartender and a lone woman seated at a table. The woman, June (Verna Bloom), turns out to be another sculptress—repetition is the rule rather than the exception in the maze-like mise-en-scène of *After Hours*— and Paul's unlikely savior. June turns him into a papier-mâché sculpture like the contorted imitation Munch (*The Scream*) Kiki was assembling. Thus encased—even his mouth is sealed, the scream of terror aborted— Paul is rendered as helplessly immobile as Jerry Langford in *The King of Comedy*. Like Alice, who grows till she shoots through the roof then shrinks till she floats in her tears, Paul cannot even control his body much less his environment. Alice is inexplicably and arbitrarily threatened by nearly everyone and everything she confronts: snubbed at the tea party, accused at the trial, insulted at the croquet game. Paul, too, is bedeviled by people and places that seem benign but turn hostile. And beginning with Marcy and ending with June, his most dangerous liaisons are with women. Odysseuslike, Paul encounters a series of women as deceptively fatal as any Circe or Calypso. And like Odysseus, he is the hero of a circular narrative that begins and ends at home. Between home and home lie a series of encounters chiefly with women that range from the merely perplexing to the actively perilous. Such adventure stories tend to be more episodic than organic: scrambling the episodes need not subvert the entire narrative. Still, episodes are conventionally arranged in ascending order of "difficulty." Caught up in a series of unfamiliar even unreal situations, the hero must prove himself by "passing" progressively more arduous "tests." Success depends upon adaptability, which in turn depends upon personal development. Alice, for example, enters Wonderland passive but emerges assertive: she has learned to take arbitrariness in her stride. The rap against Paul is that he is a self-absorbed representative of 1980s yuppie culture who goes home no wiser than when he left. Yet Timothy Corrigan argues that Paul's "adventures in SoHo teach him that. . . . survival in contemporary life means having a performative relationship with the contingencies that overtake any sense of control." Paul learns, in other words, how to handle himself in SoHo much as Alice learns how to handle herself in Wonderland. Further, Corrigan implies that SoHo demands of Paul the same responsive fluidity achieved by Alice. "As long as he maintains the traditional centrality and reality of a simple point of view in a contemporary city, as long as he inhabits the city as a reflection of himself, the relay of events and images necessarily support both persecution and paranoia," and he becomes a victim of the kaleidoscopically shifting milieu he is trapped in. "His escape occurs only when he learns to perform himself as a changing identity and figure in the images, scenes, and art objects that appear randomly to invade his life with a life of their own."[6] Corrigan's claim that Paul learns to "perform its [SoHo's] images in order to survive them" would be more convincing if some shock of (self-)recognition demonstrably occurred. Paul "finds his way out of SoHo by recreating himself," concludes Corrigan, finessing the fact that it is June who recreates him. In the end, Paul seems more lucky than enlightened, a Keystone Kops character spewed out of SoHo by the same capricious fate that swept him up.

Time and again, Paul is victimized by women who are initially sympathetic but eventually threatening. After his contretemps with Marcy he wants only to go home. That escaping is not as easy as entering SoHo becomes quickly apparent when Paul tries to catch an uptown train only to discover that his last 97 cents will not cover the newly raised fare. By now desperate to get home, he wanders into a bar where the kindly bartender, Tom (John Heard), offers to lend him the fare. But the key to the cash register is in Tom's apartment, so he gives his keys to Paul and holds Paul's for security. Connoisseurs of (slapstick) comedy who have already sensed an omen in Kiki's hurtling keys intuit misadventure in the latest key business. Leaving Tom's apartment, Paul is chased by irate tenants who take him for the thief who has been working the neighborhood. Henceforth the chase motif takes over, and the imperatives of going home and dodging the mob converge. Paul makes it back to the bar, but (naturally) it is closed and he cannot retrieve his keys. Enter Julie (Terri Garr)—another version of the femme fatale embodied earlier by Marcy and Kiki—the waitress he met at the bar, who invites him to her place. Now it becomes clear that Paul is trapped in a pattern of ominous recurrence forecast by Kiki's keys and climaxed by June's sculpture. Mousetraps ring Julie's bed; the telephone number she gives him lacks a digit; she breaks into sudden hysterics; and she displays one of Kiki's bagel-and-cream cheese sculptures—all identify her with the absurd world into which Paul has fallen and which threatens to engulf him. Wracked by repetition—the bar alternately opens and closes; the pursuing mob alternately picks up and loses his trail—Paul grows more and more desperate but less and less able to find his way home.

After escaping Mohawk day at the Club Berlin, he races back to Kiki's, snatches his lost $20 bill from the faux-Munch sculpture's sticky surface, and rushes out to the street where salvation beckons in the form of a taxi. But the deus ex machina that promises to end the harrowing cycle of repetition teasingly prolongs it instead: the cabbie is the same wild driver who sped Paul downtown and who now plucks the $20 bill from his hand and speeds off. Again broke and dependent on the kindness of strangers, Paul is once more invited home by a woman. She is Gail, the Mr. Softee vendor (Catherine O'Hara), who has inadvertently cut Paul's arm—he is already bleeding from the manhandling at the Club Berlin—by opening the door on him as she exits and he tries to enter the cab. As she bandages his arm she reads on a scrap of papier-mâché newsprint clinging to his skin about an anonymous man torn apart by an irate mob. Terrified by its ominous reminders of his possible fate, Paul screams, "Stop touching me!" when Gail unsuccessfully tries to tear the paper off, and screams still more hysterically when she suggests burning it off: "Lady no lady no lady no!" As usual, the various (women's) houses that promise sanctuary prove as perilous as the street where, in headlong flight from Gail and her evil omens, Paul keeps on running as the mob closes in. Briefly eluding his pursuers, he drops to his knees in the street, peers up into the night sky and beseeches God, "What do you want from me? What have I done? I'm just a word-processor, for Christ's sake!" Paul's is the cry of the putative paranoid who thinks God has it in for him; yet it is also the plea of the relative innocent who seems more sinned against than sinner.

Running for his life, Paul glimpses a woman shooting a man behind a lighted window—a corroboration of his worst fear in its apparent linkage of sex and death. Again, he runs into a potential savior—a shy young man who mistakes Paul for a fellow homosexual and invites him home. There Paul calls the police who hang up on him when he says his life is in danger. "They're all trying to kill me," he tells the young man who has by now been turned off by Paul's nearly incoherent Walpurgisnacht story. "Why don't you just go home?" the young man replies when Paul asks to sleep on the couch. Thus ironically thrust back on the streets, Paul sees his image everywhere in "Wanted" posters Julie had photocopied from the sketch she made of him. A perfect symbol of the repetition that haunts Paul and organizes *After Hours*, Julie's infinitely reproducible sketch/poster also suggests the perfidy of women—which Gail's appearance at the head of the vigilante mob immediately ratifies. Without denying the free-floating anxiety that besets Paul, it is arguable that his fears are not always delusions of persecution (i.c., paranoia). Julie and Gail, for example, are very real persecutors whose unrelenting vendettas against him are hardly imaginary. That Paul's encounters with women reflect the sexual anxiety at the heart of *After Hours* conforms to Scorsese's maxim that "every amorous relationship is a dangerous one." Michael Henry calls the film "a vaudeville of the unconscious which associates the female sex with burning (Marcy), with trapping (Julie), with the terror of lynching, and finally with complete petrification (June)." Obstacles arise whenever Paul approaches a woman. "What amused me," explained Scorsese, "was to show how his desire is continually roused then chilled."[7] But, Marcy excepted, what Paul wants from the women he meets is not so much sex as help. Despite Scorsese's fascination with manipulating desire, there is scant evidence that Paul feels anything but panic after leaving Marcy. And even with her he probably feared sex more than he desired it. (A toilet graffito of a shark about to clamp its outsized teeth over an erect penis exemplifies Paul's castration anxiety.) Only reluctantly does he go home with Julie and Gail and then only under duress. Actually Paul's desire does not rise and fall with each woman he meets: it surges with Marcy and then subsides. As the night wears on the object of his desire mutates from sex to home. And the obstacles he encounters stand not in the way of getting laid but in the way of getting home.

Chased by the lynch mob, Paul strays (again) into the Club Berlin where June, the last of the evening's femmes fatales, "awaits" him at a table. An eerie calm envelopes the previously hectic scene, now deserted save for June who, the solitary bartender confides to Paul, is "always here." Oddly—ominously—the scheduled Conceptual Art party seems to have been canceled. Paul puts his last quarter into the juke box and out pours "Is That All There Is?," Peggy Lee's signature song about a building burning and the world going up in flames. The recording, which alternates speech and song in apparently world-weary counterpoint, invokes those elements—fire, loss, repetition—that have figured so prominently in *After Hours*. "I just want to live," Paul tells June as they dance and Peggy Lee sings, "I'm not ready for that final moment." An "older" woman, June embodies not the lover Paul fears but the mother he craves. She leads him downstairs to her studio where she cradles him in her arms and smooths his hair before encasing him in plaster. And while it is as an artist not a mother that June most directly effects Paul's salvation, the sculpture she turns him into is a symbolic expression of maternal solicitude by other means. Only when he recovers his "mother" can Paul regain his home. This condition was implied during one of the chase scenes when Paul ducks into an apartment building to elude the mob. Jabbing desperately at the buzzers, he cries "Hey Mrs. . . , Hey Mrs. . . . I went to school with your son!" And, at last resort: "Hey Mom, it's me!"

By the time the mob bursts into her studio, June has nearly transformed Paul into a papier-mâché sculpture. "Let me out, let me out," he pleads after the mob finally departs, but June stops his mouth with a final strip of paper and leaves him helplessly imprisoned. Silenced and abandoned, Paul's worst fears about women seem to have come horrifically true. Yet June is a principal player in a salvational drama that fixes maturation as the price of going home. It may be that Paul's sexual hangups are reflected in his need for a mother, and only when the apron strings he clings to are severed will he achieve full manhood.

> It might not seem that Paul wants to be silenced, but there is a horrible logic to the denouement whereby June, the most obviously maternal figure, seals his lips by pasting a strip of paper over his mouth, thus completing the process of mummification (and inverting

the trope of taking off the bandages, lifting the blindfold). It is a process that has been underway since Paul went downtown and encountered Kiki, dressed in black leather, working on a sculpture reminiscent of *The Scream*; it is a repetition that is epitomized by the "Hey Mom, it's me!" episode. All the women (and the gay man and the police) turn a deaf ear to Paul's stories, but here the maternal presence is conjured up as supremely absent.[8]

Or, if not by maternal absence, June's actions may be justified by artistic necessity:

> In the final climatic sequence, he gives himself up to another woman artist (reversing the sexual dynamics that began the film) who saves him by making him into a version of the sculpture that he had helped construct at Kiki's. He becomes a piece of energized flotsam, a post-modern work of art to be stolen and circulated indiscriminately (like all the money in the film) merely a material object who has come to recognize that (in the apocalyptic words of the juke box song of this sequence) "That's all there is." Greeted by his computer after his touristic nightmare, Paul knows better then ever the irrelevancy of traditional humanistic authorities and unified social myths.[9]

Whether Paul must learn to do without a mother or without a stable persona or without both is debatable. A larger issue is whether Paul learns anything at all from his season in (feminine) Hell. Minion's original script "had Paul going out to buy an ice cream for June down in the basement, and that was it," recalls Scorsese. "I felt something was missing there and we needed an ending that had magic." Magic aside, the ice cream ending is as inconclusive as it is arbitrary. Minion then came up with the idea of June ballooning in size so that Paul could disappear into her womb: "He just disappears off the bottom of the frame. . . and then you cut to him born naked, curled up on the cobblestones in the middle of 57th Street. The camera is looking down on him; he gets up and then runs like hell home."[10] By combining the return-to-the-womb and rebirth motifs, this version both incorporates and interprets Paul's adventures. And in its surreality and circularity, Minion's alternate ending is faithful to the style and rhythm of the overall design of the film. But David Geffen, whose company wound up financing *After Hours*, disapproved. Scorsese then closed the film with Paul, still encased in plaster, being driven off by the thieves (Cheech and Chong). Of course this was as inconclusive as Minion's original ending and, at Michael Powell's suggestion, Paul falls out of the truck in front of his office at dawn. Apparently Powell felt that his ending invoked the same Kafkaesque (il)logic that drives the entire narrational machinery of *After Hours*, and, though Scorsese claims not to have read Kafka, he finally took Powell's advice. Scorsese's disclaimer notwithstanding, Robert Philip Kolker reads *After Hours* and particularly its ending as a takeoff on Kafka:

> In his subjugation to the illogical, Paul becomes lesser kin to Franz Kafka's Joseph K., and Scorsese sees the relationship not only through Kafka's novel *The Trial,* but through Orson Welles's film of the novel. . . .The gates that close behind Paul as he leaves his office and open again the following morning when, after his terrible night, he is dumped out of the truck, wrapped up like a George Segal sculpture, echo the gates of the Law in Kafka's parable "Before the Law," which appears in the novel and is recited by Welles at the beginning of his film (accompanied by animated images of the gates, the gatekeeper, and the supplicant). . . .The labyrinthine streets of Manhattan's SoHo, the hidden and underground apartments that let out to unexpected places, the women who try to seduce or abduct or hurt Paul, the entire narrational apparatus of a man trapped for reasons unseen and unknown reverberate back to Kafka and Welles.[11]

When Paul is dumped unceremoniously but serendipitously outside his office at dawn, the nightmare is over. Like his heroic forebears (Odysseus, Heracles, Theseus) he has survived the descent into Hell and regained familiar ground. Although the "Good morning, Paul" that flashes on his computer screen could be read as an ironic reminder that he has merely exchanged one form of imprisonment for another, the greeting seems more hopeful than despairing. "I just want to live," Paul told June, and his wish has been granted. Like Scorsese's protagonists from J.R. to Rupert Pupkin, he has received absolution in the form of a second chance. Born again, Paul "has a better sense of life," according to Scorsese. "He has learned something. . . . To a certain extent he is disturbed by the materialism of our society, by its frenzied consumerism, by its neglect of spiritual values."[12] Because *After Hours* "was like a rebirth" for Scorsese, he may be reading his own experience into Paul's. After the box-office failure of *The King of Comedy* and the front-office abortion of *The Last Temptation of Christ,* the Cannes Film Festival's Best Director award advertised that with *After Hours* Scorsese's career was back in high gear.

After Hours not only exorcised Scorsese's personal demons but proved that he could still create film art even within the confines of a skimpy budget and a tight shooting schedule. No sooner was it wrapped up than he elected "to test myself further" by directing "Mirror, Mirror," a twenty-four-minute television episode of Steven Spielberg's *Amazing Stories* series on NBC. Although it was his "first excursion into horror,"

"Mirror, Mirror" traversed familiar Scorsese territory: the pathology of urban paranoia; the shallowness of media-made celebrity culture; the pitfalls of rampant materialism. He then stretched himself still further by playing Goodley, a Manhattan jazz club manager, in Bertrand Tavernier's *Round Midnight* (1986). A frequent bit player in his own movies, Scorsese had not previously tackled so meaty a role. As usual, popular success eluded him: *After Hours* eked out a modest profit, but despite glowing reviews "Mirror, Mirror" was barely noticed, and *Round Midnight* bombed at the box office.

The *Color of Money* (1986), his next feature film, represented "another challenge" for Scorsese. Never before had he made a sequel or worked with two major stars or enjoyed a (relatively) lavish budget. Paul Newman had long wanted to revive the "Fast" Eddie Felson role he had played twenty-five years earlier in Robert Rossen's classic *The Hustler* (1961). A *Raging Bull* fan, Newman may have sensed the affinities between Eddie Felson and Jake LaMotta when he invited Scorsese to direct *The Color of Money*. And Newman may also have sensed that the sequel would give him a shot at the Best Actor Oscar that had eluded him despite his many nominations, including one for *The Hustler*. What *Alice Doesn't Live Here Anymore* did for Ellen Burstyn, he intuited—correctly as it turned out—*The Color of Money* could do for him. Given Newman's status and Tom Cruise's presence, studio heads figured to be lining up to back the movie. Yet Twentieth Century–Fox and Columbia rejected it before Touchstone Pictures, the "adult" division of Disney Productions, approved it on the condition that Newman and Scorsese put up one-third of their salaries in case the film ran over budget. By this time, Scorsese's financing hassles were par for the course. Still, they reveal sad truths about Hollywood in the 1980s. Clearly, the 1970s era of challenging personal filmmaking by a bevy of talented young directors was passé. So prevailing was the current bottom-line mentality that even a project that featured a top-flight director (Scorsese), a legendary actor (Newman), and a popular heart throb (Cruise) proved hostage to the momentary whims of studio executives. When *The Color of Money* came in at $13 million—well below its $14.5 million budget—it was "the stuff sainthood is made of in Hollywood," Scorsese quipped.

OK'd at last by the money men, *The Color of Money* still lacked a working script. Walter Tevis, who wrote both Eddie Felson novels, made a love story of the sequel. But after reading *The Color of Money*, Scorsese felt that it would not make his kind of movie. Junking everything in the novel except its title, he brought in novelist–screenwriter Richard Price whose view of the material matched his own. Together they turned Tevis's bittersweet love story into a redemptive odyssey in the manner of *Raging Bull.* According to Scorsese, *The Color of Money* is about a man's struggle toward self-knowledge: "The film concerns a being who changes his lifestyle, who alters his values. His arena is a billiard room, but what it is does not matter. The film concerns delusion then charity, perversion then purity."[13] As the smoke from a burning cigarette wafts above the opening titles Scorsese's voice-over asserts that "luck plays a part in nine-ball, but for some players luck itself is an art." Top players make their own luck, but Eddie Felson's ran out twenty-five years ago when, at the peak of his game, he quit shooting big-time pool. *The Hustler* ends with Eddie beating Minnesota Fats (Jackie Gleason), the legendary king of the pool sharks, but losing his soul in the process. Like Faust, Eddie made a pact with Mephistopheles—the slimy Bert Gordon (George C. Scott)—who backs him in exchange for 75 percent of his winnings. And like Othello, who chooses evil (Iago) over good (Desdemona), Eddie listens to Bert and destroys Sarah (Piper Laurie), the woman he loves. "You've gotta' be hard, Eddie," advises Bert. So, Othellolike, Eddie makes his (evil) choice, and Sarah winds up committing suicide. Subsequently Eddie becomes unbeatable, as impervious to his rivals as was Faust during the period of his infernal contract. "How can I lose?" he asks sardonically, making another impossible shot against Minnesota Fats. But Eddie knows that the price of winning at pool is losing at life: "I loved her, Bert. I traded her in on a pool game." Too late, Eddie wises up to his Iago: "You're a loser, Bert, 'cause you're dead inside."

Twenty-five years later traces of Bert appear in Eddie. Although he is neither as reptilian nor as Machiavellian as his former mentor, Eddie likewise becomes an exploiter of young talent. Now a prosperous liquor salesman, he offers to stake talented but flaky Vincent Lauria (Tom Cruise) to six weeks on the road for 60 percent of the take. Vincent can even take along his sultry girlfriend Carmen (Mary Elizabeth Mastrantonio) just as Eddie once took Sarah along on a similar odyssey. *The Hustler* and *The Color of Money* are morality plays that employ the novice, the tempter, the girlfriend, the past, and the journey as counters in the battle of good versus evil. But *The Hustler* is by far the darker movie: Bert is consummately evil; Sarah is crippled, alcoholic, suicidal; and Eddie is unredeemed. Scorsese's initial inclination to shoot *The Color of Money* in the same black and white as *The Hustler* seemed tacitly to acknowledge the bond between the two films. Yet when the studio begged him not to do it, Scorsese relented, later claiming that he "didn't want to make any allusions to *The Hustler*." How a second Eddie Felson movie could help alluding to the first is a mystery. What Scorsese probably meant was that his typical theme—redemption through suffering—and his untypical ending—upbeat, even exultant—distanced *The Color of Money* from *The Hustler*.

To a degree, Eddie has survived by becoming what he hated in Bert; so just as Bert corrupted the young Eddie, Eddie sets out to corrupt young Vincent. What happens in *The Color of Money*, however, is a role exchange: by the time they arrive—separately, because Eddie has grown disillusioned with his role and has left Vincent and Carmen enough money to complete their odyssey without him—in Atlantic City, Vincent has become an accomplished hustler and Eddie has fallen (back) in love with the game. For Vincent, in other words, green is no longer primarily the color of the pool table but the color of money. "It's tough to lay down," he replied when Eddie invoked the modus operandi of the successful hustler: lose a little at first to win a lot later. In Atlantic City, however, Vincent proves so keen a pupil that he throws his tournament match against the unsuspecting Eddie in order to set up lucrative side games in the aptly named green room. Now it is Eddie—whose time away from Vincent and Carmen was spent practicing endlessly to regain his touch—who incarnates the purity Vincent has lost. No longer a stake horse feeding vicariously off the protegé who reminds him of his younger self—he gave Vincent his treasured cue stick when they first teamed up—Eddie is (again) a player. Refusing a share of Vincent's winnings and forfeiting the tournament match he had not earned, Eddie reverses the maxim he recited to Vincent when they set out on the road: "You remind me that money won is twice as sweet as money earned."

At the precise moment when Vincent informs the nonplussed Eddie that he had dumped their tournament match and hands his erstwhile patron an envelope containing $8,000, the child has become father to the man. An epiphany for Eddie, it is the moment when he realizes how well he has taught Vincent the (by)ways of corruption. Scorsese prefigures Vincent's fall from innocence when Eddie visits Child World (!), where Vincent earns his living as a toy salesman, to tempt him to quit his job and go on the road. Similarly, Eddie's fall *into* innocence is signaled by the sharper (in)sight he gains after being fitted with new glasses when he stayed behind to practice. Eddie's complicity in Vincent's fall is magnified by the father son relationship that develops between them on the road. The unholy alliance of Bert and Eddie in *The Hustler* was all business. Bert was a sleazy cynic motivated solely by personal profit and Eddie a small-time hustler eager to crack the big–time. But in *The Color of Money*, Eddie is more the nostalgic sentimentalist than the cynical profiteer: "Twenty-five years ago it was over for me before it got started," he confides to Vincent. Now the surrogate son will take up the aborted career—and the treasured cue stick—of the symbolic father. Because Vincent is far more innocent initially than Eddie ever was in *The Hustler*, his (Vincent's) fall is more precipitous. Armored neither with the young Eddie's experience nor with his guardian angel—Sarah defied the tempter, Carmen abets him—Vincent seems particularly vulnerable. Yet vulnerability may be the source of Eddie's actual, and Vincent's potential, redemption. Maybe it is Eddie's awareness of Vincent's vulnerability and of its exacerbation by their filial relationship that triggers his own rebirth. The same awareness may account for Eddie's urge to play Vincent in the green room. "I want your best game," Eddie demands, trying to get Vincent to play it straight, trying, in short, to restore Vincent to the way he was. "Hey, I'm back," exults Eddie as play commences, and the camera freezes the moment. With luck, so is Vincent.

Although *The Color of Money* is often cited as one of the most conventional and commercial and least personal and expressive of Scorsese's films—Robert Philip Kolker dismisses it as "another representative of the Hollywood anonymous style"—it contains signature items aplenty. Like *Mean Streets*, for example, *The Color of Money* casts its narrative of redemption in religious terms: Eddie's reflection in the black eight ball; the cue stick Vincent shoulders like a cross; the infernal scarlet of the titles, of the interior of Eddie's Cadillac, of the carpet in the Atlantic City billiard room; the "Society of St. Vincent de Paul" sign on the warehouse that once was a pool hall; and—most egregiously—the overhead shot of the tournament room as cathedral to the accompaniment of organ music. As in *Raging Bull*, the battle for redemption is waged in a sporting arena. And Eddie's words to Vincent—"Sometimes if you lose you win"—nearly echo Joey LaMotta's to his brother Jake. (The real Jake LaMotta, incidentally, had played a bartender in *The Hustler*). Finally, what began as a star vehicle for Paul Newman became a typical Scorsese morality play as well. In *The Color of Money* Eddie enacts the familiar gospel according to Scorsese: "he has to come to terms with himself, as a man—does he remain dead, or does he come alive again? To come alive again, he has got to face himself. He does not have to win, but he has got to play. He has got to put his balls on the line—literally."[14]

Eddie's "I'm back" is Scorsese's most flagrant concession to the Hollywood convention of the happy ending. Whether it is the logical culmination of Eddie's passage from sinner to saint or simply a shrewd commercial decision, the ending found favor with a mass audience conditioned by the heroics of a Rocky or an Indiana Jones. And to the Hollywood moguls, the popular success of *The Color of Money* meant that Scorsese could be trusted with big budget and big star pictures designed for mainstream audiences. Again in demand, he was recruited by Michael Jackson to direct "Bad," a sixteen-minute music video, and, after (finally) making *The Last Temptation of Christ*, by Woody Allen, to collaborate on an anthology film, *New York Stories*. On both projects, Scorsese renewed the partnership with scriptwriter Richard Price that had clicked so well on *The Color of Money*. For Jackson, who wanted to film "Bad" in black and white and had admired *Raging Bull*, Scorsese seemed the natural choice. For Scorsese, "Bad," which aired in August 1987 on CBS, meant media exposure and easy money. Set to a pulsating rock beat, the video tells a rags-to-riches story of Darryl (Michael Jackson), a multitalented black boy who returns to Harlem and acts "bad" with his old buddies. Dancing through the ghetto as if it were a mere ballroom, he makes living there look easy in a happy ending that is even more predictable than Eddie Felson's.

"Life Lessons," Scorsese's forty-four-minute contribution to *New York Stories*, resurrected a project that had fascinated him from the time he had first read Dostoyevsky's *The Gambler* in 1968. In 1973 Paul Schrader wrote a synopsis for a screenplay, but it came to nothing. Then Jay Cocks, a long-time friend and movie critic who would later coscript *The Age of Innocence*, gave Scorsese a 1973 Christmas present of a new translation of *The Gambler* along with the *Diaries of Paulina*, Dostoyevsky's mistress. Cocks's gift, particularly in its fleshing out of the Dostoyevsky–Paulina relationship, kept the project evergreen in the back of Scorsese's mind. How a famous writer debased himself for a shallow woman less than half his age intrigued Scorsese who over the years found elements of their relationship seeping "into my movies. In *Raging Bull*. A little bit in *Taxi*. . . . And in *New York, New York*, a lot of it! The difficulty in being with each other, the difficulty of loving."[15] Because "Life Lessons" had to be a New York story, and New York is the center of the art world, and writing is not visually exciting, Price and Scorsese made their protagonist a painter. Lionel Dobie (Nick Nolte)—fiftyish and famous, heedlessly splattering paint on his Armani tuxedo and $5,000 Rolex watch—transmutes sexual tension into powerful art. Typically, he feeds off the pain (self-)created from his relationships with the succession of nubile twenty-something women who serve as his "assistants" in exchange for painting—and life—lessons. To paint, Dobie must work himself into an emotional lather by turning up the music, by shooting baskets, and by insuring the presence of his latest assistant, Paulette (Rosanna Arquette). At the beginning of "Life Lessons" Paulette is away, and Dobie cannot paint even though he has got a major show opening in a few weeks. No sooner does she return, albeit on the condition that she will no longer sleep with him, than he is able to paint again. Fetishizing her braceleted ankle, gazing up at the lighted window behind which she is entertaining her latest one-night stand, enduring her ridicule and contempt, and swallowing his humiliations, Dobie paints furiously, filling canvas after huge canvas with the fruit of his obsession.

Despite the emotional fireworks of the Dobie–Paulette relationship, "Life Lessons" is concerned more with the nature of the creative process than with the effect of obsessive love. Because Dobie is ultimately a slave to his painting rather than to any woman, Paulette is there primarily to feed his art. By the time she finally walks out for good, he has finished the paintings for his latest show, which, as usual, will be hugely successful. At the show, lionized by worshipful admirers, he spots the next muse for his next show. Already he is fetishizing his latest find, zeroing in on her ear as he had on Paulette's ankle. Like Paulette, who once said "I feel like a human sacrifice," the new assistant must inevitably immolate her own painterly aspirations on the altar of Dobie's art. And about art—his own as well as others'—Dobie is uncompromising. When Paulette asks him if she is any good—with the unspoken promise of staying if he replies yes—he cannot lie. Art is his only morality, his consolation and his redemption. In anatomizing Lionel Dobie, "Life Lessons" also "says a lot about Marty and Marty's priorities, and about his ability to deal with, focus, and transcend his obsessions," according to Jay Cocks.

> It's quite moving. He [Scorsese] has to forgive the obsessed artist; if he didn't he'd be hanging himself in effigy. The movie is Marty's act of self-justification. It's very honest. Artists use people up in a way. He's got a nice little irony working here. Dobie uses this woman up, but for what seems to him a good reason. But he can't lie to her. His moral life is in his art. I think "Life Lessons" is a metaphor for the creative process.[16]

Beat the Devil:
Man and Superman

The artist's agony and ecstasy of creation in "Life Lessons" reflect what Scorsese went through to make *The Last Temptation of Christ (1988)*. Barbara Hershey gave him the 1955 Nikos Kazantzakis novel on which the film is based during the shooting of *Boxcar Bertha* in 1972, but it was not until he finally read most of it in 1978 that Scorsese "realized that this was for me."[1] By the fall of 1981 Paul Schrader had written a script and Scorsese had come to regard *The Last Temptation of Christ* as the one movie he had to make. After spending most of 1983 trying to get it into production only to have Paramount cancel it at the eleventh hour, he was distraught: "I'm not going to give up until I make the film," he told Barbara Hershey. Assuring him of her own commitment, Hershey said, "I was put on earth to play this (Mary Magdalene) part." To which Scorsese replied, "That's how I feel about directing it." Finally, in 1987, Universal gave him the green light and a paltry (just over $6 million) budget to shoot *The Last Temptation*, and Scorsese set to work with crusading zeal: "Our blood went into it," says Hershey.[2]

Schrader recognized *The Last Temptation of Christ* as the apotheosis of the redemptive theme that he and Scorsese had treated in *Taxi Driver* and *Raging Bull*. All three films are "of the same cloth: they're about lonely, self-deluded, sexually inactive people."[3] Schrader's startling identification of Christ with the likes of Travis Bickle and Jake LaMotta saturates the screenplay he crafted from the Kazantzakis novel. When asked in an April 1991 *Playboy* interview why the novel was so appealing to him that he never gave up trying to film it, Scorsese likewise emphasized its inclusivity: "Because it's about humanity. It deals with everybody's struggle." It was this apparent "reduction" of Christ to Everyman that

brought the wrath of religious fundamentalists down on Scorsese's head,
forcing the cancellation of the film in 1983 and sparking demonstrations
against it even before it was released in 1988. Following Kazantzakis,
Schrader's script—much rewritten by Jay Cocks and Scorsese, but intact
in its essentials—stresses Christ's humanity without diluting his divinity.
The last temptation—to live and die as an ordinary man—is the hardest
to overcome precisely because it appeals to human instinct. It is the
"metaphorical leap into this imagined temptation" that accounts for the
"greatness of the book," according to Schrader: "The great hook of *The
Last Temptation* is the idea of the reluctant God, the person whom God is
imposing himself on—that's pure Kazantzakis."[4] Not that the concept of
the reluctant God is foreign to divinity: the odd Olympian, bored with
changeless perfection and sated on nectar and ambrosia, occasionally
yearned to be human and more than occasionally cohabited with mere
mortals. But Schrader and Scorsese via Kazantzakis locate that yearning
more in fear than in desire. The film opens with Jesus (Willem Dafoe)
writhing on the ground in pain, beset by voices he cannot still calling
him to a vocation he does not want. He is the carpenter who makes the
crosses on which Romans crucify recalcitrant Jews. "You're a Jew killing
Jews," Judas spits out contemptuously. "I struggle, you collaborate," he
adds, pummeling the passive carpenter. Jesus makes crosses so that
"God will hate me" and silence the tormenting voices. But the voices
persist as do the unseen presences—"Who's following me?"—that stalk
him. To Schrader, *The Last Temptation of Christ* is centrally about this tortuous relationship between a reluctant man and a persistent God: "a psychological film about the inner torments of the spiritual life; it's not
trying to create a holy feeling. That's what the book is like, that's what
Marty wanted and that's the script I wrote. It's a tortured human struggle
about a common man possessed by God and fighting it. God is a demon
in that way."[5]

As if its stress on Christ's humanity was not enough to rile the reli-
gious crazies of America, *The Last Temptation* zeroes in on his sexuality.
Schrader's bit about "lonely, self-deluded, and sexually inactive" protagonists implies that the first two conditions result from the third. Citing
Jake LaMotta's prefight sexual abstinence, Schrader aligns it with the
pent-up celibacy of his other characters: "Yes, that's the Deadly Sperm
Backup. Marty and I call it the DSB; . . . the idea comes up again in *The
Last Temptation*, where Jesus comes outside and one of the characters
says, 'That's what happens when you don't sleep with women—your

sperm goes up to your brain and makes you crazy.' "[6] It is when Jesus tries to persuade the Nazarenes to follow him to Jerusalem that his taunter accuses him of DSB-induced self-delusion. Yet the skeptical Nazarene has got it only half-right: Jesus may suffer from DSB, but his claim to divinity is true nonetheless, as Scorsese makes clear:

> He's God. He's not deluded. I think Kazantzakis thought that, I think the movie says that, and I know I believe that. The beauty of Kazantzakis' concept is that Jesus has to put up with everything we go through, all the doubts and fears and angers. He makes me *feel* like he's sinning—but he's not sinning, he's just human. As well as divine. And he has to deal with all this double, triple guilt on the cross. That's the way I directed it, and that's what I wanted, because my own religious feelings are the same.[7]

The issue of Christ's sexuality is raised initially in the early scene at Mary Magdalene's brothel. Sitting in her outer room among the waiting clients, he watches Magdalene make love to one man after another. Displayed rather than concealed behind the diaphanous curtain that "veils" her serial couplings from the waiting onlookers, she incarnates sexual temptation par excellence. Testifying to Magdalene's allure is the endless stream of men seeking her favors: as Jesus waits patiently, declining his own turn, men of all colors bed her until the light changes, day becomes night, and only Jesus remains. Scorsese's provocative mise-en-scène dramatizes Barbara Hershey's view of the character she plays: "Magdalene was supposed to be fantastic, to warrant the fact that men would come from throughout the world to see her." The more "fantastic" Magdalene, the greater Christ's temptation. For Scorsese,

> The point of the scene was to show the proximity of sexuality to Jesus, the occasion of sin. Jesus must have seen a naked woman— must have. So why couldn't we show that? And I wanted to show the barbarism of the time, the degradation to Mary. It's better that the door is open. Better there is no door. The scene isn't done for tit-illation; it's to show the pain on her face, the compassion Jesus has for her as he fights his sexual desire for her. He's always wanted her.[8]

Hershey likewise stresses the "tone of pain"—Magdalene's as well as Christ's—in the scene. Coupling with her clients, she expresses more real pain than fake pleasure. "Watching her pain has got to kill him because he feels responsible for her being there," claims Hershey, compounding Christ's pity with a measure of guilt. As if Magdalene's naked, painted body and steamy couplings and Christ's conflicted feel-ings were not enough to highlight the brothel scene, Scorsese's camera work privileges it still further. When Magdalene and Jesus are alone at last and she looks up and sees him there, "Marty shot that in subliminally slow motion," says Hershey. In that moment, "There's that subliminal stretching of time, the kind you have in an emergency."[9] The concept of a Christ riven by sexual desire underlies the entire setup of the brothel scene. Scorsese's Christ must *see* Magdalene in (sexual) action; Kazantzakis's Christ remains outside in her courtyard sitting in front of her closed door.

As emotionally charged and elegantly composed as any sequence in *The Last Temptation*, the brothel scene reflects Schrader's and Scorsese's emphasis on the inner torments of the spiritual life. Because their Christ is tempted chiefly by sex—rather than by, say, the theologically more credible despair—the attraction between Christ and Mary Magdalene as first established in the brothel scene is all-important. Accordingly, Scorsese uses Magdalene's voice for the snake which "represents sexuality in all its forms—even in thought."[10] And she takes up the life of a prostitute, the movie implies, as a consequence of Christ's neglect. It is his inability to acknowledge, much less to consummate, their sexual relationship that at the conclusion of the brothel scene causes him to beg her forgiveness and frustrates her so much that she spits out, "You're the same as all the others, but you can't admit it—I hate you." The turning point in their troubled relationship comes about when Christ saves Magdalene from stoning—the punishment ordained for adulteresses by Jewish law—by an angry mob. "Love one another," he enjoins, and the prescription becomes an epiphany for the erstwhile prostitute who henceforth veils her face, covers her body, and penitently follows Christ. Magdalene's reformation/purification is crucial to the Devil's last temptation: a vision of Mary all in white and leading a marriage procession. No longer a sexy strumpet but a chaste bride, she is dissociated from carnal desire and identified with family values. So the last temptation is a fiendishly clever ploy of the Devil: if only Christ will forsake his Messianic destiny, he can not only achieve the sexual fulfillment he secretly yearns for but do so within the sanctified bond of marriage. A less-than-candid Jesus might even rationalize his lust as no more than the desire to have a wife and family, in short to live and die as an ordinary Jew. But then he would not be Christ.

Those who object to *The Last Temptation of Christ* as blasphemous, taking its emphasis on Jesus' humanity as a denial of his divinity, ignore the evidence of the film's title and Scorsese's stated intention.

As the son of man *and* Son of God, Jesus/Christ incorporates the double identity that his salvational role demands. He is neither man pretending to be God nor God condescending to be man. Religious fundamentalists read Scorsese's ending as they read everything—literally: Jesus lives the temptation scene instead of hallucinating it. But, of course, the sequence is a dream from which Jesus awakens to (re)place himself on the Cross and fulfill his Messianic mission. As man, he weighs the temptation; as God he transcends it. Like *New York, New York* and *The King of Comedy*, *The Last Temptation of Christ* defies genre expectations: the biblical epic conventionally accentuates Christ's divinity, not his humanity. The Christ of the Gospels stars in the greatest story ever told, adapted for the screen. Yet a fully divine Christ is a static one. By humanizing him, Scorsese follows Kazantzakis in dramatizing the mortal struggle of a man to discover his divinity. That struggle drives the first half of the film and climaxes with a recognition scene in which John the Baptist (Andre Gregory) gives Christ his blessing. Until then, Jesus is so conflicted by his dual nature and afflicted by his inner voices that he cries out, "My mother and my father and my God are fear." Scorsese calibrates Jesus' growing awareness of his calling: "I don't kill because I'm afraid" gives way to "I feel pity for everything," and then, just before his rendezvous with destiny in the person of John the Baptist, to "I wanted to kill, but I opened my mouth and out came love." Of course, it is Jesus' human side talking when he confesses to lying and hypocrisy, just as it is his human side dreaming when he "accepts" the last temptation. In neither case is he a sinner, says Scorsese, since "being God also, how can he sin?" Never questioning the divinity that makes it impossible for Christ to sin, Scorsese nevertheless wants him to feel all the psychological trauma of the human sinner: "He has to experience the guilt, experience the temptation, the feelings of anger, of lust—all these things, even the shame."[11]

Because Magdalene is the instrument of Christ's temptation, their relationship—defined in the brothel scene and refined in the dream sequences—is pivotal to Scorsese's treatment. Yet Christ's relationship with Judas is also essential, adding a sociopolitical element to the struggle. Among other things, *The Last Temptation* is a buddy movie on the order of *Mean Streets:*

> No wonder Scorsese worked and dreamed for a decade to make this picture. He knew that Kazantzakis's story could be the ultimate buddy movie. For 15 years Scorsese has been directing secular drafts

of it. Two men, closer than brothers, with complementary abilities and obsessions, who must connive in each other's destiny.[12]

And if the Jesus/Judas and Charlie/Johnny Boy connections are similar, so is what Paul Schrader calls "the central triangle" of *The Last Temptation*, "which is Jesus, Judas, and Magdalene" reminiscent of the Charlie, Johnny Boy, and Teresa setup of *Mean Streets*. Articulate and motivated where Jesus is—at least initially—tongue-tied and indecisive, Judas (Harvey Keitel) sporadically threatens to become the *real* hero of *The Last Temptation* à la Satan in Milton's *Paradise Lost.* Judas is a Jewish nationalist fighting to free his people from Imperial Rome, a rabble-rouser urging rebellion against the colonial power. There is a modern slant to the anticolonialist struggle: Jews are generally dark-skinned locals—the movie was shot in Morocco—while the Romans are invariably white; Jews sound like refugees from *Mean Streets* while Romans (and Satan!) speak with impeccable British accents. By likening Judas to a fiery leader of a modern liberation movement, Scorsese valorizes the role and raises the political stakes. So passionate is Judas's commitment to the cause of freedom that he momentarily convinces Jesus to head an armed insurrection against the Romans. But Jesus falters, helpless to attack: the moment—and the revolution—is lost.

In rejecting political activism, Jesus turns Judas around as dramatically as he turned Magdalene around in saving her from stoning. It is Jesus' betrayal of the uprising that leads Judas to betray him. Still, the point of the failed insurrection is less to give Judas cause than to expose his role in God's master narrative. At the moment when Jesus' political nerve fails, he bleeds from the hands—a sign that sacrificial death, not armed struggle, is his destiny. Not the zeal for revolution but the wish that God will let him die in battle rather than on the cross motivated Jesus to take up arms. Certain now of his fate, he divulges it to Judas: "I have to die on the cross." Not only must the crucifixion—crucial for "bringing God and man together"—occur, but Judas must instigate it. "Without you, there can be no redemption," Jesus informs him. And when the horrified Judas balks at his designated role—"Could *you* betray your master?"—Jesus replies, "No, that's why God gave me the easier job: to be crucified." This implication that Judas shares top billing with Jesus in God's scheme is theologically shocking but narratively consistent. All along, Judas has been portrayed as the stronger of the two: "Judas, I'm afraid; stay with me," Jesus pleads, and Judas passes the night cradling him in his arms.

"I have to die on the cross, and I have to die *willingly*," Jesus tells Judas even before the aborted insurrection. At first glance, the prescription seems anomalous: if the crucifixion is mandated by God, where does willingness come in? Apparently, Jesus means that God has scripted the salvific role but that he, Jesus, need not choose to play it. Volition is all: without it temptation is meaningless, and the battle between the spirit and the flesh is nonexistent. True, Jesus' instructions to Judas imply that the entire crucifixion scenario is a foregone conclusion: "Go to Gethsemane and I'll make sure that they find me there. I am going to die. But after three days, I'll come back." Still, Jesus will be free to back out at the eleventh hour, to reject the divinity that God has thrust upon him. Jesus' attempts at evading God—most sickeningly by making the crosses on which his fellow Jews are crucified—occupy the first half of *The Last Temptation of Christ.* In the second half, Christ accepts his divinity, embraces his Messianic calling, and embarks on his public ministry. The familiar Christ of the Gospels stages the miracles that establish his divinity in the minds of disciples and skeptics alike: curing the sick, raising Lazarus from the dead, turning water into wine. Inevitably the tension of the movie slackens as Christ no longer doubts his divinity but demonstrates it.

Perhaps the single most striking proof of his divine identity and preview of his sacrificial destiny occurs when Jesus tears his bleeding heart out of his body and offers it to his disciples. It is the "one scene I did add that wasn't in" Kazantzakis's book, says Schrader. "It just hit me and I loved the scene and Marty loved it."[13] Scorsese remembered his grandmother's portrait of the Sacred Heart which he associated with his earliest experience of Christ. In *The Last Temptation,* he wanted the Sacred Heart scene to level the "supernatural and the natural on the same plane." By offering them his heart, Jesus stills the bickering apostles and unites them behind him: "It's a symbol to bring them all together—especially Judas, who kisses his feet and says 'Adonai!' All of a sudden Jesus is God? Wait a second! Yes—Judas needs this. So do the others, to be convinced that this is the man."[14] The Sacred Heart scene is Scorsese's most startling recourse to the blood imagery that saturates *The Last Temptation of Christ.* Yet it would have been rivaled in shock potential by "a literal version of the Last Supper in terms of swallowing the flesh and blood of Jesus," which Schrader proposed in his first draft. This was too much even for Scorsese, and in the "second draft that scene was taken out and we went back to Kazantzakis."[15] Even in rejecting Schrader's

literalism, however, Scorsese insists on the miracle of transubstantiation. "This bread is my body; this wine is my blood," Christ informs his
disciples during the film's Last Supper. Drinking from the cup Christ
passes around, Peter realizes that the "wine" has the consistency of
blood. Bread and wine *become* Christ's body and blood in *The Last
Temptation* as they do in the Catholic Mass on which Scorsese was
reared. Christ's words—echoed down the ages by legions of Catholic
priests—mean what they say: the transformation is real not symbolic.

Via the doctrine of transubstantiation, Catholicism vivifies the sacrificial element of Christianity. At the time of his First Communion,
Scorsese recalls, he was "fascinated by images of the crucifixion and
drew endless pictures of it, which I gave to the nuns at school." So lasting
were those boyhood impressions that the adult Scorsese equates religion
with sacrifice: "Regarding ancient religions, such as in Carthage, where
they sacrificed 500 five-year-old children, or the blood sacrifices of the
Israelites, finally up to the sacrifice of Jesus on the cross, and beyond that
the sacrifice of the Mass—there has obviously been a 'civilizing' of religions, I feel, but this primal instinct towards bloodletting is still part of
our subconscious."[16] Scorsese's obsession with sacrifice and with bloodletting as its primary signifier naturally apotheosizes in *The Last
Temptation of Christ.* Christ's Passion is the ultimate expression of a theology of bloodshed that informs Scorsese's most powerful films, notably
Taxi Driver and *Raging Bull.* "The Passion"—the working title of *The Last
Temptation*—accurately reflects Scorsese's sacrificial emphasis even
though it was imposed by the studio in an effort to deflect fundamentalist brickbats.

The sufferings of Christ between the night of the Last Supper and his
death (i.e., the Passion) are etched in harsh detail: "I didn't ask you to
choose me. Do I have to die? Is there any other way?" Jesus cries out to
God in the Garden of Gethsemane. "Please give me the strength," he
prays just before Judas enters at the head of the guard to betray him with
a kiss. "Take me with you, I'm ready," Jesus tells Judas, resigned to the
physical agony that awaits him. Beginning with the condemnation by
Pontius Pilate (David Bowie) and culminating in the crucifixion, blood is
both the visible emblem and the primary religious symbol of Christ's
Passion. "I imagined this picture of Him sweating blood, just as I'd seen
it at Catholic School," says Scorsese. "But there are other times when I
enjoy just wallowing in this kind of imagery," adds the director of *Taxi
Driver* and *Raging Bull.*[17] Christ's blood flows copiously as he is savagely

beaten and crowned with thorns by the Romans. Scorsese draws out the agony of the tortured Christ bearing the cross by shooting it in slow motion to the accompaniment of wailing music. And he surrounds Christ with jeering and scowling tormentors in imitation of Bosch's harrowing painting of Christ carrying the cross: "To keep the people around him, some of them laughing and pointing at him, we had to tie them together with ropes, so they could only move one step at a time." So Christ must endure the press of the crowd and the sting of their insults along with the ravages inflicted on his body. "We took Christ's wounds from the Shroud of Turin, where the crown of thorns was not a crown but a skull-cap, and the scourging completely covered his back. If we didn't show the blood, it seemed to me to weaken the extent of his sacrifice, and diminish what it meant for him to die on the cross."[18] With the same zeal for "authenticity" that led him to the Shroud of Turin, Scorsese consulted the *Biblical Archeology Review* for evidence of an actual crucifixion. What he found—that the victim "was crucified naked, sitting sideways with his legs bent"—jogged his memory of "a fourteenth-century German wooden carving" of naked figures on the three crosses that he saw during a boyhood visit to the Metropolitan Museum of Art. Scorsese's decision to shoot Christ naked and twisted on the cross is as narratively consistent as it is historically accurate. Again, the magnitude of Christ's ordeal is rendered in harshly graphic images. And just as he intensifies the agony of carrying the cross by invoking Bosch's painting, Scorsese intensifies the agony of being crucified by imitating another Renaissance masterpiece—*The Crucifixion* (1475) by Antonello da Messina. Following da Messina, Scorsese pictures Christ nailed to the cross with the two thieves tied to trees on either side. The effect is to isolate and magnify Christ's pain and suffering.

Although the sheer agony of the crucifixion might suffice to deflect Christ from the course of martyrdom, his severest trial is not physical but psychological. Ironically, however, it is physical existence that accounts for the psychological pressure of the last temptation: a young girl appears before the crucified Christ and offers him an eleventh-hour reprieve from death. The suffering Christ takes her for an annunciatory angel whose revelation that he can climb down from the cross, marry Magdalene, and father children conforms to the not-so-secret yearnings for a normal life that Jesus harbored earlier. Of course the little girl is the Devil, and her vision of earthly delights is a scam. Having already encountered the disguised Devil in the desert and successfully resisted his temptation of power, Christ figures to be at least a little suspicious of the girl and her offer. That he is sorely tempted nonetheless reflects his partial humanity as well as the reality of the crucifixion: it is in his capacity as man that he flinches from his destiny as God. In any event, the ensuing dream sequence is the centerpiece of *The Last Temptation of Christ,* if only by virtue of its length: 35 of the film's 163 minutes. "You've done enough," the little girl tells Christ, assuring him that he is not the Messiah after all. Removing the crown of thorns, extracting the nails, and silencing the jeering crowd, she leads him away from Calvary and into "the *real* beauty of God's earth." As the last temptation sequence unfolds, Scorsese adjusts his style to reflect Christ's newfound bliss. Christ is photographed in languid long shots instead of tormented close-ups; the desert blooms, and the light softens. Scorsese even slows the pace of the sequence, perhaps to reflect the leisurely passage of some thirty-six years of Christ's imagined life. Christ duly weds a white-clad Mary Magdalene and makes love to her in a discreetly shot tableau arguably meant to contrast with the brothel scene's brutish sex. Although Magdalene dies—"God killed her," explains the little girl—Christ soon marries Lazarus's sister, Mary—"Magdalene with a different face," suggests the little girl—and rears a family. He also enjoys an adulterous fling with Martha, which the little girl justifies by stating that "there's only one woman in the world." This apparent interchangeability of the three women seems designed to excuse Christ's hasty remarriage and hastier adultery, but it may equally imply that his version of a "normal" life is a bit self-serving.

The question of Christ's motivation, momentarily finessed by the little girl's women/woman equation, surfaces more urgently in his confrontations with Paul and Judas. Meantime Jesus has achieved his goal of a normal life. "Have you any complaints?" the ageless little girl asks the aged Jesus. "No," he replies, implicitly seconding her summary of the life he has led since opting out of the crucifixion: "You've grown old; you've done well." Whether normalcy and survival constitute doing well is debatable, but Jesus is apparently content with the bargain he (unwittingly) made with the Devil. Then Saul/Paul shows up, preaching ecstatically of his epiphany on the road to Damascus and describing Christ's sacrifice on the cross. Though confronted by the living Jesus, Paul adamantly clings to the crucifixion story: it is the first indication that Jesus is "living" a dream, that he cannot outrun his fate, and that God's will has already been done. Now the dying Jesus is visited by Judas still furious at the Master who betrayed him and their cause. "Traitor," he calls Jesus. "Your place was on the cross. You broke my heart. We had the world in our hands." That Judas appears at this climactic moment and that only he has the power to explode the dream again underlines his indispensable role in Scorsese's scheme of things. Without Judas to awake him to his duty, Jesus dies peacefully in bed, the crucifixion never happens, and the world goes unredeemed. At Judas's words, Jesus bleeds anew, and a flame (Satan) springs up where the little girl previously stood. It only remains for Christ to crawl up the steps that turn into rock and reclaim his destined place back on the Cross. "It is accomplished!" he exults.

One might carp that Christ exults because he has had it both ways: joie de vivre—if only in his dreams—and Messianic fulfillment. Because of the length, the position, and the content of the last temptation sequence, there is a danger of subverting, diluting, or even negating Christ's sacrifice in the minds of the audience. Yet Scorsese rightly makes the dream as alluring as possible: if even Christ may succumb, then the temptation must be powerful indeed. And the point, of course, is that he never *really* succumbs at all. Scorsese's idea was to invoke Christ's human foibles by way of explaining the difficulty of resisting the last temptation. For if Christ is solely God, temptation is meaningless, resistance is easy, struggle is absent, and the movie loses its raison d'être. Christ triumphs on the Cross not simply because as God he can do no less but because as man he faces down his demons. This is not to say that he is not God all along; only that being God cannot absolve him from being man. In pinpointing the exact moment when Christ knows himself as God, Scorsese defines Christ's struggle and clarifies the movie's denouement:

> I wrote the scene of the raising of Lazarus myself. . . . The minute Christ raises Lazarus, he knows that He is God. And with Lazarus's hand clasping His, pulling Him into the tomb, it gave a sense of death pulling Him in, an image of the struggle between life and death. Death which He will—despite being God—have to suffer as man.[19]

Christ's is "a kind of Nietzschean superman struggle," argues Paul Schrader by way of Kazantzakis whose theology in *The Last Temptation of Christ* also included a "more mystical" element. "I skewed it towards the Nietzschean. . . .The struggle to be God, the struggle with one's own sense of divinity is an *Übermensch* problem." Thus for Schrader "the end of the film is a kind of superman triumph—calling yourself back to the Cross by force of will—and the emphasis is definitely on the man who wills himself back to the Cross rather than on the God who puts him back."[20] Another kind of superman—Christ's evil twin—wreaks psychopathic havoc as the self-fashioned avenging angel of *Cape Fear* (1991). Max Cady (Robert DeNiro), an ex-con out to get Sam Bowden (Nick Nolte), the lawyer who betrayed him, "spends his spare time reading *Thus Spake Zarathustra*, and figures himself as a kind of bargain-basement Nietzschean Superman."[21] *Üntermensch* rather than *Übermensch*, Cady turns out to be less than human, not more, despite his claim to superman status: "I spent fourteen years in an eight by nine cell surrounded by people who were less than human. My mission in that time was to become more than human."

It was the character of Max Cady that lured Scorsese into directing *Cape Fear*, a remake of a 1962 thriller about a psychotic rapist's vendetta against the man whose testimony sent him to jail. Based on John D. MacDonald's novel, *The Executioners* (1957), the original *Cape Fear* was a straightforward clash between good—Sam Bowden (Gregory Peck), respected lawyer and family man—and evil—Max Cady (Robert Mitchum), sexual sadist and implacable revenger. Wesley Strick's first script for the remake was more of the same, and Scorsese "really hated it. . . . I thought the family was too clichéd, too happy. . . . I was rooting for Max to get them."[22] But Steven Spielberg, who had initiated the project, wanted Scorsese to direct it, and De Niro wanted to play Max Cady. Spielberg agreed to let Scorsese do whatever he liked with the script, just so he preserved its happy ending. The clincher, however, was De Niro's strong conviction that, "We could *do* something with this guy (Cady)." De Niro's enthusiasm proved as infectious as it had a decade earlier when he saw himself as Jake LaMotta and talked Scorsese into making *Raging Bull*. "Bob and I hadn't worked that closely together in nine years. And so it brought back all these flashbacks," recalls Scorsese. "I thought, 'Yeah, we really *could* do something.'" Still, as in the case of LaMotta, Scorsese had to relate Cady to himself:

> I've always been drawn to the exploration of this sort of character . . . a character who will not give up, who's unrelenting, who not only tortures himself but the people around him. De Niro and I just happened to lock into that sort of thing together. I mean, we have the same kinds of feelings, the same painful reactions to a lot of this material—so painful that it gets very, very hard for us to express it in words. But we're able to act it out. In France they

asked me recently, "What would you do if you didn't have De Niro to play these parts?" I thought about it for a second and I said, "I'd do it myself."[23]

Melodrama becomes psychodrama as Scorsese complicates the simplistic agon he hated in Strick's original script. Cued by the 1962 *Cape Fear*, Strick had pitted a satanic Max Cady against a saintly Sam Bowden. Only because Bowden had been a witness for the prosecution was Cady out to get him. In Scorsese's version Bowden is not a prosecution witness but a public defender assigned to represent Cady. Confronted with evidence of Cady's victim's promiscuity, Bowden buried it to insure that the jury would not exonerate a savage rapist. Thus playing judge and jury—even God—Bowden betrayed his solemn obligation to his client. "You see, in Scorsese," Thelma Schoonmaker observed while editing *Cape Fear*, "*Everyone* is guilty."[24] During fourteen years in a brutal Georgia prison, Cady learned to read and write and discovered the suppressed evidence that might have set him free. "You gotta' learn about loss," Cady tells Bowden. When Cady laughs off Bowden's offer of $10,000 to get out of town and Bowden asks him what he wants if not money, Cady replies, "I only want what you have, counselor," a cryptic reference to the wife and daughter Bowden has but that Cady lost after he went to prison. The reference also invokes the sexual threat to Bowden's wife and daughter that underlies Cady's scheme of revenge.

Aberrant sexuality—and not only Cady's—threads through *Cape Fear* as it does in so many Scorsese movies. Bowden's infidelity in the past has created a dysfunctional family in the present. His wife Leigh (Jessica Lange), unable—or unwilling—to forgive much less to forget, seizes every opportunity to remind Sam of his lapse(s). Their daughter Danielle (Juliette Lewis), a precocious fifteen-year-old child–woman, is routinely subjected to the litany of her mother's accusations and her father's denials. Even as he faults Leigh for dwelling on his past indiscretions, Sam is carrying on an affair with Lori Davis (Illeana Douglas). It is Sam's sexual bad faith that lays the burden of guilt and suspicion on the Bowden family. And it is sexual transgression that links Bowden the adulterer to Cady the rapist. Cady's brutal assault on Lori is a macabre (sub)version of her relationship with Bowden. Tipsy and upset because Sam has stood her up, Lori proves an easy mark for Cady who savages her precisely because she is sexually involved with Bowden. The opening salvo in his war against Bowden's women as a means of revenge against Bowden himself, Cady's brutalizing of Lori is activated by yet another show of sexual bad faith on Bowden's past. By standing up Lori, Sam adds to the sum of his hypocrisies in addition to getting her nearly murdered. As Leigh's husband, as Lori's lover, and as Cady's lawyer, Sam is guilty of the betrayal that Cady has come back to punish.

Because Sam Bowden is a far cry from Gregory Peck's straight-arrow family man of the original *Cape Fear*, Cady's motive, if not his intent, gains a certain sanction. For Scorsese, "Cady was sort of the malignant spirit of guilt in a way, of the family—the avenging angel. Punishment for everything you ever felt sexually. It is the basic moral battleground of Christian ethics."[25] Certainly, Cady sees his vendetta as a religious crusade and himself as the righteous avenger. "I am your salvation," he tells Sam, reminding him that it is easier for a camel to pass through the eye of a needle than for a rich man to enter the king-dom of heaven. Conceiving his mission in Biblical terms, Cady is for-ever spouting scripture. In his original script, Wesley Strick gave Cady an evangelical fundamentalist childhood and a sprinkling of Biblical references. As De Niro developed the role he pestered Strick for more Biblical quotes, chiefly about vengeance, and cloaked a killer's psy-chotic ravings in the rhetoric of God's wrath. Moreover, Cady has inscribed on his body the twisted theology of his speech: TRUTH and JUSTICE balances scales suspended from a wooden cross tattooed on the naked back that Cady reveals while doing push ups in his cell just before his release from prison. Later, when he is hauled into the station and strip-searched, Sam Bowden and police lieutenant Elgart (Robert Mitchum) watch from behind a one-way mirror as the camera pans the full range of Cady's biblically inspired tattoos. "Vengeance Is Mine," "My Time Is at Hand," "The Lord Is the Avenger," and "Time the Avenger" typify the citations that blanket his torso, each biblical source meticulously annotated in finer print. "I don't know whether to look at him or read him!" exclaims Elgart.

Reading Cady reveals the nature and the nurture of his obsession. During his long years in prison Cady suffered the same mortification of the flesh that he intends to inflict on Bowden's women. Brutalized and sodomized, he imagines a grisly poetic justice in doing unto others what others did unto him. Textualizing his body (the flesh made Word?) arguably codifies as it symbolically reenacts the mortification of the flesh. Cady attributes Leigh's revulsion to his "too many tattoos. . . . But you see there's not a whole lot to do in prison but desecrate your flesh."

Actually, reading was what he mostly did in prison. Learning to read, he discovered his betrayal, and learning to write he inscribed on his body the language of revenge his reading spawned. Desecration becomes, then, a mode of consecration, an indelible imprimatur of vengeance. Words, for Cady, are the weapons of revenge. Normally taciturn and brooding, he waxes eloquent at those moments when language promises to serve his obsession. There is a streak of the performer in Cady that links him to Jake LaMotta and Rupert Pupkin and, less obviously, to Travis Bickle (whose body-building routine, like Cady's, prefigures obsessive violence). Two episodes in which he employs the rhetoric of seduction to disarm women reveal his performative talent.

In the bar scene with Lori, Cady plays upon her resentment at being stood up by Sam to draw her into a sexual orbit compounded of artful lies and ironic half-truths. Alternately acting the sympathetic listener and hyping his sexual charisma, Cady lures Lori into a one-night stand that culminates in a graphically violent and even cannibalistic rape scene. But he reserves his greatest performance for the ominous mock-seduction sequence with Danielle (Danny) that is arguably the center-piece of *Cape Fear*. It begins when Cady, posing as her drama teacher, phones Danny and arranges a meeting. As with Lori, feigned sympathy becomes the key to greater intimacy: Cady comes on like a New Age therapist, urging Danny to use the "negativity" created by menstrual pain and clueless parents to do her own thing. Danny's budding sexuali-ty—invoked by references to the onset of menstruation and the parental anxiety it implicitly provokes—is highlighted by the camera's caressing close-ups of the nubile body that her scanty sleepwear reveals as much as conceals. At the other end of the line is Cady, hanging upside down on a chinning bar by one hand as he dexterously cues Aretha Franklin's "Do Right Woman—Do Right Man" with the other. "Now you can trust in me cause I'm the Do-Right Man," he tells the rapt Danny, adding that the class meeting has been relocated "to the theater. I mean what better place for drama, right?"

At school the next day, Danny edges down an ominously deserted and shadowy basement corridor to the theater. There, in the bowels of the building (Hell) awaits Cady (Satan) dragging on a joint that he offers to the amazed yet fascinated girl. By enlisting her as a coconspirator in a clichéd act of rebellion against authority, the "teacher" ingratiates him-self with the pupil just as he did with the Aretha Franklin song. It is the initial ploy in a seduction campaign that continues with chitchat about

Henry Miller and thwarted adulthood. The scene is egregiously theatrical, played on stage where a lit-up set reveals a fairy-tale granny's house nestled in the woods. What with the pot smoking and sexual innuendos, even the naive Danny smells something fishy: "You're not the drama teacher, are you?" "Maybe I'm the Big Bad Wolf," suggests Cady, casting her in turn as Little Red Riding Hood in a scenario that he has (pre)arranged and that the setting has evoked. After (falsely) reassuring her that he had not killed the family dog and gaining her permission to put his arm around her, Cady ups the sexual ante by caressing her face, slipping his thumb past the barrier of her braces into her mouth, and finally kissing her lingeringly and passionately. Although certain versions of "Little Red Riding Hood" climax with a putatively innocent but possibly attracted girl being eaten by the Big Bad Wolf, this one ends with Cady simply walking out of the auditorium. Like some Riding Hoods, Danny is both frightened and fascinated at the prospect of being (sexually) devoured. With Lori, Cady's sexual appetite morphed into cannibalism: the sickening image of Lori's bitten cheek mediates the tender caress of Danny's face. This time, however, Cady contents himself with the simulated fellatio and the passionate kiss before exiting the stage. Yet despite their very different outcomes, the "seductions" of Lori and Danny similarly invoke the psychosexual subtext of *Cape Fear*. Cady is "competing" with Bowden for the women—wife, mistress, daughter—in Bowden's life. Their competition comes to a head when Cady goes after Leigh and Danny in the movie's harrowing finale.

At Cape Fear, where the Bowden family tries futilely to elude Cady—he clings to the underside of their car—on their houseboat, Scorsese orchestrates the animal and scriptural signifiers that mediate the movie into a crescendo of luridly savage and melodramatically exaggerated violence. As the family drives unknowingly toward their rendezvous with terror, a roadside sign asks ominously, "Where will you spend eternity?" When he corners them on the houseboat, Cady screams at Leigh and Danny, "Take off your clothes. Down on your knees. Tonight you're going to learn to be an animal and to die like one." Of course he has already played the Big Bad Wolf with Danny and warned Lori to stay sober—'cause I'm just one hell of an animal"—prior to savaging her animalistically. Less than human, Cady called his fellow prisoners, and his first act of vengeance against the Bowden's was to kill their dog. If his "mission" was to "become more than human" in jail, it is to reduce the Bowdens to less than human on the houseboat. Cady apparently sees no contradiction between his scriptural injunctions and his bestial actions. "Every man has to go through Hell to reach his paradise," he told Danny in the "Little Red Riding Hood" scene. "I sentence you to the ninth circle of Hell," he shouts at Sam just before the houseboat splinters on the rocks. Thus passing judgment—as Sam once did on him—Cady enacts the ultimate superman role that he claimed for himself after beating up the three thugs that Sam had hired to scare him off: "I am as large as God," exulted Cady. During and after his interminable knock-down-drag-out fight with Sam, Cady *does* seem superhuman: torched and drowned, he keeps resurfacing until, the water finally closing over his head, he gurgles his parting words: "Who'll come with me? I'm bound for the promised land."

Max Cady's end is as histrionic as any opera character's, a cinematic *Götterdämmerung* in which he "dies" again and again. In Scorsese's over-the-top mise-en-scène—houseboat pitching, water roiling, women screaming, blood spurting—scary thriller and Gothic horror show intersect. Cinematographer Freddie Francis, who had directed many British horror films in the 1960s and 1970s, gave *Cape Fear* its aura of "malevolent vitality" that Scorsese was after. The very elements are made to reflect the turbulence generated by Cady: crimson water washes over the opening credits; a blackly boiling artificial sky backgrounds Cady's exit from prison; wind and rain machines churn the watery ooze of Cape Fear into a maelstrom during the titanic battle of the finale. Special effects, jagged cutting, oblique angles, startling close-ups, frenetic pacing, and expressionistic color and lighting deliberately blur the generic boundary between thriller and horror film. For Scorsese is not so much remaking *Cape Fear* as retrofitting it for deeper water. Retaining the basic plot, the key actors (Mitchum becomes a no-nonsense lawman, Peck a smarmy lawyer), and the (rescored) soundtrack, Scorsese reprises his source even as he revises it. Retooling personalities, complicating moral issues, multiplying religious signifiers, and shuffling generic markers, he (re)fashions a scary thriller into a harrowing psychodrama. "I have to ground everything in a bedrock of spiritual motivation," he explained on the eve of shooting *Cape Fear*. A project concocted for mass appeal and commercial profit turned out to be an unlikely repository of his obsessions and one of Scorsese's "most Catholic" pictures.[26]

Millennium Approaches: Something(s) Old, Something(s) New . . . .

In *GoodFellas* (1990) Scorsese returns to the familiar terrain of *Mean Streets*, but with a difference:

> *Mean Streets* is much closer to home in terms of a real story, some-what fictionalized, about events that occurred to me and some of my old friends. [*GoodFellas*] has really nothing to do with people I knew then. It doesn't take place in Manhattan, it's only in the boroughs, so it's a very different world—although it's all interrelated. But the *spirit* of it, again, the *attitudes*. The morality—you know, there's none, there's none.[1]

It is the *Mean Streets* world of organized crime, insular and amoral, that Scorsese anatomizes in *GoodFellas* and again, in *Casino* (1995). The two 1990s films are companion pieces of sorts: true stories drawn from Nicholas Pileggi books and shot in semi-documentary style. For the first time since *Mean Streets*, Scorsese put his name on a script, sharing credit with Pileggi for *GoodFellas* and again, for *Casino*. Although Scorsese calls *GoodFellas* "a nostalgia piece from the early 1960s, when I grew up," it is set as well in the 1970s and early 1980s, like *Casino*. In both movies, Robert De Niro and Joe Pesci play gangland buddies whose rise and fall roughly conforms to the fate of the Mob. *GoodFellas* and *Casino* comprise a volatile mix of easy money, illicit drugs, and violence, which makes and breaks the featured gangsters.

GoodFellas is based on Pileggi's *Wise Guy: Life in a Mafia Family* (1985), a nonfiction treatment of the life and times of mobster Henry Hill. A ghostwritten workup of Hill's reminiscences, *Wise Guy* takes a documentary approach—evident in its subtitle—that appealed to

Scorsese. *Italianamerican* is to *Mean Streets* as *American Boy* is to *Taxi Driver* as *The Last Waltz* is to *New York, New York*—documentary companions to the feature films. For Scorsese, documentaries embody the narrative "clarity" he is after in his features. *GoodFellas* and (especially) *Casino* rely heavily on documentary techniques—voice-overs, place and date captions, historical references—to carry the storyline. "I wanted the style to kind of break down by the end," says Scorsese, "so that by his [Henry Hill's] last days as a wiseguy, it's as if the whole picture would be out of control, give the impression he's just going to spin off the edge and fly out. And then stop for the last reel and a half." Wanting to "get as much movement as possible" and "overwhelming" the audience "with images and information" at the same time, he shot most of the movie at runaway speed. Often, however, it is when the onrushing camera suddenly freezes a moment that maximum drama occurs. While admitting that the "freeze frames are basically all Truffaut," Scorsese maintains nonetheless that the technique comes from documentaries. "Images would stop: a point was being made."[2] In *Casino*, Scorsese would push the documentary style of his feature films to its outer limits.

In Robert Warshow's classic formulation, movies like *GoodFellas* and *Casino* recall Greek tragedy: "The gangster movie . . . is a story of enterprise and success ending in precipitate failure."[3] The hero's fate is conventionally foreshadowed if not sealed by a seminal event—Oedipus murders his father, Agamemnon sacrifices his daughter—most often a violent one. Before the *GoodFellas* credits roll, Tommy De Vito (Joe Pesci) viciously stabs and Jimmy Conway (Robert De Niro) methodically shoots the bleeding and still twitching torso of Billy Batts whom they have beaten nearly to death and stuffed in their car trunk. But Batts was a "made man," a member of the Gambino inner circle; his murder violates the Mob taboo against internecine killing. Consequently the bosses invoke their own brand of poetic justice: calling Tommy, who instigated the murder, with the news that he is to become a "made man" himself, they brutally slaughter him when he shows up for his "initiation." Instead of enjoying the ritual of initiation, Tommy is subjected to the ritual of revenge in an eye-for-an-eye enactment of the code he has violated. Jimmy flies into a violent rage when he learns of his buddy's fate, but Henry Hill (Ray Liotta), who had watched Tommy and Jimmy dispatch Batts, reflects that "There was nothing we could do about it. Batts was a made man and Tommy wasn't. And, we had to sit still and take it. . . . They even shot Tommy in the face so his mother couldn't give him an open coffin at the funeral." That Batts's murder is a watershed in *GoodFellas* is not readily apparent in the opening sequence, which is titled simply "New York 1970," and which comes across more as black comedy than as dire portent (Batts is stabbed and shot enough to kill a platoon before he finally dies, and his death throes no sooner end than Henry Hill observes that "I always wanted to be a gangster"). The importance of the scene is clarified when it is repeated and expanded later in *GoodFellas*.

This time, a caption pinpoints the fatal date—June 11, 1970—when the supervolatile Tommy, incensed by Batts's insults, all but murders the "made man." Accompanied by Jimmy and Henry, Tommy then dines at his mother's (Catherine Scorsese's) house where he borrows the formidable kitchen knife he used to finish Batts off in the opening sequence and now wields again as the mayhem replays. Tommy embodies the random violence that interferes with making money, the raison d'être of the Mob. "That's why, in *GoodFellas*, Tommy is killed," reasons Scorsese. "After a while he was making more noise than money. He started killing people for no reason. So they had to get rid of him. He was messing up the whole plan."[4] An outburst of violence as senseless as the Batts imbroglio occurs when Tommy murders Spider. Playing cards with the boys, Tommy blows up when Spider forgets his drink order. Brandishing a gun and ordering the hapless young gofer to dance "like they do in cowboy movies," Tommy shoots at the floor but hits Spider in the foot. When he badgers the kid again in a second card game scene, Spider, his foot heavily bandaged, retorts, "Why don't you go fuck yourself, Tommy?" At this, the other players jeer Tommy who promptly pulls out his gun and pumps six slugs into Spider's chest. Tommy's (over)reaction shocks even the implacable Jimmy. Again Tommy has violated the order of things: murdering a harmless kid is as insane as murdering a "made man." If it weren't that Scorsese leavens the brutal murders with comedy routines about disposing of the bodies—"OK, you killed him [Spider], you gotta dig the hole"—Jimmy tells Tommy—Tommy's hair-trigger temper could pass for the "tragic flaw" that precipitates disaster. But *GoodFellas* is not Greek tragedy: its calculated juxtaposition of the terrible and the banal ironically punctures the wise guy mystique. It is Scorsese's antidote to the romanticized Mafia of *The Godfather*.

Henry Hill, whose voice-over narration shapes *GoodFellas*, believes in the myth. From his first confession—"I always wanted to be a gangster"—uttered with no trace of irony only moments after Batts's murder—to his last regret—"The hardest thing for me was to leave the life"—Henry was married to the Mob. Although he works his way up from all-purpose gofer for neighborhood capo Paulie Cicero (Paul Sorvino) to full-fledged mobster, Henry cannot ever be a "made man" because, like his idol and mentor Jimmy Conway, he is not "family" (i.e., not one hundred percent Sicilian). That Henry is not a big-time Mafioso accords with his function in *GoodFellas*: to anatomize a collective lifestyle in chronicling an individual life. Scorsese depersonalizes Henry, denying him an independent existence apart from the Mob. By pluralizing Pileggi's book title, Scorsese locks his focus on the ethos of the group rather than on the identity of the individual. (*Wise Guys*, the working title, had already been used for a movie, so Scorsese opted for *GoodFellas*.) Henry Hill's cinematic status as a window on the Mob is established in the extended flashback that succeeds the opening scene of Batts's murder. Fittingly, a point-of-view shot captures young Henry (Chris Serrone) gazing through an open window—as Scorsese himself did as a boy—at the street scene below. Soon, he is Paulie's gofer, at thirteen "making more money than many of the grownups in the neighborhood." By the time he meets his hero, Jimmy Conway—"one of the most feared guys in the city"—Henry is already an apprentice gangster. After his first run-in with the law, Jimmy congratulates him for keeping his cool and reminds him of the mobster's credo: "Never rat on your friends. And always keep your mouth shut." His apprenticeship successfully served, Henry becomes a full-time gangster in earnest.

When *GoodFellas* fast-forwards to "Idlewild 1963," (now Kennedy Airport) a typical Scorsese restaurant scene of raucous male camaraderie establishes Henry as one of the boys. Now twenty-something, debonair in natty clothes and flashy accessories, he has apparently achieved the lifestyle of his dreams. What this lifestyle consists of is clarified in Robert Warshow's account of the movie gangster:

> Success is conceived as an increasing power to work injury, it belongs to the city, and it is of course a form of evil. . . . The peculiarity of the gangster is his unceasing, nervous activity. The exact nature of his enterprises may remain vague, but his commitment to enterprise is always clear, and all the more clear because he operates outside the field of utility. He is without culture, without manners, without leisure, or at any rate his leisure is likely to be spent in debauchery so compulsively aggressive as to seem only another aspect of his "work." But he is graceful, moving like a dancer among the crowded dangers of the city.[5]

Henry's moves translate into sexual allure for Karen (Lorraine Bracco) whose initial aversion—exacerbated when he stands her up on a date—melts in a Copacabana seduction sequence. Staged by Henry and choreographed by a vertiginous handheld shot of the couple's labyrinthine route into the club, the Copa sequence demonstrates how status is conferred by the Mob and reflected in flunkies fawning over a twenty-year-old kid. Henry's warm reception at the fabled nightclub, the largesse he scatters to obsequious minions, the special ringside table that he graciously accepts as his due wow Karen. That even a respectable Jewish girl from the suburbs falls for Henry's macho cool and shallow charm suggests that the easy money and explosive violence—Henry viciously pistol-whips a neighbor boy who tried to rape Karen—of "the life" add up to sexual attraction. When Henry and Karen marry, it is Paulie who throws a lavish reception and his cohorts who rain cash on the newlyweds whose *real* family henceforth will be the Mob.

Although gangsters are theoretically at odds with the "normative" culture they prey on, Scorsese sees them as more emblematic than aberrant:

> Yeah, the lifestyle reflects the times. In the early Sixties, the camera comes up on Henry and he's waiting outside the diner and he's got this silk shirt on and he hears "Stardust." And he's young and he's looking like all the hope in the world ready for him and he's going to conquer the world. And then you just take it through America—the end of the Sixties, the Seventies, and finally into the end of the Seventies with the disillusionment and the state of the country that we're in now. I think his journey reflects that.[6]

Flushed with cash and happily married—"We always did everything together," says Karen—Henry cruises through the sixties in style. But the new decade—ominously heralded by the 1970 Batts murder—exposes the fault lines that ultimately destroy the Mob. As representative man, Henry enacts the disenchantment of the seventies as he had enacted the ebullience of the sixties. No longer does he do "everything" with Karen, instead splitting his time between home and the apartment where he has set up his sluttish mistress, Janice (Gina Mastrogiacomo). That Karen's scenes of rage—storming into Janice's apartment, threatening Henry with a gun—are intercut with Tommy's attacks on Spider symptomize the spreading degeneracy of the seventies. Ostentatious sex and rampant violence violate the code and threaten the stability of "the life." When Henry and Jimmy get ten years for roughing up a mobster whose sister turns out to be a former FBI typist, what might have been a harmless escapade in the sixties proves to be a costly error in the seventies.

True, Henry serves only four years of his jail sentence, but when he comes out he is a compulsive pillpopper and confirmed drugdealer. Lying about his drug trafficking to Paulie who has expressly forbidden it, Henry draws Tommy and Jimmy in with him. While clandestine drug-peddling is hardly the rebellion against King Arthur and defection from the Round Table that a similar episode suggests in *The Godfather*, it does symbolize the breakdown of Mob discipline. "The Seventies sequence is about losing control, about disintegration," interviewer Gavin Smith suggested to Scorsese, who agreed:

> Totally. Henry disintegrates with drugs. With Jimmy Conway, the disintegration is on a more lethal level, the elimination of [every-body else]. Earlier there's so many shots of people playing cards and at christenings and weddings, all at the same table. If you look at the wedding, the camera goes around the table and all the people at that table are killed by Jimmy later on.[7]

What is ironic about the mutual disintegration of Henry and Jimmy—and of Tommy as well—is that it is preceded by and precipitated by the Mob's most conspicuous success: "The biggest heist in American history." They net six million in cash, "more than enough to go around," but they cannot stand prosperity. Henry goes on dealing drugs, Jimmy begins eliminating everybody else connected with the robbery, and Tommy is executed for whacking Batts. There is an inevitability built into their decline: Tommy gives a wiseguy eight or nine years of high living before he winds up dead or in jail. And his notion that the days of wine and roses are fleeting also applies to society at large. By the seventies, postwar American consumer culture degenerates in tandem with the Mob. Cultural degeneration is so palpable in *GoodFellas* that "even the music becomes decadent," according to Scorsese. "Unchained Melody," nearly "unrecognizable" in its "Italian doo-wop" rendition starkly reflects "the decadence of what happened in the Seventies and the Eighties."[8] Like *Taxi Driver* and *The King of Comedy*, *GoodFellas* evokes an overripe consumer culture whose popular heroes are as likely to be killers, kidnappers, or gangsters as not. That *GoodFellas* ends not with a bang but a whimper may be Scorsese's way of deglamorizing "the life." Busted by the narcs, dismissed by Paulie, and terrified by Jimmy, Henry rats on his fellow mobsters. His defection in 1980 parallels the Batts murder of 1970: both decades begin with portents of the Mob's demise.

Another deglamorizing tactic is to deny Henry the moral conflict much less the remorse attached to betraying his buddies. After he decides to play ball with the FBI, he is untroubled by matters of conscience and concerned solely with matters of comfort (e.g., negotiating his relocation to a warm climate once he joins the Federal Witness Protection Program). Whether dickering with the Feds, fingering Paulie and Jimmy in court, or, especially, vegetating in a colorless suburb courtesy of the Witness Protection Program, Henry exudes the banality of evil. The swaggering wiseguy has morphed into "everyone else. . . . I'm an average nobody. I get to live the rest of my life like a schnook." Maybe it is in being a schnook that Henry incarnates a more devastating put-down of postmodern American society than he ever did as a wiseguy. As "an average nobody" he represents the mass culture that spawns and sustains the mobster he was.

Casino is *GoodFellas* removed to Las Vegas. So striking are the films' similarities that *Casino*'s raison d'être seems unclear. "I don't know what to say, I can't defend myself," a discomfited Scorsese replied to Bernard Weinraub's question about recycled themes and techniques. "I'm attracted to the same territory," Scorsese added. "I'm attracted to characters because they play right on the edge. There's life and death in every decision they make." What fascinated him about Las Vegas was its aura of excess: "Where there's excess, there's danger. Any place that pushes people to the edge—and Las Vegas does that—creates great drama."[9] Certainly Scorsese strives mightily to apply his formula in *Casino*, pushing people to—and over—the edge as readily as he had in *GoodFellas*. And Las Vegas, the clichéd embodiment of American excess, figures to be the ideal site for the pushing to occur. Yet places do not automatically create "great drama," no matter how much pushing they inspire. Budgeted at more than $50 million—double what *Goodfellas* cost—and running nearly three hours, *Casino* suffers from the disproportion between its epic intentions and its commonplace conflicts. That *Casino* may sink under the weight of its own portentousness is already apparent when the final chorus of Bach's *St. Matthew Passion* accompanies the opening credits. (Because the movie begins and ends with the same car blast that sends its protagonist flying through the air, the Bach sounds again over the closing credits). The free-floating figure is mobster-casino boss Sam (Ace) Rothstein (Robert De Niro), and the film backtracks to reveal how he got to this point. While Rothstein (Frank "Lefty" Rosenthal in real life) is *Casino*'s putative hero, Las Vegas is its actual subject. The first hour of the film, with its voice-over explanations of the intricacies of skimming millions of dollars of casino profits into the Mob's coffers, plays like a documentary. Details such as how to convert mountains of coins into bills that can be crammed into suitcases for weekly delivery to the Mob in Kansas City pile up ad infinitum. And when Rothstein's old Chicago buddy, Nicky Santoro (Joe Pesci in still another of his mad-dog-killer roles) shows up in Las Vegas, adding his to the endless stream of voice-overs, the documentary machinery of *Casino* threatens to mangle whatever human interest the plot contains. Replete with Vegas lore, *Casino* subverts the delicate balance between history and character that *GoodFellas* sustains.

What human interest *Casino* generates is largely confined to the games that sometime hooker Ginger McKenna (Sharon Stone) plays with various men. Ace is smitten at first sight like one of those film noir heroes who are instantly devastated by the sexy femme fatale. That he actually falls in love with her image as captured by a TV security camera—a freeze-frame hypes the effect—presumably illustrates Ginger's high-voltage sex appeal. Wooing the reluctant call girl, who is loath to give up her profession or her long-time pimp, the sleazy Lester Diamond (James Woods), Rothstein finally makes her an offer she can't refuse: the key to his safety-deposit box in addition to the usual cars, jewels, clothes, and house with swimming pool. So she marries him and for Ace it is mostly downhill from there. Punctuated increasingly by screaming fights, the marriage predictably unravels. Ginger abuses drink and drugs, kidnaps her own daughter, takes up again with Lester, and even betrays Ace with Nicky. Yet Ginger's predictable infidelities and Nicky's still more predictable bursts of violence—like squeezing a thug's head in a vise—seem staged for histrionic effect (Stone's emoting garnered a Best Supporting Actress nomination) rather than compelled by narrative logic. *Casino* is convincing in documenting the (d)evolution of Las Vegas and the arcane workings of casinos, less so in dramatizing the human factor.

Whether *Casino* is saved by its documentary insights or scuttled by its dramatic bathos is debatable. Less debatable is its remoteness: Scorsese is reprising familiar themes but on unfamiliar territory. "I don't really understand the games and it's not really my kind of place," he says of Las Vegas.[10] Not that he had not made great movies on similarly uncongenial subjects—boxing, for example. But in the case of *Raging Bull*, Scorsese was inspired by a perceived link between Jake LaMotta and himself. No such rapport with his central character is apparent in *Casino*. Moreover, the Ace Rothstein role is itself a remote one, according to James Kaplan. Noting *Casino*'s thematic affinity—"a true-life morality play about the consequences of crossing rules"—with other Scorsese films, Kaplan goes on to cite Rothstein's character as the source of the movie's difficulty:

> [*Casino*] is also a somber reflection on the limits of power. But power—as concentrated in the remote central character, the gambler Ace Rothstein . . . is the main reason *Casino* fails to be great. Scorsese's greatest pictures—*Mean Streets* and *Taxi Driver* and *Raging Bull* and *Last Temptation* and *GoodFellas*—are about the strivings of powerless heroes; *Casino* is about the struggle of a powerful hero to hold on. The conclusion is forgone.[11]

Kaplan's contrast between the "powerful" Rothstein and Scorsese's "powerless heroes" may be too pat. Are Christ and Travis Bickle equally powerless? And is Rothstein all that powerful? As a Jew, he is even more of an outsider than the Irish Jimmy Conway was in *GoodFellas*. Ace, a former bookmaker and gambler and a wizard with numbers, is installed as casino boss by the Mob. And what the Mob gives, it can as easily take away: Ace's "power" lasts only so long as he proves useful. When his private life—like Santoro's mayhem—spins out of control and gets in the way of business, Rothstein is finished. His end is reminiscent of Henry Hill's in *GoodFellas*: exile as the price of survival. Still useful to the Mob as a numbers man, Rothstein is "retired" to Florida after he miraculously survives the car explosion.

GoodFellas made a lot of money and won a slew of critical awards, while *Casino* struggled to break even and won mixed reviews at best. Yet despite their divergent popular and critical receptions, the films are two sides of the same coin. According to Scorsese, *GoodFellas* differs from his previous work primarily in its ending. Instead of showing moral conflict and/or character development,

> Here I tried to use exposition as a device to distract the audience. To get through the film, a two-and-a-half hour film, very quickly and then gamble on the resonance of the actions of the characters to reveal the characters, to reveal the moral character, if there is any. But you're sure there is no moral conflict. They just do it for fun and they deal with it. And that's the experiment in the film. And to people who know that world, it works.[12]

The "gamble" Scorsese took in *GoodFellas* he takes again in *Casino*. If the gamble pays off better in *GoodFellas*, it is because the "resonance of the actions" and the viability of "that world" diminish in *Casino*. Or maybe it is because *GoodFellas* carries the gangster movie about as far as it can go. The long farewell to the Mob that shapes the narratives of both films could be Scorsese's own farewell to the genre. In any event, *GoodFellas* will remain a tough act to follow.

GoodFellas and *Casino* are valedictories to the Mob—and to the era of Mob rule. By the 1990s, the omnipotent Mafia of *Mean Streets* had grown sclerotic if not moribund, its salad days long past. The wiseguys like Ace Rothstein and Nicky Santoro who pillaged and terrorized Las Vegas are no more, and the town they ruled they would no longer recognize. Modern Las Vegas has (d)evolved into just another Disneyland, a family theme park where gambling itself has been largely reduced to pulling the handles of the ubiquitous slot machines. Even Scorsese's home turf grows barely recognizable: Little Italy is a misnomer, and 42nd Street threatens to become a cordon sanitaire à la the Vegas strip. As his world fades into ancient history, the danger of its cinematic recapitulation becoming increasingly remote (a common rap against *Casino*) heightens. Had *Casino* immediately followed *GoodFellas*, Scorsese might have been diagnosed as suffering from the disappearance of his habitual characters and settings. Of course movie genres may survive the demise of their subject matter(s)—witness the Western—but as their subject matter recedes, genres eventually atrophy or at least adapt—again, the Western. The gangster movie, Scorsese's favorite genre, is a case in point. Moviemakers like himself are "on the way out. At least I think I am," he says. Quentin Tarantino's postmodern gangster films, for example, treat as ironic the violence that for Scorsese is real. "I *couldn't* do what Quentin does," Scorsese adds, explaining his own alienation from what is new(s).[13] Between *GoodFellas* and *Casino*, however, came *The Age of Innocence* (1993)—powerful evidence that Scorsese's art transcends violence and genre and that he is emphatically not "on the way out." And if the two gangster movies exploit familiar terrain, *The Age of Innocence* and *Kundun* explore new territory.

That *The Age of Innocence* confounds Scorsese's plaint that his want of irony renders him virtually passé is itself ironic. Invoking Paul Schrader's distinction between the existential hero of *Taxi Driver* and the ironic heroes of Tarantino movies, Scorsese accounts for his own *tristesse*: "Schrader feels that the world today deals more with the *ironic* hero, and that's the hero of the twentieth-century, where we're not taken seriously anymore, or won't be. . . . Maybe I'm an old twentieth-century guy . . .

on the way out."[14] How ironic, then, that Scorsese "reverts" to the *nine-teenth*-century world of Edith Wharton, ironist par excellence, whose Pulitzer Prize winning *The Age of Innocence* (1920) features Newland Archer, as ironic a hero as Schrader—or Tarantino—could hope for. Of course the implication that the ironic hero is a late twentieth-century invention is patently absurd. Moreover, postmodern irony verges on the banal and/or what Henry James, the supreme ironist and Wharton's mentor, disdainfully called the vulgar. So faithful is Scorsese to Wharton's vision that he edited *The Age of Innocence* to synchronize with Joanne Woodward's voice-over narration. And Woodward's lapidary reading perfectly captures the cool detachment and acidic irony of Wharton's prose. To re-create 1870s New York as authentically as possi-ble, Scorsese researched the era obsessively and brought in experts to adjudicate matters of setting, costume, and etiquette. That it was a soci-ety grounded in binding rituals and nuanced behavior mandates his fanatical attention to detail: "It's really important. Because all those details are ultimately what kept those people in check and imprisoned them."[15] These all-important rituals were enacted in formal events—notably dinner parties—which were themselves highly ritualistic. Engraved invitations, rigid seating protocol, rich place settings, lavish food and wine presentations, sumptuous floral arrangements, and more expressed the social status of hosts and guests alike. As Wharton's mouthpiece, Woodward decodes Scorsese's images, lacing them with irony in the process. "The prose is important, the way the words are put together. And the irony in the content of the prose," maintains Scorsese in defense of the running voice-over. "Hearing the prose and seeing the images create a certain world. . . complete, almost. I was experimenting here, trying to make it somewhere between the literary and the visual."[16] It is no small achievement on Scorsese's part to evoke images exquisite enough to stand up to Wharton's jeweled prose.

What attracted the admittedly unliterary Scorsese, who was given *The Age of Innocence* in 1980—it took him seven years to read it—was the story of unconsummated love. Would-be lovers Newland Archer (Daniel Day-Lewis) and the Countess Ellen Olenska (Michelle Pfeiffer) repress their sexual yearnings and squander their sexual opportunities, hedged in by conventions they claim to disdain but dare not disobey. It is pri-marily this theme of sexual frustration that links the apparently anom-alous *The Age of Innocence* to Scorsese's other films. From *Who's That*

Knocking? to *Casino*, Scorsese's male protagonists are racked by sexual longing. And the women they yearn for—"the girl" in *Who's That Knocking?*, Betsy in *Taxi Driver*, Vicki in *Raging Bull*, Ginger in *Casino*—are, like Ellen Olenska, usually blonde goddesses who function as Scorsese's femmes fatales. Generally, Scorsese's men fall in love at first sight, and whether, like Jake LaMotta and Ace Rothstein, they get their women, or, like Travis Bickle and Newland Archer, they do not, all of them incarnate thwarted desire. A recurring final shot zeroes in on the hero alone: Travis driving off in his cab, Jimmy Doyle turning away from the phone booth, Rothstein rusticating in Florida—and Newland Archer retreating from the square where Ellen lives in Paris.

The brief Paris finale conflates the many ironies of *The Age of Innocence*. Newland Archer, now a fifty-seven-year-old widower, has been dragged off to Paris by his son Ted (Robert Sean Leonard). Strolling with his father in the Tuileries, Ted blithely alludes to Newland's "secret" passion for the Countess Olenska. Earlier, the voice-over's running commentary had revealed that in 1870s New York society what Newland thought he was so masterfully concealing was regarded as common knowledge. Now it turns out to his amazement that even his supposedly naive wife was in on the "secret." Moreover, the rituals that governed love and marriage in the upper-crust society of the 1870s are all but forgotten a generation later. Ted's engagement to a daughter of the disgraced Julius Beaufort, for example, would have been scandalous if not impossible then but is unremarkable now. To dispose so casually of those "rules" that people formerly lived by suggests the emptiness both of the "rules" and their adherents. That Newland Archer, at bottom a most conventional man, had imagined himself above the conventions for which he occasionally voiced contempt is as ironic as the demise of the conventions themselves.

It is this gap between what Archer says and what he does that accounts for much of the irony of *The Age of Innocence*. Despite his self-professed craving for intellectual and amatory stimulation, he shares the beliefs and performs the rituals of his society. The opening sequence—a brilliantly filmed night at the opera—establishes the stylized social drama of Old New York and Archer's role in it:

> The choreographing of looks between members of the audience, the overlaying of the operatic voices with whispered gossip, as well as the narrator's voice–all this suggests that the players in this fiction are not confined to the stage. Going to the opera clearly

> constitutes a ceremonial event for this society, a way of ritualistical-
> ly defining spatial and social parameters. But as well as the social
> dimension, the routine of conventions to be observed, we are alert-
> ed to the hothouse atmosphere of this world. Sensations, momen-
> tary intensities, trajectories of desire that connect people and
> images, across unimaginable spaces, are rendered cinematically,
> and burnt into memory.[17]

Wharton's prose underlines the ceremonial behavior of the audience,
including Archer, noting that it was "not the thing" to arrive early at the
opera. Afterward, New York society adjourned to the Beauforts whose
annual ball "invariably happened in the same way." Even after his
involvement with Ellen ostensibly defies social taboo, Archer remains at
heart a creature of his milieu. A telltale shot tracks ranks of men somber-
ly—and identically—clothed in black, clutching their derbies against the
wind, and lockstepping in slow motion, before resting on Newland
Archer, indistinguishable from the masses.

Ellen Olenska is the nonconformist Archer imagines himself to be.
Her attendance at the opera marks her return to New York and to the
"polite" society she forsook for Europe and marriage to a dissolute
Polish count. This first public appearance is staged to demonstrate that
Ellen, far from being a social pariah, is securely cocooned amidst the
Mingott clan. Yet she is first sighted through the several opera glasses
that are trained on the Welland box where the scandalous spectacle of
the wayward wife upstages the Faustian spectacle of the opera. And
when Archer makes a beeline for the box, it is unclear whether he is
magnetized by Ellen or, as Wharton observes, he wishes to see his
fiancée, May Welland (Winona Ryder) "through whatever difficulties
her cousin's anomalous situation might involve her in." In the novel,
Ellen's remembrance of things past—"I see everybody here in knicker-
bockers and pantalettes"—shocks Archer in its "unseemly . . . picture of
the august tribunal before which, at that very moment, her case was
being tried." Ellen either blindly or blithely disregards the social deco-
rum so essential to Archer—"Nothing could be in worse taste than mis-
placed flippancy," he concludes about her innocent raillery. When Ellen
crosses the drawing-room at a party to talk to Newland, she commits a
faux pas that inscribes her as "different," as Wharton's barbed commentary makes clear: "It was not the custom in New York drawing-rooms for
a lady to get up and walk away from one gentleman in order to seek the
company of another. Etiquette required that she should wait, immovable

as an idol, while the men who wished to converse with her succeeded each other at her side."

Faithfully reproduced in Woodward's voice-over, Wharton's sly aside turns an innocuous social gaffe into an incisive social critique. At first glance, Ellen's transgression only spotlights another of the innumerable social codes that, like arriving late at the opera, defy logic. In this case, however, she has unwittingly (?) challenged not merely the arbitrary strictures of society but its elemental structures as well. Not that a woman fresh from the salons of the European haut monde could be expected to stay rooted to her chair in a New York drawing-room. But walking across that room turns acquiescence into action, social determinism into self-determination, containment into freedom. Like many of Wharton's protofeminists, Ellen instinctively rebels against the master narrative that enshrines patriarchal hegemony. By the moral calculus of Old New York, a Julius Beaufort's sexual dalliance is amusing while an Ellen Olenska's abandonment of a dissipated husband is scandalous. True, society can be magnanimous—the Mingotts and the Wellands close ranks around Ellen at the opera and the lordly van der Luydens invalidate the snubs of lesser social arbiters by pointedly and repeatedly making her their guest. But social protection exacts the price of social conformity. Beyond the social pale lies the contingent world that Ellen invokes in a key exchange with Newland about their future together. "We're near each other only if we stay far from each other," she tells him, rejecting the alternative of "trying to be happy behind the backs of the people who trust [us]." Newland groans, "Ah, I'm beyond that." "No, you're not," corrects Ellen. "You've never been beyond. And *I* have . . . and I know what it looks like there." Perhaps she fears a repetition of the social isolation she has known; or perhaps she simply knows her man.

Once the love triangle and its social context are established, the issue of Newland Archer's character dominates *The Age of Innocence*. And while Scorsese's reading of Wharton's text is faithful, even reverential, his reading of Archer may, intentionally or not, be more flattering than hers. No sooner does Archer enter the novel than his character is X-rayed by Wharton's mercilessly ironic prose. After first explaining his late arrival at the opera as "the thing" to do, Wharton adds a second reason for his delay: "He had dawdled over his cigar because he was at heart a dilettante, and thinking over a pleasure to come often gave him a subtler satisfaction than its realization." Dilettantism hints at shallowness, and the suspicion that Archer is something of a lightweight hero haunts the novel. And if he *is* a dilettante *and* a social conformist, the chance that Archer will risk all for love is pretty slim. He may yearn for Ellen Olenska, but the yearning is mediated by a mind-set that privileges cogitation over consummation. For Scorsese, however, the yearning is all: Newland's love for Ellen is an obsessive passion, not a mere habit of mind. Of course, the love is genuine—and mutual—in the novel as well; it is only that Wharton's initial characterization of Newland may stack the deck against its consummation. In the film, the renunciation of love comes across more as a noble sacrifice than as a failure of nerve. Whether this results primarily form Scorsese's reading of Wharton or from the romantic personae of Daniel Day-Lewis and Michelle Pfeiffer and the lush mise-en-scène is a moot question.

Two scenes, the second a variation on the first, nicely illustrate Scorsese's reading of Wharton. A year and a half after he and Ellen had last met prior to his marriage, Newland and May arrive in Newport where "the Wellands always went" in summer. Newland—who had tried unsuccessfully to coax May into spending the summer on a remote island off the coast of Maine—is now more than ever a prisoner of the social rituals he thought to escape with Ellen. When the Newland Archers call on Granny Mingott, it turns out that Ellen has come to spend a day with the old lady. Asked to fetch her back to the house, Archer follows Ellen's path toward the shore and spots her from afar standing at the end of the pier and gazing out to sea. "If she doesn't turn before that sail crosses the Lime Rock light I'll go back," he thinks. The sailboat duly glides past the lighthouse, the figure on the pier does not turn, and Newland retraces his steps. Picking up on Wharton's imagery—a "long-drawn sunset was splintering into a thousand fires, and the radiance caught the sail"—Scorsese gives the scene the look of an Impressionist painting. The play of light, the shimmer of water, the grouping of pier, lighthouse, sailboat, and solitary woman holding aloft a parasol and facing out to sea conjure up an impossibly romantic mise-en-scène. In a film rich with the recurring imagery of desire—even Ellen's gloves and fans and parasols become sexual signifiers—it is this scene that best expresses what Ellen ultimately embodies for Archer: "She had become the composite vision of all that he had missed." When he sits "for a long time on the bench in the thickening dusk, his eyes never turning from the balcony" some thirty years later in Paris, Newland envisions Ellen "sitting in a sofa corner near the fire, with aza- leas banked behind her on a table." She is in his imagination as she was the long-ago evening when he visited her little house on 23rd Street, and they fell into each other's arms. "It's more real to me here than if I went up," Archer thinks, and turning away from the apartment as he had once turned away from the pier, he walks back to his hotel alone.

As Wharton writes it, Archer remains to the end a man who relishes experience more in the anticipation than in the consummation. Although his love for Ellen is sincere, it is also shallow. Near the beginning of the Newport sequence, Newland remembers his passion for her as a "momentary madness" and his dream of marrying her as "almost unthinkable." Now safely married to "one of the sweetest-tempered and most reasonable of wives," Archer recalls Ellen "simply as the most plaintive and poignant of a line of ghosts." Wharton more than implies that he is not a man to be swept away by passion. When he advised Ellen against divorcing Olenski, for example, Archer revealed his true colors: the fear of scandal overpowers the wish that she be free. His vows that he would have married her "if it had been possible for either of us" is greeted "with unfeigned astonishment" by Ellen: "And you say that when it's you who've made it impossible." In the novel, Archer's grand passion is constantly subverted by Wharton's ironic asides on his essential conventionality. Because she sanctifies marriage in her novels about as much as Scorsese does in his films, Wharton typically has little sympathy for characters who marry for the wrong reasons. That Archer is comfortable in a marriage that he himself characterizes as "a dull association of material and social interests," like most of the others he knows, belies his all for love pronouncements to Ellen.

Imaging Wharton's key scenes and voicing them over with her prose, Scorsese invokes the letter, and even the spirit of her text. Yet one of his most inspired touches is "missing" from the novel. As Archer sits gazing up at Ellen's balcony in the final scene—of the book and movie—Scorsese revises Wharton's version of what Archer remembers. Imagining Ellen in her Paris apartment, he sees her not reclining on a sofa surrounded by azaleas but standing by the water that luminous day in Newport. It is the exact tableau that Archer saw before but with one all-important difference: this time she turns around—not in the distance but in medium close-up—and she smiles. When Ted, incredulous at his father's hanging back, asks him what he should say to Madame Olenska, Archer replies, "Say I'm old-fashioned: that's enough." Newland prefers to remember Ellen as she was rather than to confront her as she is. Gilding memory, by "seeing" her turn around and smile is his way not only of preserving Ellen as she was but as she *ideally* was. Archer's achingly poignant (re)vision apotheosizes the yearning that for Scorsese lies at the heart of *The Age of Innocence*. As usual, Scorsese illustrates his attraction to a particular theme by referring to its conceptualization on film. He often cites the image in William Wyler's *The Heiress* (1949) of Montgomery Clift banging on the door and not being allowed in as the inspiration for his own images of frustration. *The Heiress*, based on Henry James's *Washington Square*, casts Clift as a man who throws over a woman who wanted him only to be thrown over in turn by the same woman years later when he wants her. And James, like his disciple Wharton an ironic specialist in out-of-sync relationships, limns the consequences of failing to seize the day. But *Washington Square* is "missing" the key image that in *The Heiress* had such an unforgettable impact on Scorsese. Clift's door-banging revises James in the same way that Ellen's turning and smiling revises Wharton: both images intensify the frustration of unconsummated desire.

It is in terms of the frustration he has dramatized so powerfully in his films that Scorsese invariably views his own career. The endless struggle for personal expression in the face of commercial imperatives; the feeling that his brand of filmmaking is passé; and the failure to win a Best Director Oscar lie behind his June 23, 1996, remark to *60 Minutes* interviewer Lesley Stahl: "I've been in a bad mood for twenty-five years." Yet this is the same filmmaker whom no less an authority than Steven Spielberg lauded on the same program as America's best— "because he's the most honest"—director. And as the millennium approached, even the habitually pessimistic Scorsese had to admit that the 1990s had been good to him. Although still haunted by the fear that the lean years of the mid-eighties might return, he was, in the mid-nineties, amply cushioned against impending disaster by a lucrative four-year, three-picture deal with Disney. Ensconced in a sumptuous Upper East Side townhouse outfitted with a state-of-the-art viewing room, and rarely emerging into a society he claims no longer to belong to, Scorsese lives, and lives for, cinema. Single-mindedly devoted to his art, he makes time for little else: "I have no life-style. I just make these movies—that's *it*."[18] Actually, Scorsese not only makes movies but produces, preserves, restores, re-releases, and acts in them as well. The consummate cineast, he has almost single-handedly prevented vast swatches of film history from being lost even as he continues to make film history himself. A crusade against fading color film stock he began at the 1979 New York Film

Festival prodded Kodak to improve its film. At the same time he was thus enhancing the prospects of the future, Scorsese was salvaging the legacy of the past. In 1990, along with other prominent American directors, he founded the Film Foundation "dedicated to ensuring the survival of the American film heritage." By the mid-nineties, Scorsese had achieved near-iconic status among film aficionados. Fêted from Hollywood to New York, showered with awards (save for that elusive Oscar), and honored with retrospectives, he had won mainstream success without sacrificing his personal vision.

That vision remains, above all, religious. How to live a Christian life in a fallen world is the recurring theme of his major films. Those films express the religious passion of a director still under the spell of Catholic ritual long after leaving the Church. "He's got movie making and the Church mixed up together; he's trying to be the saint of cinema," Pauline Kael said of Scorsese apropos of *Raging Bull*.[19] What Kael regards as confused intentions is, for better or for worse, Scorsese's modus operandi—and his modus vivendi. In the spring of 1996, he was off to Morocco to shoot *Kundun* (The Presence), the first picture in the Disney deal. *Kundun*—an epic about the selection of the fourteenth Dalai Lama and the Chinese takeover of Tibet—would seem to be a pretty far-out project for a director of Scorsese's background. Maybe he is bidding to join the pantheon of those great directors who, as he has often stated, could make any type of movie. *Kundun* has obvious affinities with *The Last Emperor* (1987), another Asian epic that marked a similar career departure for one of Scorsese's idols, Bernardo Bertolucci. More likely, however, *Kundun* appeals to the same religious impulse that drove Scorsese to make *The Last Temptation of Christ* against all odds. What he said about *The Last Temptation* may finally apply to a picture as apparently anomalous as an Asian epic, and indeed, to his entire oeuvre:

> I made it as a prayer, an act of worship. I wanted to be a priest. My whole life has been movies and religion. That's it. Nothing else.[20]

Notes

Chapter 1: Flashbacks: An Auteur is Born

1. Paul Schrader, *Schrader on Schrader,* ed. Kevin Jackson (London: Faber and Faber, 1990), 133.

2. David Bordwell and Kristin Thompson, *Film Art: An Introduction,* 3d ed. (New York: McGraw-Hill, 1990), 400.

3. Annette Insdorf, *François Truffaut,* (New York: Touchstone, 1989), 20.

4. Michael Pye and Lynda Myles, *The Movie Brats: How the Film Generation Took over Hollywood* (New York: Holt Rinehart Winston, 1979), 192.

5. Mary Pat Kelly, *Martin Scorsese: A Journey* (New York: Thunder's Mouth, 1991), 11.

6. Diane Jacobs, *Hollywood Renaissance* (New York: A.S. Barnes, 1977), 129.

7. Martin Scorsese, "In the Streets," in *Once a Catholic: Prominent Catholics and Ex-Catholics Discuss the Influence of the Church on Their Lives and Works,* ed. Peter Occhiogrosso (Boston: Houghten Mifflin, 1987), 98–99.

8. Ibid., 97.

9. Paul Schrader, *Taxi Driver* (London: Faber and Faber, 1990), xxi.

10. Quoted in Jacobs, *Hollywood Renaissance,* 129.

11. Scorsese, "In the Streets," 93.

12. Ibid., 92.

13. Martin Scorsese, *Scorsese on Scorsese,* ed. David Thompson and Ian Christie (London: Faber and Faber, 1989), 3.

14. Pauline Kael, *For Keeps* (New York: Dutton, 1994), 455.

15. Scorsese, *Scorsese on Scorsese,* 54, 60.

16. Bella Taylor, "Martin Scorsese," in *Close-Up: The Contemporary Director,* ed. Jon Tuska, Vicki Piekarski, and David Wilson, (Metuchen, N.J.: Scarecrow Press, 1981), 298.

17. Scorsese, *Scorsese on Scorsese,* 6.

18. Ibid.

19. Peter Biskind, "Slouching toward Hollywood," in *Premiere* (November, 1991), 68.

20. Scorsese, *Scorsese on Scorsese,* 20.

21. Amy Taubin, "Blood and Pasta: Martin Scorsese's Cinema of Obsessions," in *Village Voice* (September 18, 1990), 38.

22. Kael, *For Keeps,* 510.

23. Ibid., 375.

24. Scorsese, *Scorsese on Scorsese,* 14–15.

25. Ibid., 31.
26. Kelly, *Martin Scorsese: A Journey,* 68.
27. Scorsese, *Scorsese on Scorsese,* 14.
28. Ibid., 21.

Chapter 2: Our Gang: From Elizabeth Street to *Mean Streets*

1. Anthony DeCurtis, "Martin Scorsese," in *Rolling Stone* (November 1, 1990), 64.
2. Ibid., 65.
3. Kelly, *Martin Scorsese: A Journey,* 15.
4. Scorsese, *Scorsese on Scorsese,* 113–14.
5. Mary Pat Kelly, *Martin Scorsese: The First Decade* (Pleasantville, N.Y.: Redgrave, 1980), 16.
6. David Rensin, "*Playboy* Interview with Martin Scorsese," in *Playboy* (April, 1991), 68.
7. DeCurtis, "Martin Scorsese," 65.
8. Scorsese, "In the Streets," 98.
9. Michael Bliss, *Martin Scorsese and Michael Cimino* (Metuchen, N.J.: Scarecrow Press, 1985), 47.
10. Scorsese, "In the Streets," 100.
11. Kelly, *Martin Scorsese: A Journey,* 71–72.
12. Scorsese, *Scorsese on Scorsese,* 48.
13. Kael, *For Keeps,* 507.
14. Robert Phillip Kolker, *A Cinema of Loneliness,* 2d ed. (New York: Oxford University Press, 1988) 168.
15. Rochelle Reed, ed., *Dialogue on Film: Martin Scorsese.* Vol. 4, no. 7. (Los Angeles: American Film Institute, April 1975), 17.
16. Les Keyser, *Martin Scorsese* (New York: Twayne, 1992), 40.
17. Ibid, 46.
18. Reed, *Dialogue on Film: Martin Scorsese,* 17.
19. Ibid., 18.
20. Ibid., 17.

Chapter 3: The Way West: Making It in Hollywood

1. Scorsese, "In the Streets," 2.
2. "*Playboy* Interview with Martin Scorsese," 58.
3. James Monaco, *American Film Now* (New York: Zoetrope, 1984), 152.
4. Jonathan Rosenbaum, "The Way It Was," in *Chicago Reader,* Section 1 (August 12, 1994), 10.
5. Monaco, *American Film Now,* 152–53.
6. Stephen Talty, "Invisible Woman," in *American Film* (September/October 1991), 44.
7. Taylor, "Martin Scorsese," 315.
8. *Ibid.*
9. Scorsese, *Scorsese on Scorsese,* 30.
10. Biskind, "Slouching Toward Hollywood," 62.
11. Kelly, *Martin Scorsese: The First Decade,* 19.
12. Taylor, "Martin Scorsese," 317.

13. Pye and Myles, *The Movie Brats,* 199.

14. Seth Cagin and Philip Dray, *Born to be Wild: Hollywood and the Sixties Generation* (Boca Raton, Fl.: Coyote, 1994), 40.

15. Lee Lourdeaux, *Italian and Irish Filmmakers in America: Ford, Capra, Coppola, and Scorsese* (Philadelphia: Temple U. Press, 1990), 239.

16. Scorsese, *Scorsese on Scorsese,* 36.

17. Taylor, "Martin Scorsese," 320.

18. Scorsese, *Scorsese on Scorsese,* 39–41.

19. Reed, "Dialogue on Film: Martin Scorsese," 10–11.

20. Taylor, "Martin Scorsese," 331.

21. Pye and Myles, *The Movie Brats,* 203.

22. Richard Dyer, "Stars," excerpted in *Film Theory and Criticism,* ed. Gerald Mast, Marshall Cohen, and Les Braudy, 4th ed. (New York and Oxford: Oxford University Press, 1992), 626.

23. Reed, "Dialogue on Film: Martin Scorsese," 22.

24. Kelly, *Martin Scorsese: A Journey,* 84–85.

25. *Ibid.,* 85.

26. Reed, "Dialogue on Film: Martin Scorsese," 21.

27. *Ibid.*

28. Taylor, "Martin Scorsese," 339.

29. Michael Ryan and Douglas Kellner, *Camera Politica: The Politics and Ideology of Contemporary Hollywood Film* (Bloomington: Indiana University Press, 1988), 141.

Chapter 4: Apocalypse and After: God's Lonely Man

1. Schrader, *Schrader on Schrader,* 27, 117.

2. Keith McKay, *Robert De Niro: The Hero behind the Masks* (New York: St. Martin's, 1986), 49.

3. Schrader, *Schrader on Schrader,* 126.

4. Ibid., 126, 116.

5. Scorsese, *Scorsese on Scorsese,* 53, 62.

6. Pye and Myles, *The Movie Brats,* 208.

7. Scorsese, *Scorsese on Scorsese,* 62.

8. Robin Wood, *Hollywood from Vietnam to Reagan* (New York: Columbia University Press, 1986), 52. It's Wood who calls the New York of *Taxi Driver* "the excremental city."

9. Scorsese, *Scorsese on Scorsese,* 54, 60.

10. Schrader, *Schrader on Schrader,* 122.

11. Robert B. Roy, *A Certain Tendency of the Hollywood Cinema, 1930–1980* (Princeton, N.J.: Princeton University Press, 1985), 359–60.

12. Wood, *Hollywood from Vietnam to Reagan,* 54.

13. Christopher Sharrett, "The American Apocalypse: Scorsese's *Taxi Driver,*" in Christopher Sharrett, ed., *Crisis Cinema: The Apocalyptic Idea in Postmodern American Film* (Washington, DC: Maissoneuve Press, 1993), 227.

14. Ibid., 230.

15. Scorsese, *Scorsese on Scorsese,* 63, 66.

16. Schrader, *Schrader on Schrader,* 87–89.

17. Sharrett, "The American Apocalypse: Scorsese's *Taxi Driver,*" 233–34.

18. Schrader, *Schrader on Schrader,* 122.

Chapter 5: The Sound(s) of Music: From the Bands to The Band

1. Kelly, *Martin Scorsese: A Journey,* 109.
2. Pat Hackett, ed., *The Andy Warhol Diaries* (New York: Warner Books, 1989), 60–61, 134.
3. Kelly, *Martin Scorsese: A Journey,* 109.
4. Ibid., 104.
5. Scorsese, *Scorsese on Scorsese,* 69.
6. Ibid.
7. Gerald Mast, *A Short History of the Movies,* 5th ed., revised by Bruce F. Kawin (New York: Macmillan, 1992), 302.
8. McKay, *Robert De Niro: The Hero behind the Masks,* 73.
9. Mast, *A Short History of the Movies,* 5th ed., 303.
10. Kelly, *Martin Scorsese: A Journey,* 111–12.
11. Richard Lippe, "*New York, New York* and the Hollywood Musical," in *Movie* 31/32: 100.
12. Ibid.
13. Biskind, "Slouching Toward Hollywood," 68.
14. Scorsese, *Scorsese on Scorsese,* 73–74.
15. Kelly, *Martin Scorsese: A Journey,* 116.
16. Ibid., 117.
17. Biskind, "Slouching toward Hollywood," 68.

Chapter 6: That's Entertainment: Performance as Destiny

1. Kelly, *Martin Scorsese: The First Decade,* 202.
2. Schrader, *Schrader on Schrader,* 133.
3. DeCurtis, "Martin Scorsese," 61.
4. Biskind, "Slouching toward Hollywood," 68.
5. Scorsese, *Scorsese on Scorsese,* 77.
6. Kelly, *Martin Scorsese: A Journey,* 141
7. Wood, *Hollywood from Vietnam to Reagan,* 245. My ensuing discussion of the "homosexual subtext" is indebted to Wood's analysis.
8. Joyce Carol Oates, *On Boxing* (Garden City, N.Y.: Dolphin/Doubleday, 1987), 30.
9. Wood, *Hollywood from Vietnam to Reagan,* 257.
10. Oates, *On Boxing,* 25.
11. Schrader, *Schrader on Schrader,* 133.
12. Kelly, *Martin Scorsese: A Journey,* 121.
13. Schrader, *Schrader on Schrader,* 131, 133.
14. David Friedkin, "Blind Rage and 'Brotherly Love': The Male Psyche at War with Itself in *Raging Bull,*" in Steven G. Kellman, ed., *Perspectives on Raging Bull* (New York: G. K. Hall, 1994), 130.
15. Kael, *For Keeps,* 978–79.
16. Scorsese, *Scorsese on Scorsese,* 92.
17. McKay, *Robert De Niro: The Hero behind the Masks,* 112–13.
18. Wood, *Hollywood from Vietnam to Reagan,* 266–67.
19. Timothy Corrigan, *A Cinema without Walls: Movies and Culture after Vietnam,* (New Brunswick, N.J.: Rutgers University Press, 1991), 206.
20. Ibid., 209.
21. Mackay, *Robert De Niro: The Hero behind the Masks,* 122.

Chapter 7: Staying Alive: Other People's Projects

1. Michel Cieutat, *Martin Scorsese* (Paris: Rivages, 1986), 197. My translation from the French.
2. Kelly, *Martin Scorsese: A Journey*, 183.
3. Ibid, 185.
4. Keyser, *Martin Scorsese*, 151.
5. Salman Rushdie, *The Wizard of Oz* (London: British Film Institute, 1992), 44.
6. Corrigan, *A Cinema without Walls: Movies and Culture after Vietnam*, 95, 96.
7. Cieutat, *Martin Scorsese*, 200. My translation from the French.
8. Lesley Stern, *The Scorsese Connection* (London: British Film Institute and Bloomington: Indiana University Press, 1995), 112.
9. Corrigan, *A Cinema without Walls: Movies and Culture after Vietnam*, 97.
10. Scorsese, *Scorsese on Scorsese*, 100.
11. Kolker, *A Cinema of Loneliness*, 2d Ed., 233, 234.
12. Cieutat, *Martin Scorsese*, 207. My translation from the French.
13. Ibid, 216.
14. Kelly, *Martin Scorsese: A Journey*, 193.
15. Chris Hodenfield, "Martin Scorsese: The Art of Noncompromise," in *American Film* (March 1989), 50.
16. Kelly, *Martin Scorsese: A Journey*, 247.

Chapter 8: Beat the Devil: Man and Superman

1. Richard Corliss, "Body . . . and Blood," in *Film Comment* 24, no. 5 (September/October 1988), 38.
2. Kelly, *Martin Scorsese: A Journey*, 205, 213.
3. Schrader, *Schrader on Schrader*, 140
4. Ibid., 135.
5. Ibid., 136.
6. Ibid., 133.
7. Corliss, "Body . . . and Blood," 36.
8. Ibid., 42.
9. Kelly, *Martin Scorsese: A Journey*, 226.
10. Ibid., 227.
11. Michael Morris, "Of God and Man: A Theological and Artistic Scrutiny of Martin Scorsese's *The Last Temptation of Christ*," in *American Film* 14 (October 1988), 45.
12. Corliss, "Body . . . and Blood," 42.
13. Schrader, *Schrader on Scorsese*, 136.
14. Corliss, "Body . . . and Blood," 36.
15. Scorsese, *Scorsese on Scorsese*, 118.
16. Ibid.
17. Ibid., 126.
18. Ibid., 138.
19. Ibid., 143.
20. Schrader, *Schrader on Schrader*, 137, 139.
21. Stern, *The Scorsese Connection*, 173.
22. Biskind, "Slouching toward Hollywood," 73.
23. Owen Gleiberman, "Martin Scorsese: America's Greatest Director," in *Entertainment Weekly* (December 6, 1991), 33, 34.

24. Stephan Talty, "Invisible Woman," in *American Film* (September/October 1991), 47.

25. Biskind, "Slouching toward Hollywood," 73.

26. Rensin, "Playboy Interview: Martin Scorsese," 64.

Chapter 9: Millennium Approaches: Something(s) Old, Something(s) New . . .

1. Gavin Smith, "Martin Scorsese Interview," in *Film Comment*, September/October 1990, 28.

2. Ibid., 30.

3. Robert Warshow, "Movie Chronicle: The Westerner," in *Film Theory and Criticism*, 4th ed., 453.

4. Kelly, *Martin Scorsese: A Journey*, 262, 263.

5. Warshow, "Movie Chronicle: The Westerner," 453.

6. Smith, "Martin Scorsese Interview," 29.

7. Ibid., 30.

8. Ibid., 29.

9. Bernard Weinraub, "Martin Scorsese, Attracted to Excess, Still Taking Risks," in *The New York Times*, November 27, 1995, B4.

10. Ibid.

11. James Kaplan, "The Outsider," in *New York*, March 4, 1996, 34.

12. George Hickenlooper, *Reel Conversations: Candid Interviews with Film's Foremost Directors and Critics* (New York: Citadel Press, 1991), 32.

13. Kaplan, "The Outsider," 40.

14. Ibid., 34.

15. Bill Cosford, "Scorsese Masters Wharton's High Parlors with Ease, Grace," Knight-Ridder/Tribune News Service, September 30, 1993.

16. Ibid.

17. Stern, *The Scorsese Connection*, 223.

18. Kaplan, "The Outsider," 37.

19. Kael, *For Keeps*, 878.

20. Kelly, *Martin Scorsese: A Journey*, 6.

Select Bibliography

Biskind, Peter. "Slouching Toward Hollywood." *Premiere*, December 1991, 60–73.

Bliss, Michael. *Michael Scorsese and Michael Cimino*. Metuchen, N.J.: Scarecrow Press, 1985.

Cieutat, Michel. *Michael Scorsese*. Paris: Rivages, 1988.

Corliss, Richard. "Body and Blood: An Interview with Martin Scorsese." *Film Comment*, October 1988, 36–42.

Corrigan, Timothy. *A Cinema Without Walls: Movies and Culture After Vietnam*. New Brunswick, N.J.: Rutgers University Press, 1991.

De Curtis, Anthony. "Martin Scorsese." *Rolling Stone*, 1 November 1990, 58–65, 106, 108.

Jacobs, Diane. *Hollywood Renaissance*. South Brunswick, N.J.: A. S. Barnes, 1977.

Kael, Pauline. *For Keeps*. New York: Dutton, 1994.

Kellman, Steven, ed. *Perspectives on Raging Bull*. New York: G. K. Hall, 1994.

Kelly, Mary Pat. *Martin Scorsese: A Journey*. New York: Thunder's Mouth Press, 1991.

———. *Martin Scorsese: The First Decade*. Pleasantville, N.Y.: Redgrave, 1980.

Keyser, Les. *Martin Scorsese*. New York: Twayne, 1992.

Kolker, Robert Philip. *A Cinema of Loneliness*. 2d ed. New York: Oxford University Press, 1988.

Lourdeaux, Lee. *Italian and Irish Filmmakers in America: Ford, Capra, Coppola, and Scorsese*. Philadelphia: Temple University Press, 1990.

McKay, Keith. *Robert De Niro: The Hero Behind the Masks*. New York: St. Martin's, 1986.

Morris, Michael. "Of God and Man: A Theological and Artistic Scrutiny of Martin Scorsese's *The Last Temptation of Christ*." *American Film*, October 1988, 44–50.

Pye, Michael, and Lynda Myles. *The Movie Brats: How the Film Generation Took over Hollywood*. New York: Holt, Rinehart & Winston, 1979.

Ray, Robert B. *A Certain Tendency of the Hollywood Cinema, 1930–1980*. Princeton, N. J.: Princeton University Press, 1985.

Reed, Rochelle, ed. *Dialogue on Film: Martin Scorsese*, vol. 4, no. 7, April 1975. Los Angeles: American Film Institute, 1975.

Rensin, David. "*Playboy* Interview with Martin Scorsese." *Playboy*, April 1991, 57–74, 161.

Schrader, Paul. *Schrader on Schrader*. Edited by Kevin Jackson. London: Faber & Faber, 1990.

———. *Taxi Driver*. London: Faber & Faber, 1990.

Scorsese, Martin. "In the Streets." In *Once a Catholic: Prominent Catholics and Ex-Catholics Discuss the Influence of the Church on their Lives and Works*, edited by Peter Occhiogrosso, 88–101. Boston: Houghton Mifflin, 1987.

————. *Scorsese on Scorsese.* Edited by David Thompson and Ian Christie. London: Faber & Faber, 1989.

Sharrett, Christopher, ed. *Crisis Cinema: The Apocalyptic Idea in Postmodern American Film.* Washington, D.C.: Maissoneuve, 1993.

Stern, Lesley. *The Scorsese Connection.* London: British Film Institute, 1995.

Taylor, Bella. "Martin Scorsese." In *Closeup: The Contemporary Director*, edited by Jon Tuska, Jr. Metuchen, N. J.: Scarecrow Press, 1981.

Von Gunden, Kenneth. *Postmodern Auteurs.* McFarland, 1991.

Major Films Directed by Martin Scorsese

Who's That Knocking at My Door? (Joseph Brenner Associates, Trimod Films, 1969)

Woodstock (Warner Brothers, 1970) Assistant Director and Editor

Boxcar Bertha (American International Pictures, 1972)

Mean Streets (Warner Brothers, 1973)

Alice Doesn't Live Here Anymore (Warner Brothers, 1974)

Taxi Driver (Columbia Pictures, 1976)

New York, New York (United Artists, 1977)

The Last Waltz (United Artists, 1978)

Raging Bull (United Artists, 1980)

The King of Comedy (Twentieth Century-Fox, 1982)

After Hours (Double Play, the Geffen Company, 1985)

The Color of Money (Touchstone, 1986)

The Last Temptation of Christ (Universal Pictures, 1988)

"Life Lessons" in *New York Stories* (Touchstone, 1989)

GoodFellas (Warner Brothers, 1990)

Cape Fear (Universal, 1991)

The Age of Innocence (Columbia, 1993)

Casino (Universal, 1995)

Index